Communication and Culture

Communi

An Introductio

Tony Schirato a

Los Angeles | London | New Delhi
Singapore | Washington DC

nia 91320

cations India Pvt Ltd
B 1/I 1 Mohan Cooperative Industrial Area
Mathura Road
New Delhi 110 044

SAGE Publications Asia-Pacific Pte Ltd
33 Pekin Street #02-01
Far East Square
Singapore 048763

British Library Cataloguing in Publication data

A catalogue record for this book is available
from the British Library

ISBN   978-0-7619-6826-9
ISBN   978-0-7619-6827-6(pbk)

Printed and bound in Great Britain by
CPI Antony Rowe, Chippenham, Wiltshire
Printed on paper from sustainable resources

Foreword

Communication and Culture is an introductory text, one that attempts to signpost a field of enquiry, and to provide some basic tools and understandings for negotiating that field. In this, the book is to be distinguished from the many other kinds of cultural studies readers. It provides an introduction to the field in a way that those readers do not, an introduction of a kind that has not really been attempted since John Fiske's *Introduction to Communication Studies* (Methuen 1982) and Gunther Kress (ed.) *Communication and Culture* (NSW University Press 1988). Like those books this one focuses on communication as an essential part of cultural studies. Like recent readers it also inevitably constructs its own version of cultural studies, one that includes an earlier Australian tradition of social semiotics, and places an important focus on textual studies. This book is an excellent introduction to a number of the theories and debates that inform current arguments in the field and it has the very considerable advantage of introducing them in ways that will be manageable for beginning students.

It is also a book which is truly interdisciplinary, recognising the need for certain kinds of basic literacies, derived from many different disciplinary locations and theoretical positions, and acknowledging the need to theorise subjectivity and otherness and to provide access to theories about these things even in the introductory stages of a cultural studies curriculum. The authors range widely in their choice of textual examples. The themes and issues these examples raise always engage with global issues of subjectivity, gender, race and ethnicity, with issues of ideology and intertextuality, and with issues of value. The book provides an introudction to communication in cultural studies as international and comparative practice (Morris & Muecke 1995:2), and it faces squarely the need to teach about language, written text structures, and the values attached to different textual performances in different contexts, as part of that practice. The book does this in the process of teaching that communication is much more complex than language or verbal text alone.

Communication and Culture does not build disciplinary or anti-disciplinary fences within the interdisciplinary space of cultural studies. It allows semiotics, textual studies and philosophy, social and critical theory to talk to one another and shows how useful it might be to let them. It makes it clear throughout that men and women *do* cultural studies and that men and women, of all kinds, need to be addressed *by* cultural studies. That, it seems to me, is an important place to begin. Beyond that beginning, an introduction to the field which reaffirms the importance of communication and cultural literacy in cultural studies is what this book seeks to provide. This book has been rewritten to provide the most up-to-date accounts of recent developments in the three areas of spoken, written and visual communication which are its primary focus, and to make the book relevant to an international audience in a global context. It will be extremely valuable as a text wherever issues of cultural value, communication, cultural capital and cultural literacy are on the teaching agenda, and it offers, in accessible and challenging ways, the tools that are needed to understand and to engage with current debates.

Terry Threadgold

REFERENCES

Halliday, M.A.K. 1978 *Language as Social Semiotic: The Social Interpretation of Language and Meaning*, Edward Arnold, London
Morris, M. & Muecke, S. 1995 'Editorial', *The UTS Review* 1(1): 1–4

Contents

Preface

This book aims to provide readers with a set of perspectives, approaches and analytical techniques for understanding the range of practices which are labelled 'communication'. We understand communication as the practice of producing and negotiating meanings; a practice which always takes place under specific social, cultural and political conditions. If we take communication to be a set of situated practices, we need to adopt approaches to studying these which do not idealise communication. It follows that there are a number of choices we as authors have made about what to include in this book.

It is important that we state clearly what this book is not: it is not a historical account of the development of either communication studies or cultural studies. It does not claim or attempt to provide a comprehensive account of current research in these fields. Nor is it a book about 'effective communication' or a 'how to . . . (write reports, make public speeches)' book. Useful as that kind of book is, our purpose here is to present the study of communication in a way that moves beyond the immediately pragmatic to equip readers with the means to reflect on and analyse a broad range of communication practices. That is, this book aims to develop the reader's critical understanding of communication in terms of:

- what is happening;
- how it is happening; and
- what the consequences are of particular communicative acts and specific types of communicative practices.

We see this goal as pragmatic in the wider sense of equipping readers with flexible literacies which will be transposable from one context to another. It is important to signal clearly the way in which we have used the much-abused term 'literacy' in this book. We define 'cultural literacy' as a knowledge of meaning systems and the ability to negotiate those systems within different cultural contexts. We use the term 'cultural literacy' to include questions of cross-cultural perspectives, but we want to distinguish our use of the term from the formulaic or elitist notions of what might constitute such forms of 'literacy'. We explicitly reject moves such as E.D. Hirsch's regressive attempt to entrench a dominant version of a specific (Western) culture's privileged meanings and knowledges.

Literacy, then, is a key term; this book aims to render visible (as opposed to transparent and naturalised) the forms of literacy which all members of a culture use in negotiating their daily lives. In doing so, it aims to help readers develop their own communicative and cultural literacies.

Both cultural studies and communication studies have historically been interdisciplinary areas. In order to address the questions posed above, we call upon a range of theoretical approaches. We move between a number of theoretical positions and disciplinary areas, including cultural theory, semiotics (both 'classical' and 'social'), linguistics, media studies, psychoanalysis and Marxism.

The approaches we have selected, however, are linked by a commitment to the notion of communication as a contextualised practice. While we provide a brief introduction to basic concepts of classical structuralist semiotics, particularly the sign, we move on from this paradigm fairly quickly, because of its limitations in dealing with contexts. (Instead of the sign, we will treat the basic units of meaning making as texts or more broadly practices.) Social semiotics and related linguistic approaches are introduced for their usefulness in linking the analysis of texts to social contexts. Bourdieu provides a set of concepts for understanding practice and literacies in terms both of specific situations and more general cultural systems. Marxist and neo-Marxist work on the relation between communication and ideology provides ways of understanding how specific communication practices are valued and deployed for political means (that is, for social groups to obtain or maintain power). Cultural theory derived from psychoanalysis enables us to make the important link between meaning making practices and the ways in which people are assigned cultural identities; identities which have cultural values and ideological effects. These are the theoretical strands which inform this work.

The book focuses on three areas of communication practice which could be considered 'primary' systems of communication: spoken, written and visual communication. We use these categories not as 'pure' categories, but as starting points for examining the complexities of the uses to which these mediums are put, including practices which exhibit 'hybrid' characteristics and make use of 'new' technology. Spoken, written, visual and multimodal are used to introduce and exemplify theoretical concepts and modes of analysis. Examples are taken from a wide range of contexts, including spoken conversation, films, plays, magazines, Internet discussions, TV shows, classroom interaction, workplace negotiations, paintings, newspapers, politics, advertising, history, photographs, law courts, riddles and cartoons.

HOW THIS BOOK IS ORGANISED

The chapters are organised into a sequence so that later chapters build on concepts explained in earlier chapters. Generally speaking, the first half of the book introduces and demonstrates a set of important concepts for understanding and analysing communication practices (Chapter 1 to 7). The second half of the book discusses specific practices, genres and mediums (Chapter 8 to 10). However, it is possible to read the book out of order, by using the glossary where necessary to supplement your understanding of new concepts.

Chapter 1 introduces the fundamental concepts of communication, culture and literacy, and discusses the limitations of popular understandings of communication. We argue that the study of communication needs to recognise 'difference' as intrinsic to communication contexts.

Chapter 2 discusses theories of signs and meaning (or semiotics). Picking up on the concept of difference, we look at the ways in which communication attempts to resolve or mask differences, demonstrating the political and contested nature of meaning.

Chapter 3 outlines a theory of cultural/communication practice, and demonstrates how it can be used to illuminate and explain the dynamics of communication practices in particular contexts. This chapter covers concepts such as cultural field, capital and habitus.

Chapter 4 provides an account of the framing devices which structure communication practices and in turn cultural meanings; concepts such as intertextuality, narrative, genre and discourse. We discuss the ways in which the context of culture produces and also constrains communication practices.

Chapter 5 examines influential theories of ideology and their application to communication practices. The chapter also deals with the ways in which globalisation has shifted the 'ground rules' in relation to the working of ideology, and demands new ways of theorising ideology.

Chapter 6 introduces the concept of subjectivity, and examines the ideological character of the processes of producing subjectivities, or identities. The chapter highlights the importance of gender and sexuality as defining 'markers' of identity, but also as 'markers' or signs which are culturally produced or 'performed'.

Chapter 7 focuses on the relationship between texts and contexts, and develops a framework for analysing this relationship. It emphasises the interdependence of textual practices and the contexts in which they take place, and identifies how aspects such as power, capital and field are negotiated through language and other forms of communication.

The next three chapters examine the genres and literacies specific to the mediums of speech, writing and the visual. Chapter 8 contrasts the spoken and written mediums, and the ways in which the culture both values and under-values speech. In this chapter, we also look at the dialogic nature of all communication, and more specifically at the dynamics of spoken dialogue.

Chapter 9 discusses recent shifts in the function of the written word, and the changing literacies demanded by the technological/information revolution. We look at the social functions and cultural values of different written genres, and writing's place in relation to the public and private spheres.

Chapter 10 argues that the visual has become the dominant medium in contemporary Western cultures, and focuses on the various genres and mediums which deploy visual signs. We discuss the supposed objectivity of the visual, as well as the ideological functions of visual texts and the ways in which subjectivity can be visually produced.

Acknowledgments

This book arose out of our need to develop material for use in teaching a first year subject in communication and cultural studies. To a large extent, the approach we have taken in this text has been directed by the responses to and feedback about the unit which our students gave us.

We gratefully acknowledge the feedback we've received from our colleagues Andrew Wallace, Geoff Danaher, Philippa Bright and Nick Szorenyi. Pat Goon provided illustrations which are valuable supplements to the written text.

We would also like to thank Elizabeth Weiss, Colette Vella and Alison Forsyth at Allen & Unwin for their sound advice and exemplary professionalism.

Finally, grateful acknowledgment is made to the following copyright holders for permission to reproduce material: *The Australian* for 'Philosopher's art escapes duty of reality' and for 'A history of invasion ignores more balanced school of thought'; News Limited for the photograph of Andrew Williams; Pan Books for the extract from *The Restaurant at the End of the Universe* by Douglas Adams; Elizabeth Johnston (Brisbane-based freelance journalist) for 'Evonne goes back to the beginning'; *The Australian Magazine* for 'In the case of Pat O'Shane'; *Dolly* magazine for the contents page from *Dolly* and for 'Why he thinks you're desperate'; Sony Australia for the Sony ad; Methuen for the extract from 'Last to Go' by Harold Pinter; Albion Books for the extract from *Netiquette* by Virginia Shea; Allen & Unwin for the extract from 'Contesting domestic territory' by Virginia Nightingale; Judyth Mermelstein for 'Technology, publishing and on-line communities' (electronic message); *New Woman* for 'The (office) politics of pregnancy'; *Morning Bulletin* for the photographs 'Week's leave, 50 years' service', 'Firefighters get funds', 'Exchange student off to Germany' and 'Mobile screening unit near'.

Every effort has been made to obtain permission from copyright holders; if there are any errors or omissions please contact the publisher, and we will aim to rectify this in subsequent editions.

TONY SCHIRATO AND SUSAN YELL
OCTOBER 1999

Chapter 1

Communication and culture

This chapter addresses the relationship between communication, culture, and the concept of cultural literacy. Meanings are not to be found or understood exclusively in terms of acts of communication, but are produced within specific cultural contexts. What do we mean by the terms communication, culture and cultural literacy?

- *Communication* can be understood as the practice of producing meanings, and the ways in which systems of meaning are negotiated by participants in a culture.
- *Culture* can be understood as the totality of communication practices and systems of meaning.
- *Cultural literacy* can be defined as both a knowledge of meaning systems and an ability to negotiate those systems within different cultural contexts. It is virtually impossible to describe and analyse what is happening in any communication context or practice without using the concept of cultural literacy.

The notion of communication as a cultural practice requiring various forms of cultural literacy is strongly influenced by the work of Pierre Bourdieu. Bourdieu's ideas are particularly useful to our understanding of communication because of his suggestion that practice, or what people actually do, is both constrained by, and develops as a response to, the rules and conventions of a culture.

One way to understand the relation between culture and practice is through Bourdieu's metaphor of the journey and the map (Bourdieu 1990b). Cultures are both the maps of a place (the rules and conventions) and the journeys that take place there (actual practices). Cultural literacy can be understood, then, as a 'feel' for negotiating those cultural rules

Pierre Bourdieu is a French sociologist and cultural theorist who has written extensively on the relationship between cultural structures and practices. His earliest works were anthropological studies of Algerian people and culture, and include *The Algerians* and *Outline of a Theory of Practice*. He wrote important texts on the way education systems help reproduce certain cultural values and practices (such as *Reproduction in Education, Society and Culture*, with Jean-Claude Passeron), but his most influential work has dealt with the relationship between **cultural fields**, **capital** and power. These texts include *Distinction*, *The Logic of Practice*, *Language and Symbolic Power*, *In Other Words*, *The Field of Cultural Production*, *Practical Reason*, *On Television and Journalism* and *The Rules of Art*.

and systems—for 'making your way' through a culture. And practice can be understood as the *performance* of cultural literacy.

Every communication practice (speaking to one another, wearing certain types of clothing) constitutes an additional part of those cultural maps. Communication and culture are not separate entities or areas. Each is produced through a dynamic relationship with the other.

An example of the relationship between communication, context and cultural literacy can be found in the example of the way the *Challenger* disaster (the explosion of the US space shuttle *Challenger* in 1986 over Cape Canaveral, and the death of the seven astronauts, including a number of civilians, on board) has been interpreted and explained. One technical communication textbook wrote that: 'The *Challenger* was not an engineering disaster; it was a communication disaster . . . [which shows that] good communication—especially for technically trained people—is essential' (Pattow & Wresch 1993:11).

Now according to this (probably reasonably representative) account, the *Challenger* disaster occurred, not simply because there were engineering problems (the O-rings didn't set in place) but because the engineers involved couldn't adequately communicate the problem to management groups of both the company involved (Thiokol) and NASA. The account given in the textbook, however, makes clear that the engineers did make several attempts, the night before the disaster, to alert management to the potential danger. The textbook assumes, because engineers were communicating to management, that the problem was a 'failure of communication'. In a sense they were right, but not in the way they think.

The textbook account of the disaster mentions a variety of contexts that could be brought to bear on why *Challenger* blew up:

- there had been engineering problems with NASA launches going back eight years;
- both Thiokol and NASA were anxious to prove their capabilities and competence, which were under question; and
- this launch was important to the US space program, which had been dogged by postponements and technical failures.

There may also have been other political contexts, such as the prestige that politicians and the government wished to gain from a successful launch. The textbook mentions most of these factors, but in the end ditches them all in favour of the 'failure of communication' line.

Let's consider an alternative explanation—one which takes these contexts into account. Thiokol and NASA management knew about the potential danger, but they were under pressure to launch the shuttle anyway. When Thiokol and NASA engineers tried to convince management to postpone, they ran into a stone wall: as one engineer described it, 'Arnie actually got up from . . . the table, and . . . put a quarter pad down . . . in front of the management folks, and tried to sketch out . . . what his concern was . . . and when he realized he wasn't getting through, he just stopped' (Pattow & Wresch 1993:8).

Management obviously didn't have the same agenda as the engineers. The engineers communicated effectively in a technical sense, but what they lacked was a wider cultural literacy. For the engineers to convince management to postpone the flight, they needed to take a different tack and concentrate not on technical problems, but on the possible ramifications of those technical problems, and how these might tie in with the agendas and interests of management. The engineers could have made the point, for instance, that a postponement might be a considerable setback (for NASA, Thiokol, the President), but that decision makers should also consider the consequences of the shuttle blowing up in front of a huge television audience, with the prestige of NASA, Thiokol and the President on the line (which is exactly what happened).

Had the engineers had that wider cultural literacy, they would have known that any attempt to sway management needed to involve treating the launch not as a technical problem, but as a PR exercise. We may think we understand what's going on in a situation (we understand the relevant rules, regulations and conventions), but what happens in practice is often informed, and even determined, by agendas that aren't up front, and sometimes can never be publicly articulated. The ability to negotiate between the rules of a culture and what happens in practice is what we have called cultural literacy.

THE PROCESS MODEL OF COMMUNICATION

Gunther Kress, writing in *Communication and Culture* (Kress 1988a), points out that when the term communication was first used regularly— in the nineteenth century, in Europe—it mainly referred to the physical means of communication, such as roads, railways and shipping. It was only in the later part of the nineteenth century, with the development of other means of passing information, that communication came to refer to the print media, and later still to radio, film, television, video and computers.

Kress argues that although the old-fashioned notion of communication as a 'thing' was gradually replaced by the notion of communication practices, processes and mediums, this 'thingness', this notion of communication being based on the model of, say, goods being transported by barge or train, persisted in contemporary process models. In other words, communication practices are still largely understood, in process theories, the media, and everyday culture, in terms of the model of Sender–Message–Receiver.

From this perspective, communication is very much like the postal service. First, something is made or composed (written, spoken, signalled), then it is addressed, mailed and delivered (I speak, write or gesture to somebody), and finally the 'thing' is received and taken into possession (the message is read, decoded, accepted by somebody).

At the beginning of this chapter we suggested that three components were essential to any understanding and analysis of communication practices. These were:

1. the relationship between communication and culture;
2. the notion that meaning and practice are context specific; and
3. cultural literacy.

All three of these points are absent from the process school model, which is mainly used in texts that describe, theorise and teach communication practices in business, scientific and technical contexts. This model is largely derived from various American theories of communication that were developed in order to improve and explain communication practices within large organisations such as corporations. These various theories of communication were taken up in a diluted form and passed into everyday and, importantly, media culture. As a result they became the contemporary 'commonsense' idea of communication. We won't be dealing with the specific developments of this approach; an excellent (contextualised) account can be found in Mattelart's *Mapping World Communication* (1994).

We can illustrate the limitations of this model through reference to an example that often appears in process model texts: drawings or cartoons of two figures with 'bubbles' that contain their thoughts or messages (see Figure 1). The cartoon suggests that communication has been effective when both bubbles contain exactly the same content. In this cartoon, for instance, the symbols in the bubble sent by the person on the left correspond to those in the bubble belonging to the person on the right.

It is interesting to examine this commonly used style of cartoon and ask:

- what does it presume about communication; and
- what does it not take into account?

The first point that needs to be made is that in this example, and in the process model generally, communication is almost completely decontextualised. In other words, most background or relevant information, most contextualising detail, is left out. Secondly, it presumes that communication involves the same message being transmitted intact from the sender to the receiver.

Let's consider the cartoon in some detail. It suggests that the same message went from one brain to another, and was understood—received—exactly as was intended. This seems plausible enough, because

Figure 1 The process model of communication

Illustration by Pat Goon

the two characters look the same and presumably think along similar lines.

These two cartoon figures are in some ways marked as different, however, insofar as one is sending, and the other is receiving, a message. How do we know this is what is happening? Well, we can't say for sure, but if we employ our cultural literacy, we could say that the body language being employed by the two figures directs us to that interpretation. For instance:

- Reading from left to right (as we usually do in western culture), one figure 'comes before' the other.
- The first figure is standing 'at ease' and holding out a hand, presumably 'communicating' something to the second, who stands at attention, listening.
- The mouth of the first figure is open (we presume this signals 'speaking'), while the mouth of the second is closed (this signals 'silence').
- The first figure's head is tilted so that the gaze is directed above the head of the second figure, whose gaze is fixed, straight ahead (to check this claim, draw a straight line from the line of where the tips of their respective noses are pointed).
- Finally, the first figure's bubble seems to be emanating from a mouth, while the second figure's bubble comes from the head.

There is a very useful term that comes out of linguistics—**binary**—which refers to the way meaning is produced through a relationship between two different concepts. Binaries will be discussed in more detail in Chapter 2. It is sufficent to point out that the two concepts that constitute a binary:

- are normally read as a hierarchy; and
- only make sense, only come to mean, in terms of one *not being the other*.

An example of a binary is man/woman. Conventionally, the term 'man' can be understood, and comes to mean and have value, because it is *not* 'woman', among other things ('man' could also be understood, of course, as 'not boy', or 'not youth'). Historically the man/woman binary has usually been constituted as a natural hierarchy that values men over women; that is to say, the values of the two terms, and the relation between them, have historically been ideologised. There is a detailed description of the notion of ideology in Chapter 5.

Let's return to our cartoon and try to describe and analyse the binaries we can identify there. With the first figure, the following first terms of certain binaries might apply:

- manager or boss;
- active;
- in control;
- knowing;
- casual.

The second figure could be read in terms of the other aspect of each binary:

- subordinate;
- passive;
- being controlled;
- relatively uninformed;
- formal and attentive.

These binaries seem to characterise the relationship between the two figures in terms of difference; and yet the details which signal those binaries are hardly prominent in the cartoon. On the contrary, the cartoon in some ways does its best to 'play down' difference. Notice, for instance, the absence of distinguishing features in either figure. Their bodily features (hair style, shape of head, height, weight) are almost exactly the same, as are their clothes. We could reasonably assume that the two figures share backgrounds, cultural literacies and values, and think along the same lines. And yet as we noted earlier, this cartoon also makes use of what we could call *markers* (or **signs**) of difference. It 'tells the story' of a boss effectively communicating orders or information to an attentive, comprehending and docile subordinate.

COMMUNICATION AND DIFFERENCE

The cartoon needs to both mark and de-emphasise difference if it is to work. Why? Because there are differences and hierarchies in all organisations. On the other hand, if those differences are made too prominent, or are given too much emphasis, then the process theory of communication, which argues that messages are sent and received by people who are more or less the same, wouldn't really make sense.

What if we were to place greater emphasis on the markers of difference in this cartoon? What if we were to use the notion of difference as our departure point, and read a number of possibilities of illiteracy, disagreement, dissatisfaction, jealousy, resentment, cross-purposes, and competing or mutually exclusive agendas into the figures in the cartoon? In other words, what if we starting thinking about the almost infinite number of contexts that could be brought to bear on reading this cartoon, or the numerous cultural contexts that these two people don't have in common?

This is not to say that people don't understand what is being said to them, or that people don't communicate effectively. What it means is that markers of communication (words and gestures, for instance) will be read and evaluated differently by different people, depending on the cultural contexts they bring to any communication practice, and on the specific contexts in which that practice takes place.

Let us read the cartoon in terms of possible work relationships between the two figures. First of all, they are not on an equal footing: one of them is probably more powerful than the other, at least in this work context. One gives orders, the other receives them. One evaluates the other's responses and work, and is in a position to recommend whether that worker keeps a job or is fired or promoted. There is a power relation between the two which largely determines what they can say to one another and how they treat one another.

This power relation is not, of course, fixed. In certain work areas (technical work, for instance) the subordinate may become the more experienced, competent, and knowing of the two. In a non-work context, say at a squash club, the subordinate, who might be an A-grade squash player, will have much more status and prestige than the boss, who might be a D grader. Again, this will work to redefine the power relations between them, which may remain fluid across different contexts.

Let us take a more specific example of how different contexts determine what happens in communication practices. The cartoon might suggest that the two people are more or less the same, but generally people differ from one another in terms of:

- gender;
- sexual preference;
- age;
- religion;
- occupation;
- wealth;
- political affiliations;
- entertainment interests;
- social values;
- ethnicity;
- educational qualifications;
- cross-cultural experiences.

Let us pick up on one apparently small point of difference—age—and see where it could take us.

Let us presume that the boss is fifty and the subordinate is twenty years old. The 'message' in the boss's bubble is 'We need someone to clean out the toilets. Go and do it now, and have it finished in thirty minutes. And don't play that stupid loud music—it will stop everybody else in the place from concentrating on their work.' Now, according to the process theory of communication, that is what appears, without qualification, in the subordinate's bubble. However, while the subordinate might hear everything that was said, 'what was said' won't mean the same to both persons.

For the boss, the orders that were given were fair and reasonable. For the subordinate, however, the orders are an insult. The subordinate didn't take on this job (as an apprentice, say) to clean toilets. Traditionally cleaning public toilets is low-status work, normally reserved for unskilled workers. Moreover, it is a dirty, smelly and (usually) unpleasant job that is unlikely to do anything but lower a person's sense of worth or self-esteem.

Our twenty-year-old knows this. Through his familiarity with various texts (films, television shows, novels), he is aware that cleaning toilets is demeaning. This reaction is produced, of course, out of a particular set of cultural values and literacies specific to this twenty-year-old. On the other hand, the boss, our fifty-year-old, has worked at a variety of jobs, including cleaning toilets. The boss does not understand that cleaning the toilets might seem demeaning to the apprentice. Cleaning toilets is, for the boss, a sign of your versatility, a sign you are down to earth, a sign that you obey instructions and therefore in all likelihood are a good and valuable worker.

There might be various other points of contention which stop the boss's message from making its way, with its meaning intact, to the subordinate's bubble. The boss walks in and sees the twenty-year-old apparently idle. The boss 'knows' twenty-year-olds are lazy and easily distracted, 'knows' they 'don't like hard work', and have 'no respect for authority'. From this context, the boss cannot see anything in a twenty-year-old but disrespect and a disinclination to work. The twenty-year-old, on the other hand, hears the boss's words with a mixture of annoyance and practical objections. He is 'in the middle of an important job, and can't leave it at the moment'. Anyway, 'cleaning the toilets takes more than half an hour, and where are the cleaning materials and equipment?'

We could choose any number of examples of different contexts for our cartoon which would demonstrate that what appears in one bubble need not automatically appear in the other, no matter how clearly or concisely the message might be communicated. And we haven't even moved into the potentially more difficult and contentious area of cross-cultural communication. The process model of communication only

Jean Baudrillard is a French cultural theorist who has achieved considerable fame and perhaps even greater notoriety. Baudrillard's earlier works (such as *The Mirror of Production* and *For a Critique of the Political Economy of the Sign*) provided extremely important critiques and developments of Marxist versions of the relation between political economy and sociocultural contexts. From the publication of *Simulations* Baudrillard's work began to emphasise the ways in which (post)modern culture and technology erase reality and replace it with simulations, with what he chose to call the 'hyperreal'. Baudrillard has increasingly come to be seen—even within postmodernist circles—as a maverick, and his work a scandal. His perhaps intentionally provocative remarks about contemporary (non)reality (such as 'the Gulf War never happened') have made him a favourite target for writers critical of poststructuralist and postmodernist theories of meaning.

makes sense, then, as long as the differences we have referred to are more or less edited out of its diagrams and theories.

BAUDRILLARD AND CONTEXTS

We have been arguing that the various meanings and communication practices within a culture are produced because different contexts are brought to bear to frame signs and events differently. We take the position that meaning is always context specific; or, as Jacques Derrida might phrase it, 'there is nothing outside the (con)text' (Derrida 1988). We mentioned, however, that the process model of communication has passed into everyday use and acceptance, and dominates the way meaning making and communication are understood in important cultural institutions, such as the media.

Let's look at an example of how these two conflicting positions were played out when the print media reported on a visit to Australia by the French 'postmodernist' Jean Baudrillard.

Figure 2 shows one article, taken from the *Australian*, which was particularly sceptical of Baudrillard's Gulf War statement.

What Baudrillard argues in his book on the Gulf War is that much of what happened—the military movements, the air strikes—didn't make much sense in terms of military strategy. Rather than these activities being directed towards specific military goals—destroying the enemy, reclaiming territory—Baudrillard argues that much of what went on in the Gulf War was intended to create the scenario, the event, the theatre

Figure 2 'Philosopher's art escapes the duty of reality'

The French Government and its protégé, rogue philosopher Monsieur Jean Baudrillard, could hardly take official offence when Australian Customs impounded his photographic exhibition, pending payment of duty, after rejecting it as art—under his philosophy, the photos may not even exist.

In fact, under M. Baudrillard's radical 'hyper-reality' philosophy, we're all victims of cultural orgasm and mass-media hype and the Customs service itself along with this newspaper—and you who think you're really reading it—may not exist.

So it has to be said a 'hyper-real' international incident was averted after last-minute federal/State ministerial intervention secured the release of the 50 photographs only hours before the exhibition was due to open in Brisbane.

The man and his photographs are real enough for Brisbane's Institute of Modern Art to be outraged that Customs does not deem any photographs as art.

These events, if they ever took place, began when Brisbane's Griffith University and the institute convinced the acclaimed French theorist and philosopher-turned-artist to bring his photographs to Australia, with the sponsorship of the French Ministry for Foreign Affairs.

M. Baudrillard duly turned up in Brisbane last month with 50 photographs, for an Australian tour, which will include a two-day symposium on his philosophies in Brisbane this weekend.

Nevertheless, his entire Brisbane exhibition, titled The Ecstasy of Photography, was deemed merely photographs and not art by Customs in Brisbane, and demanded excise duty of almost $16,000.

In desperation the Institute of Modern Art turned to Queensland's Minister for the Arts, Mr Wells, who in turn contacted the federal Minister for Customs, Senator Schacht.

A 'facilitation' was reached under which the photographs were released after the institute lodged a surety of almost $16,000, essentially guaranteeing the exhibition was art, was here for public display and would not be sold in Australia.

M. Baudrillard—who wrote a book denying the Gulf War happened and believes mankind has burnt itself out since the cultural orgy of the 60s—was more philosophical.

'Maybe it's not art, not at all. Maybe it's not art in the sense that they are not aesthetic objects,' a bemused M. Baudrillard said modestly.

M. Baudrillard took up photography—after being given a camera five years ago—even though he believed art and just about everything else is dead.

As Griffith University's Dr Nicholas Zurbrugg, who is researching M. Baudrillard's legacy for the 90s, said: 'The man who said art was dead then became (a photographic) artist, but when his art got to Australia the Customs said "Your art isn't art". Perhaps they've read him.'

© *The Australian*. Robbins 1994:6

of war. That is, various military activities were performed in order to produce the illusion of a conventional war narrative or story.

In considering Baudrillard's argument, it is worthwhile mentioning two other contexts, or **intertexts**, that might help us understand his claim that the Gulf War was largely produced for western audiences by the American military and media acting in concert. First there is the belief, in America, that the Vietnam War was lost 'back home'; that is to say, it was lost because the images and reports that were sent back to American audiences did not correspond to the official explanations and stories put out by the Pentagon. Official narratives were imposed upon material sent from Vietnam, but gradually alternative readings of that material emerged which challenged the notion that the Vietnam War was a 'just war' which 'made sense'. Viewed from this context, Baudrillard's claim that the Gulf War 'didn't happen' could be read as an argument that much of the activity that took place in the Gulf was aimed not at winning the war in the desert (that was more or less assured), but at winning a war of conflicting stories and meanings. Paul Patton makes this point in his introduction to a text containing Baudrillard's essays on the Gulf War:

> It was not the first time that images of war had appeared on TV screens, but it was the first time that they were relayed 'live' from the battlefront. It was not the first occasion on which the military censored what could be reported, but it did involve a new level of military control of reportage and images. Military planners had clearly learnt a great deal since Vietnam: procedures for controlling the media were developed and tested in the Falklands, Grenada and Panama. As a result, what we saw was for the most part a 'clean' war, with lots of pictures of weaponry . . . and relatively few images of human casualties, none from the allied forces. In the words of one commentator, for the first time, 'the power to create a crisis merges with the power to direct the movie about it . . . Desert Storm was the first major global media crisis orchestration that made instant history'.

> Patton in Baudrillard 1995a:3

The second context that might help us frame Baudrillard's statement is the United Nations 'invasion' of Somalia in 1994. When American troops poured on to Somalian beaches, they were met, not by the enemy, but by hordes of journalists and photographers who 'shot them' with their cameras. The dramatic night-time landing had no military significance in any conventional sense—the Somalian troops were elsewhere, and the Americans could have paddled in on surfboards in the middle of the day and still achieved the same result. The invasion was almost pure performance, designed to produce a 'result' . . . back home.

For Matt Robbins, Baudrillard's claim that the Gulf War 'didn't happen' could be framed in terms of only one context—here was an ivory-tower philosopher talking nonsense. Robbins knew that during the Gulf War bombs were dropped, people were killed, and battles won and lost, and yet Baudrillard seems to be suggesting that there was no physical reality to the Gulf War—no blood or bodies or battles. He doesn't consider the possibility that Baudrillard's comments could be contextualised differently. What Baudrillard could have been suggesting was that the events in the Gulf were about the creation of a coherent war narrative. This is not the same as saying 'nothing happened'. Rather, it might be suggesting that events—physicality and materiality—have no natural meaning. The Gulf War, for Baudrillard, could be read as a conflict not about national boundaries but about meanings—and their contexts. That such conflicts of meaning cause blood to be spilled demonstrates just how serious a matter meaning is.

A second example, in this article, of how meaning is both context-specific and tied up with the notion of cultural literacy, is to be found in the way in which Robbins approaches the question of whether or not Baudrillard's photographs are 'art'. Baudrillard suggests that they are 'not art in the sense that they are not aesthetic objects', a position the customs officials seem to have agreed with, since we are told they do 'not deem any photographs as art' (Robbins 1994:6). The customs officials probably evaluated Baudrillard's photographs in terms of a perspective that allows certain objects (paintings, statues) to be designated as art, but disallows this claim when confronted with more everyday objects (photographs, video stills, t-shirts).

When Baudrillard writes that 'art doesn't exist', he could be suggesting that the distinction between one set of objects (say, paintings) and another (photographs) based on the notion of aesthetic value (this is valuable, this isn't) is impossible to maintain because there is no natural or disinterested basis for this distinction. A number of objects, genres and mediums (for example, cartoons, jazz music, film) which weren't previously considered art are now objects of study in schools and universities, exhibited in galleries and museums, and marketed and sold as aesthetic objects.

It could be argued that the context in which an object is placed or located determines whether or not it is evaluated as art. There is an episode of *Doctor Who* in which the Doctor's spaceship, the Tardis, lands in the French art gallery the Louvre. When the Doctor (Tom Baker) and his companion eventually return to the Tardis they find an art critic (played by John Cleese) standing in front of the spaceship and explaining to his companion why it is a wonderful piece of art. Its status as art is produced by its (physical) context: it is an object in the Louvre, and it doesn't have any obvious function (it isn't a toilet or a cafe), so therefore it must be a 'work of art'. Of course if the art critic's cultural literacy had extended to the *Doctor Who* series, this would have introduced another context and changed the way the Tardis was read.

The main point that we have been making in this section is that meanings and communication practices are always informed by, and produced out of, different contexts. What we will do now is to look more closely at the notion of context in terms of the relationship between communication and cultural literacy.

CONTEXTS AND CULTURAL LITERACIES

We have suggested that communication practices are always produced, read and negotiated in terms of specific contexts, but what is a context? We have made the point that communication and meanings are not 'things'. What about contexts?

It is often assumed that contexts are stable sets of circumstances. Contexts are often understood as being a simple amalgam of cultural features such as:

- meaning systems (fashion codes, professional codes, body language codes or religious codes, for instance);
- material conditions (say, urban or rural); and
- participants or members (based on categories such as class, gender, age and race).

It is easy to presume that any specific combination of those different cultural features (that is to say, a context) can be used to read and explain communication practices. There are at least two problems with this presumption:

1. the perception as to what constitutes a particular context is not likely to be shared by everyone; and
2. the meaning of those communication practices will change across persons, places and time.

Consider the following example. In the US in 1992, Professor Anita Hill claimed that she had been sexually harrassed by Judge Clarence Thomas, who was at the time President Bush's nominee to the US Supreme Court. Hill and Thomas were questioned by (male) members of the Senate as part of the process of establishing if Thomas was fit to sit on the Supreme Court. Thomas reacted to this questioning by becoming emotional, and claimed that he was undergoing a 'high-tech lynching'. Hill remained cool and impassive, and handled questions in a competent and professional—and not emotional—manner.

The male senators believed Thomas, not Hill; and the Hill–Thomas affair, as it came to be known, was contextualised as a huge failure for the American feminist movement. Numerous feminists mulled over what had happened and why. There was a strong suggestion that Hill had failed to 'perform' as a victim—which allowed the men who questioned her to dismiss her as cold and calculating. Hill's communication practices were deemed ineffective by many because they didn't convince her immediate audience—American male senators.

In subsequent political elections in the United States, the number of women standing for office increased substantially, as did the number of voters willing to elect women to political office. In the wake of those results, feminists and other interested parties began to reassess the Hill–Thomas affair. Rather than being seen as a failure for American feminism, it was reasoned that the senators' disdainful treatment of Hill and her accusations had aroused strong feelings among women throughout the country. Feminists and political commentators were forced to recontextualise the affair: it became a significant moment in the advancement, rather than the failure, of American feminism.

How can we say that communication practices must be understood in terms of specific cultural contexts if there is no such thing as a completely stable context? There are at least two ways in which we can talk about stable contexts.

First, we could point out that in some contexts (the army, for instance) communication genres and interpersonal relations are very clearly delineated and regulated (the most frequent speech genres used, for instance, are likely to be 'commands' and 'compliance'). This doesn't really allow much room for negotiation (it is unlikely that a private would tell a captain that s/he didn't feel comfortable standing at attention).

Second, it is important to note that even in reasonably flexible **cultural fields** we often act as if contexts were stable. Certain ideas, stories and meanings come to be naturalised, and accepted without question—this is called 'ideology'.

An example of how ideology stabilises contexts can be seen in the way certain events—Churchill's speech about the British never surrendering to Hitler, or the Eureka Stockade revolt—are mythologised and pass 'beyond contestation'. In 1990 a group of Australian veterans of the ANZAC landing at Gallipoli went back to Turkey, accompanied by politicians and journalists, to commemorate the battle fought there in the First World War. Australian journalists reported these events in terms of particular **genres** (reminiscences, celebrations, appreciations) and **discourses** (again mainly military, but also patriotic); they were all about Australians commemorating a heroic and significant moment in their history.

The problem with this version of events was that it was natural only as far as most Australians were concerned. When curious Turkish journalists filed their stories they wrote about Australians coming to apologise for their invasion of Turkish soil. Australian journalists reacted with shock and horror. How could anyone 'misread' these events? The Gallipoli landing constituted almost a sacred narrative within Australian culture. But in Turkey the landing was part of a very different story.

How is it that contexts remain open to different readings and practices if cultural rules and ideologies work to stabilise them? One of the defining characteristics of cultural literacy is an ability to recognise the rules that apply in a context, and to negotiate them. Let's consider some examples of these literacies at work. A lawyer in a courtroom is prosecuting a rape case. At the same time the lawyer is dealing with a judge who thinks that raping a prostitute is not as serious a crime as raping an 'ordinary' person. The lawyer might wish to tell the judge that he is a misogynist, a bigot, a fool and fifty years out of date in his thinking. The speech genre to be employed is, say, 'criticism'—but how is this to be done?

It might be unwise, at least in this context, to use 'feminist' terms (misogyny, patriarchy, sexism) for two reasons. First, the institution of the law courts more or less demands that professional members adhere to a certain type of language, what we might call legal discourse. Second, it is possible that the judge will either not understand what is being said or, worse, will treat such comments as insulting, or as symptoms of scandalous politicising of the law, and react negatively.

To point out that the judge's attitudes are dangerously out of date by making use of appropriate legal discourse (references to recent precedents, for instance), or to put that same proposition respectfully to the jury (and hence bypass the judge), would be to demonstrate considerable literacy.

Players are supposed to abide by the official rules of a game, but in practice it is often a person's ability to move outside legitimate rules and moves that makes a difference. Consider the following example. Two people are playing a game of chess and 'black' is about to win. The player using white pieces 'accidentally' knocks the table, the pieces are overturned, and the game ends as a draw.

The rules of chess are straightforward enough, but there are all kinds of other rules—'unofficial rules'—that come into play and can be used in order to win, or to avoid losing, a game. The losing player makes a move that is not in the rule book—and gets a draw; after all, it would be 'bad form' to accuse your opponent of cheating.

Official rules obviously constrain the kinds of moves that can be made in any game—or communication practice, which is largely the same thing—but at the same time players can take advantage of those constraints. The rules of chess, and of every other cultural activity, from football to tax returns, more or less presume that people will respect the 'spirit' of those laws or rules—which leaves a great deal of scope for all kinds of 'illegitimacies'.

Consider this example. Two friends from Australia were teaching in Papua New Guinea many years ago and were asked to invite a young student, who was soon to visit Australia on a cultural exchange program, to dinner. The school principal wanted the student to learn Western table manners, and they were supposed to tutor her in these cultural conventions and 'rules'. What they explained, however, was not so much the rules of dining, but how the student could use those rules to her own benefit.

As the dinner proceeded, they explained to the student that when there was only one piece of potato or cake left on a plate, the student should ask, in as disinterested a voice as possible, if anybody wanted the last piece. The rules of etiquette more or less disallowed answers in the affirmative, which meant that the student could then say: 'Well, if nobody wants it, I may as well have it.' The student ate very well in Australia.

These two apparently different notions of cultural rules and conventions—as constraints, and as opportunities—are addressed very acutely in the works of the French cultural theorist and sociologist Pierre Bourdieu. His work will be discussed again, in greater detail, in Chapter 3.

SUMMARY

In this chapter we have argued that:
- communication practices are always informed by and produced within cultural contexts; and
- that cultural practices, and the contexts that produce and constrain them, are closely connected to the notion of cultural literacy, which can be understood as both:
  — a familiarity with the rules and conventions of a culture; and
  — a feel for negotiating those rules and conventions.

FURTHER READING

Baudrillard, J. 1995, *The Gulf War Did Not Take Place*, trans. P. Patton, Power Publications, Sydney

Mattelart, A. 1994, *Mapping World Communication: War, Progress, Culture*, trans. S. Emanuel and J. Cohen, University of Minnesota Press, Minneapolis

——1996, *The Invention of Communication*, trans. S. Emanuel, University of Minnesota Press, Minneapolis

Chapter 2

Signs and meaning

This chapter deals with the relationship between signs and meanings. Meanings are not just 'out there' waiting to be identified or discovered, but are 'read into' signs. This process of reading signs and making meanings is not arbitrary, but is what we call an **ideological** process.

In the previous chapter we suggested that meaning was context-dependent, and that factors such as cultural literacy determined the kinds of meanings available to different individuals and groups within a culture. We pointed out that thinking about and analysing communication using notions such as context and cultural literacy means there are many things we can't take for granted. For example:

- meanings don't pass unproblematically from the brain of a sender to that of a receiver;
- contexts are never identical for, or completely shared by, participants; and
- communication cannot be completely controlled by the intention of the sender.

This does not mean, of course, that people don't claim to know what things truly mean. On the contrary, people frequently claim that everyone agrees, say, about what a word means, and behave as if that meaning is natural or beyond question. Consider the word 'violence'. Bill Clinton and other American politicians argue that the representation of violence on television 'does a violence' to children. This issue is taken up in an episode of *The Simpsons*, where Marge Simpson, horrified by what her kids are watching on the cartoon 'Itchy and Scratchy', mobilises community opinion to force the network to censor the violence. Instead of Itchy and Scratchy blowing each other up, they sit in rocking chairs on the verandah drinking lemonade and being 'nice' to each other. As far

Ferdinand de Saussure made a revolutionary contribution to the study of language and meaning in the lectures he gave to students at the University of Geneva in the first decade of the twentieth century. These lectures were recorded by his students and published under the title *Cours de Linguistique Générale*, or *Course in General Linguistics*. Saussure's insight that meaning was produced through the relation between different terms in a language influenced major theorists in the fields of structuralism and semiotics.

as Marge (and President Clinton) is concerned, cartoon violence produces 'real violence'. As far as Bart and Lisa Simpson are concerned, censoring 'Itchy and Scratchy' does 'a violence' to children ('it sucks'). Marge is convinced that she is right and her children are wrong. But when a section of the community mobilises to force the local art gallery to 'cover up' Michaelangelo's nude statue of David, Marge thinks that . . . a 'violence' has been done—which makes her reconsider the censorship of 'Itchy and Scratchy'.

There are two points that we are introducing, and dealing with, here:

1. words do not function as labels that can be unproblematically attached to things or acts or experiences; and
2. despite this, people do use words to label things and acts or experiences. However, what those words 'really' mean is usually a matter of negotiation, disagreement or conflict.

MEANING AS A SYSTEM OF RELATIONS

There is a 'commonsense' notion that things have an obvious and natural attachment to words. But theories were developed in the early part of the twentieth century which challenged the way meaning had been understood as the authentic reflection, in language, of a thing or of the world.

What happened was the development of new theories about meaning, called **semiology** (or the science of signs). These theories are now usually referred to as semiotics, and were initially proposed by the Swiss linguist Ferdinand de Saussure (Saussure 1989).

The key to Saussure's revolutionary view of language was the notion that meaning is *relational* rather than *substantive*. What this means is that there is no innate meaning attached to a language's terms, only differences. All meaning is produced through 'language systems' based on a notion of difference, rather than identity.

Saussure was primarily interested in what he called the linguistic sign, which he divided into three aspects:

1. **signifier;** *[handwritten: Communicator Physical form of representation]*
2. **signified;** *[handwritten: Concept]*
3. **sign.** *[handwritten: Word]*

What did he understand by these terms? The 'signifier' is the physical form of the sign, for example the written word or the spoken sound (the word 'elephant', for example). The 'signified' is the concept that is 'evoked' (the idea of elephantness). The 'sign' is the combination of the signifier and the signified.

A particular mark or sound 'means' something, according to Saussure, only because an *arbitrary* relation has been established (and institutionalised) between itself and something else. This is borne out by the fact that different cultures have different words for the same thing or concept. Saussure points out that the French use the word 'boeuf', the Germans use 'Ochs', and the English use 'ox' to refer to more or less the same thing (Saussure, quoted in Innis 1985:37)—although a Hereford is not the same as a Charolais or a Friesian. The meaning of each sign does not come from the thing referred to, but from the relation between the sign (boeuf, Ochs, ox) and the sign system (the French, German or English language).

Let's look at the question of how a semiotic system works to produce the 'meaningful' linkage between, say, words and things. Saussure insisted that a 'linguistic sign is not a link between a thing and a name, but between a concept and a sound pattern' (Saussure 1989:66). He used the term signified to refer to the concept, and the term signifier to refer to the sound pattern (or other material form).

For Saussure, the sign is the product of an arbitrary relationship between the signifier and the signified. For example, the signifier 'tree' (or 'arbre' in French) and the concept of a tree, when taken together, constitute a sign. This relationship of a signifier to a signified, which produces the sign, is worked out within the language systems that users have to deal with in their everyday communication practices. According to Saussure, there was always a complete linguistic system available which more or less determined what kinds of things people could do with language. Further, since the relationship between signifiers and signifieds was arbitrary—that is to say, not natural or logical—those relationships tended not to change, precisely because this self-contained relational system could not be 'reasoned' with.

Saussure's theories turn conventional notions of language and meaning upside down. Taking this insight further, structuralists and semioticians argued that semiotic systems were not produced by, or in response to, 'the world' (as a reflection or labelling of what was 'outside there'). Instead they edited out the world, and at the same time 'produced' the world, as and through a series of self-contained systemic relationships. The word 'tree' was not produced by the green leafy thing; on the contrary, the green leafy thing came to be understood, to be seen, and to mean in terms of semiotic systems.

Saussure's work has been extremely useful and influential, but is not without its problems. The most obvious difficulties concern the issues of the signified, intentionality and the arbitrariness of meaning. First, the signified. How, we might ask, is the signified different from the signifier? The answer is . . . that it isn't! The word 'elephant' is a signifier, but the concept it evokes (elephantness) is just another signifier (a picture in our mind, or the idea of a large animal that is supposedly scared of mice, or the smell associated with elephants; these are all new signifiers). Every time we use a sign, it gets translated into another sign. At no stage do we get the 'real' elephant, or a concept of elephantness that isn't produced through a sign system. Saussure more or less overlooked this point.

Second, Saussure presumed that every sign had to be 'put together' and sent by someone, and he strongly, if implicitly, emphasised the role of the sign sender. It is easy to see, however, that there are plenty of signs that are not intended. If you put on the only clean shirt you have, without caring what is on the front of it, you are not intending to act as a walking sign. This does not stop people from reading you in terms of your shirt ('Save the Gastric Brooding Frog', 'Kurt Lives', 'I am an idiot'). Further, we read the moon, the sunset and a lake as signs, and yet nobody produced those signs to communicate to other people.

Eco (1979) suggests that the American theorist C.S. Peirce overcomes this problem of intentionality in Saussure's semiotics by defining a sign as 'something which stands to somebody for something in some respect or capacity' (Peirce quoted in Hawkes 1977:126). This explicitly allows communication to be thought of as both intentional and unintentional, and is able to account for the ways in which meanings are read into the natural world.

The third problem with Saussure's work was tied up with the issue of the arbitrariness of meaning. We previously made the point that the link between words and things or acts was not natural; there was nothing essentially elephantish about the word 'elephant'. But there is a second, related point that must also be taken into account; although the use of words to designate or describe things or acts is arbitrary, it is also *motivated*. What this means is that the ways in which words are used and deployed, and the meanings they come to suggest, do not occur accidentally. Rather, meaning is always political. We could say, following

Lang not arbitrary

the lead of the German philosopher Nietzsche, that the production of meaning is always, first and foremost, a sign of power (Nietzsche 1956).

Let's consider these points in more detail. Saussure's theory of the sign does not entirely stand up to close scrutiny, mainly because of problems with the distinction he employs between signifiers and signifieds (or, more specifically, between sound image and concept). We can agree that a signifier—the word 'woman', or the word 'man', for instance—only comes to mean through its relation to other signifiers (what are known as **binaries**) in a semiotic system. The signifier 'man', for instance, can be understood as 'not woman', or 'not boy'. What about the concept, however, that supposedly goes with it? If I were to speak or write the word 'man', there is no single concept, or single thing, not even a particular biology, which corresponds exactly to that signifier. As an example, let us consider Figures 3 and 4.

Figure 3 shows a youngish man who who some people might describe as a 'hunk'. But is a hunk a 'real man'? If the criteria for maleness are exhausted by this representation, then most of the biological specimens that tick the 'male' box on forms aren't 'real' men. Do most men have muscle-bound bodies, jaws seemingly hewn out of rock, and tight, taut stomachs? Not really. And yet most audiences would identify

Figure 3 'Is this a man?'

Andrew Williams,
Courtesy of News Ltd

Figure 4 'Is this a man?'

Bill Ketteringham, Courtesy of
Bill Bachman/Guide Book Company

non-hunkish men as . . . men. They appear to have all the bits and pieces, in the right places, shapes and sizes, to qualify as men. But now look at Figure 4: is this a man?

Consider the response we got when we showed a first-year university class these images. We showed an overhead projection of the first photograph and asked 'Is this a man?'. The responses ranged from sniggers to 'oohs' and 'aahs' and whistles. We then showed the second photograph and asked the same question. Almost as one, the audience burst out laughing.

What this demonstrated was that not all men are men; or again, that what counts as maleness changes depending on the relations between different signifiers, and the context of those relations. Had we shown a series of photographs of older, working-class men, to a group of older men (or women), then inserted the second photograph and asked, 'Is this a man?', it is unlikely that anyone would have laughed.

The point is that there are no natural concepts that automatically and naturally 'attach' themselves to signifiers. If someone says the word 'man', people do not read this signifier the same way. What they do, in fact, is respond to the first signifier by producing another signifier, or series of signifiers. These signifiers are not necessarily shared by other people, and are different from the first signifier.

Meanings might be produced within semiotic systems, but why are different meanings produced? Semiotic systems do not, of course, produce and reproduce themselves. The influential role of Saussure's theories, and in particular the crucial distinction he makes between *langue* (the language system) and *parole* (actual speech), however, caused many later theorists to emphasise the study of the rules of semiotic structures, as opposed to the study of semiotic practices.

Saussure knew that semiotic practices were a mess, hard to make sense of, and difficult to categorise or systematise. Semiotic structures, on the other hand, lent themselves to a neat, controlled scientific approach. As Saussure wrote:

> The linguist must take the study of linguistic structure as his primary concern, and relate all other manifestations of language to it. Indeed . . . linguistic structure seems to be the one thing that is independently definable and provides something our minds can satisfactorily grasp.
>
> Saussure 1989:9

Saussure drew an analogy between language and semiotic systems and practices, on the one hand, and the rules of the game of chess and chess moves, on the other. The rules of chess, like the rules and categories of semiotic systems, are always complete and internally logical. Of course both chess rules and semiotic systems undergo changes, and can be studied *diachronically*, that is, across history. Diachronic changes tended to be viewed by Saussure and other like-minded linguists, however, as irrational forces 'distorting the logical purity of the language system' (Volosinov 1986:61).

Let us recap for a moment. Saussure's work and theories were extremely influential, and produced a kind of linguistic revolution, because they changed the way that people came to understand how meaning was produced. Instead of seeing language and semiotic systems as containers into which the natural meanings of the world were poured, Saussure made the point that meaning was relational; that is to say, meaning was produced, and the world was read, understood and seen, in terms of how signifiers were related to each other within semiotic systems. Further, each semiotic system was an abstract entity, which was complete and self-logical at any moment, and it was the rules and logics of those systems (*langue*), rather than the changes that took place within them across time, or individual semiotic practices (*parole*), that was the proper concern of linguistics and semiology.

We have already noted one effect of this Saussurean approach, which is that you end up writing about meaning and meaning making as if you were dealing with an autonomous and anonymous semiotic machine which arranged rules, categories and meanings in a neutral and dis-passionate way. There are a number of problems with this approach, the most obvious of which is that the production of meaning always involves, at some level, questions of power and politics.

Saussure was not particularly interested in how or why the signifier 'woman' could come to be understood as part of a binary such as woman/human, nor would he have been interested in the way in which that same signifier tended to be associated with 'negative' valuations (not reasonable, not intelligent, not responsible). Because of Saussure's pref-erence for the study of *langue* over *parole*, he would simply have rejected the questions we posed above as unscientific, illegitimate, or pointless. And this is not even to begin to take into account the equally crucial question of how the material effects of reality and the world are filtered or produced through semiotic systems.

SIGNS, HISTORY AND CONTEXTS

Saussure's theories of semiotics overturned the notion that language simply reflected reality in a natural and unmediated form. But if this was the case—if semiotic systems determined the way we saw the world—then it is not difficult to understand that the control of how and what meanings were produced was an extremely important political

V.N. Volosinov was a Russian linguist who wrote within what has come to be called the Bakhtin School. This school was made up of a group of writers, mainly active in the 1920s and 1930s, who wrote on a wide variety of areas including linguistics, literature and folk culture. Although the school wrote out of what could be called a Marxist perspective, the Stalinist context in which its members worked was intolerant of anything that diverged from strict official doctrines. As a result the school's members were persecuted, and the exact authorship of their texts, including Volosinov's *Marxism and the Philosophy of Language*, is in dispute. This text, which has been ascribed to Volosinov remains, however, the first, and perhaps the best, attempt to understand language practices in terms of specific socioeconomic contexts.

question. It is at this point that we need to turn our attention to the critique of Saussurean linguistics provided by V.N. Volosinov.

Volosinov was a Marxist linguist with a very different approach from Saussure's. His main criticism of Saussure's theories was that they constituted languages as idealised, abstract machines which edited out questions of language practice. In other words, Saussure's models were very much like the clean, smoothly running, perfect hospital in the British comedy series *Yes, Prime Minister*, which only ran effectively because it refused to take in patients.

Volosinov turned some of Saussure's major insights against him in order to demonstrate that there was no such thing as an autonomous language system, except perhaps in the mind of the occasional deluded Swiss linguist. If, as Saussure suggested, all meaning was relational, then the notion of *langue*, or a *synchronic* (that is to say, unchanging) semiotic system, did not correspond to any reality, but produced a reality. More to the point, the notion of *langue* and synchronicity could only be understood in terms of what they were not in a semiotic system—in this case *parole* and diachronicity.

Volosinov made just this point, but in a very practical way. How, he asked, could there be such a thing as a perfect, autonomous semiotic system? Since that system was constantly in use, and therefore constantly changing, it was never the same as itself. Moreover, as we discovered in the previous chapter, the production of meaning—the way people read things—is in no way strictly portable or pre-ordained. Volosinov had three important contributions to make on this point:

1. 'What is important for the speaker about a linguistic form is not that it is a stable and always self-equivalent signal, but that it is an always changeable and adaptable sign' (1986:68).

2. 'Words are always filled with content and meaning drawn from behaviour and ideology' (1986:70).
3. 'The meaning of a word is determined entirely by its context. In fact, there are as many meanings of a word as there are contexts of its usage' (1986:79).

Let's look at these three propositions and see how they help us to move out of the 'structure without mess, practices or people' that was the legacy of Saussurean linguistics. In other words, how does Volosinov help us to address the gender politics, say, of the history of the signifier 'woman'?

The three propositions we took from Volosinov can be summarised as:

1. signs are adaptable and changeable;
2. words—signifiers—have a history of meanings; and
3. the meanings that are read into signifiers, the meanings that are activated from a variety of potential meanings, depend on the specific context.

Now, this is a long way from Saussure's 'hospital without patients'. Volosinov implicitly accepts Saussure's proposition that meaning is produced through semiotic systems, but rather than seeing this as a natural and neutral process, Volosinov insists that the meanings are always the result of ideological struggles. That is to say, different groups in a culture—groups predicated on notions of, say, class, race, ethnicity, gender, age, profession or religion—work to try and ensure that 'their' meanings are accepted. Because signs are, in Volosinov's terms, adaptable, carry a history of meanings, and can be used in different ways in different contexts, the production of meaning is always open, always a struggle.

The signifier 'woman' has been the site of a number of ideological battles, of course, particularly during the past thirty years. In some ways we could say that the various feminist movements that have fought against sexism and patriarchy have been fighting not only for equal pay or social equality, but even more fundamentally to reclaim and renegotiate what is meant by the signifier 'woman'.

Why is the meaning of a word as important as changing material conditions? Because, as Saussure pointed out, reality, the world, and material conditions are not given, but rather are produced as meaningful through signs. What this means is that there is an important relationship between the dominant value or meaning of the signifier 'woman', and the way women are treated in a culture. If 'woman' is associated with emotionality, lack of reason, unprofessionalism and domesticity, then it is very difficult to change the material conditions in which women find themselves, difficult to help women gain access to different areas of a culture (government, professions, the public sphere) which supposedly require qualities such as reason and professionalism. And, consequently, it is difficult to get a culture to revalue those tasks traditionally performed by women (domestic duties, for instance). This is because, as the (circular) logic would have it, those tasks are performed by women, women are emotional and lack reason, therefore those tasks are not valuable.

THE POLITICS OF MEANINGS

A good example of this 'politicising of meaning' is to be found in the feature article shown in Figure 5, concerning the question of whether Australia was settled or invaded by Europeans, which appeared in a metropolitan newspaper. The background to the story was that primary school social studies syllabuses in some Australian states were now referring to a European 'invasion' of Australia, whereas previously they had referred to a 'settlement'. This change was disputed by some state governments, who attempted to restore the reference to a settlement. The article comments on this dispute as to the naming and meaning of this particular period of Australian history; we have included it here because it both discusses and aggressively participates in the politics of naming and meaning. Right Wing Journo. Not historian

On one level the author of the article, P.P. McGuinness, seems to be putting forward the suggestion that meaning is indeed contingent and tied up with politics, and not reducible to simple truths or easy answers. He asks the question about invasion/settlement, and states, in his first paragraph, 'There is no clear answer to this question'. His discourse clearly locates meaning and the writing of history within the domain of politics. There are references to the 'struggle to own our history' (paragraph 2) and the Orwellian notion that 'Who controls the present controls the past' (paragraph 7), both of which tie in with Volosinov's suggestion that meaning is always produced through conflict. And towards the end of the article he acknowledges the difficulty of teaching a 'sophisticated and balanced account of what happened in our history' (paragraph 19).

These references to the political nature of meaning making are replaced, however, with the notion that meanings or positions I agree with are somehow disinterested and beyond politics, while the views of those I disagree with are politicised. So while the article seems committed to the position of undecidability ('There is no clear answer to this

Figure 5 'A history of invasion ignores more balanced school of thought'

[1] Was Australia 'invaded' by Europeans, or was it 'settled'? There is no clear answer to this question, since any sensible discussion of the issues involves looking at the complex history of Australia since 1788 and indeed before that, and comparing it with the history of invasions and settlements in other countries.

[2] That is, it is a serious historical question to which there will never be a clear answer. But the recent row over the proposed new primary school syllabus in NSW which proposes to adopt a vocabulary which is not entirely categorical as to what happened in our history is not at all about history. It is about the struggle to own our history.

[3] Partly it is the indoctrination of little children in a view of what we, and they, are doing here and what they should think about it. This is the essence of the ferocious attack on the quite reasonable modifications of the syllabus which the Minister for Education has required of the Board of Studies.

[4] There is a generation of historians and school teachers who now act like the worst of trade unions, and who insist that their 'hard won gains' of the last 25 years should now be defended down to the last comma and the last dogma.

[5] The generation of Australian historians of the 1970s and 80s spent much of its time determinedly rewriting the history of Australia and especially the history of European–Aboriginal relations in Australia, from the point of view of the kindergarten Marxism which gained influence in the universities in those decades. Colonialism, imperialism, exploitation, genocide, invasion, conquest are all key words in this view.

[6] The up and coming historians, and the teachers, journalists and others who popularised their views, have now become the establishment of Australian history (along with the advocates of women's studies, gay studies, and so on) and they are vociferously defending the orthodoxy which they have managed to disseminate widely. Any historian who disagrees with them is either relegated to the sidelines, or, like Geoffrey Blainey, subjected to a sustained campaign of abuse and denigration.

[7] The new establishment is now concerned to insist that the very partial and biased view of Australian history which they have foisted on the educational system should be treated as the unquestioned and unqualified truth. They have espoused the Orwellian thesis: Who controls the present controls the past, and who controls the past controls the future.

[8] It is a system of thought control which, by forbidding the use of vocabulary which suggests that there are alternative views, prevents (it is hoped) the formulation of different programs or interpretations.

[9] Did Europeans invade Australia? Yes, in the sense that they arrived and occupied land. Did they consider it an invasion? No, not really, since they assumed that they had the right to take what seemed to them a largely unoccupied and unused country, to care for it, and to take account of the welfare of its 'savage' occupants.

[10] The British settlers–invaders were far less brutal in their approach to the whole process than were most other groups, anywhere in the world. They considered themselves settlers, and the British government on numerous occasions gave instructions as to the protection of the welfare of the Aboriginal inhabitants, and even respect for their land rights.

[11] It was later generations of settlers and native-born Australians, in particular, who often enough under the slogans of national independence and even

republicanism rejected the civilising influence of the Westminster administration and engaged in sometimes brutal policies towards the Aborigines.

[12] Possibly the worst offenders were the religions, who believed that they were saving the souls of the Aborigines by destroying their culture and traditions. Were the missionaries invaders?

[13] And of course the pre-1788 history of Australia was a history of successive waves of immigration by the precursors of present-day Aborigines, of internecine warfare over hunting lands, of violent conflict and the disappearance of many tribes or bands.

[14] Who invaded Australia first? Even the smallpox epidemic which seems to have killed many of the pre-1788 population seems more likely to have come from trading contact with Asia than from the Europeans.

[15] Invasion or no invasion, the history of the European presence in Australia has been one just as much of settlement, of cultivation, of investment and of the building of an infrastructure of government, industry and urbanisation. The impact of this on the Aboriginal population was in many cases harmful; in many cases beneficial.

[16] It is clear that the Aboriginal cultures, no more than the indigenes of the Americas, could not come to terms with the impact on them of European civilisation and religion: the Europeans usually had not the faintest idea of what they were dealing with, any more than did the indigenes. But again the history of Australia is not nearly so bloody or so brutal as that of the Americas, particularly those parts of the Americas which were faced with Spanish, Portuguese, and French imperialism.

[17] There is absolutely no doubt that one European power or another would have invaded, annexed, occupied, settled—choose your terminology—Australia if the British had not staked their claim first. La Perouse nearly made it first; had it not been for the French Revolution France might in any case have displaced the tiny British enclave; any other of the various hungry imperial powers of the 19th century would have moved in given a chance.

[18] The simple truth is that, given the alternatives of the times, the Aborigines were extremely lucky that it was the relatively gentle British (relatively— the Irish thought otherwise) who got here first.

[19] Now, of course, it is difficult to teach a sophisticated and balanced account of what happened in our history without taking into account the European impact on the indigenes, since many things which were done in its course by the Europeans to the Aborigines were, and are in retrospect, horrifying. But this is not the whole of Australian history, as many of the Aborigines themselves are perfectly aware.

[20] Many of the things which were done to the Aborigines were not about genocide or racism, as is now so frequently pretended, but were the social policy orthodoxies of their day. The removal of children from single mothers and their institutionalisation was a cruelty inflicted on whites, in quantitative terms, much more than on blacks.

[21] The notion that Australian history should be taught, to little children in schools and colleges, as the history of an invasion is the product of a political propagandistic version of history. Our history does not belong to an undistinguished syllabus committee of pedants but to the community as a whole.

The *Australian*. McGuinness 1994:15

question'), at the same time it makes clear that there is a clear, disinterested answer, or series of answers (the author's) and a politicised answer (the 'invasion' position).

How does the author move from undecidability and complexity to clear answers? First, he sets the stage for valuing one position over another by appealing to categories and criteria which are supposedly neutral; examples of this are the categories of, and criteria for, a 'sensible discussion' (paragraph 1) and 'the simple truth' (paragraph 18). A sensible discussion is supposedly what is happening in this article, and after that 'discussion', we will be able to identify 'the simple truth'.

We referred earlier in this chapter to the notion of binaries; in other words, each term in a signifying system is related to another term, and meaning is produced through identifying what that term is not; 'good', for instance, is not 'bad'. If this article constitutes a 'sensible discussion', what other terms are deployed to constitute binaries here? A sensible discussion would presumably not involve 'indoctrination' (paragraph 3), 'ferocious attacks on . . . reasonable modifications' (paragraph 3), 'dogma' (paragraph 4), 'vociferously defending . . . orthodoxy' (paragraph 6), 'abuse and denigration' (paragraph 6), a 'partial and biased view' (paragraph 7) and 'a political propagandist version of history' (paragraph 21). In this way, the article takes the first step towards replacing the notion that meaning is political with the notion that 'I am sensible, and the other is political'.

This is first step in the production of the binary 'sensible/political'. The second step is to denigrate the term political, and those who hold 'political' views; in other words, the author's 'sensible discussion', having castigated the 'invasion' camp for their 'abuse and denigration', quickly moves to denigration. 'There is a generation of historians and school teachers,' he writes, 'who now act like the worst of trade unions' (paragraph 4), who have rewritten history 'from the point of view of . . . kindergarten Marxism' (paragraph 5); they constitute 'an undistinguished syllabus committee of pedants' (paragraph 21). 'Trade unions', 'Marxism' and 'syllabus committee' are all used pejoratively here; just to make sure this is understood, however, these terms are accompanied by less equivocal terms of 'abuse' ('worst of', 'kindergarten', 'undistinguished', 'pedants').

The author's 'sensible discussion' is supposedly based on taking into account the complexities and undecidability of history (What constitutes an invasion? Would things have been worse if another country had settled/invaded Australia?). The 'invasion' camp does not take this into account, he argues, because they are politically motivated: they are casually explained as 'the products of kindergarten Marxism' who have 'become the establishment of Australian history (along with the advocates of women's studies, gay studies, and so on)' (paragraph 6). The 'invasion' group are located on the other side of a 'sensible discussion' because they are abusive and have no sensitivity for complexities.

The first part of the struggle over meaning in this article revolves around establishing the binary sensible/political, with the author occupying the positive side, and 'invasionists' the negative side. The author has opened the way for the acceptance of his version of events by discrediting his opponents, and emphasising how different he is from them. The second step is to tell 'the simple truth' about settlement/invasion. This means denying, or at least questioning, the validity of the Aboriginal claim that their people were the victims of European violence.

We pointed out, towards the beginning of this chapter, that the word 'violence' was one of the most important and contested of signifiers; the right to decide what constitutes violence is, of course, a very powerful weapon. The author is aware of this point, and he moves to question the charge of European violence:

> Did Europeans invade Australia? Yes, in the sense that they arrived and occupied land. Did they consider it an invasion? No, not really, since they assumed that they had the right to take what seemed to them a largely unoccupied and unused country, to care for it, and to take account of the welfare of its 'savage' occupants (paragraph 9).

What strategies of argumentation are being employed here? The question of settlement/invasion seems to be reduced to a simple relativism:

- yes, the British more or less did invade, but no they didn't because they didn't know anyone was here; and
- anyway, the people who were here were savage; and
- the British only wanted to care for the land and those savage people (who weren't really there).

This reduction relies on two ploys:

1. Any notion of violence is more or less removed from the idea of 'invasion'. There is no reference to mass slaughter, rape or depopulation; the British simply 'arrived and occupied land'.
2. It wasn't an invasion because the British acted on the best of intentions: the country was unoccupied, and they felt duty bound to help out those people who didn't occupy it.

Leaving aside the obvious contradiction in the second rationale, we can focus on two crucial moves in this paragraph which repeat the tendency to depoliticise and naturalise those meanings the author is trying to promote:

1. if there was an invasion, it wasn't such a bad thing, since it is produced here as bloodless (the British 'arrived and occupied'); and
2. perhaps more important, the failure of the British to 'see' that the country was occupied, and their assumption of the burden of taking care of the 'savages', are made to seem innocent and depoliticised.

The author doesn't wish to address the notion, for instance, that failing to treat other groups as human, or assuming that a group needs taking care of, is predicated on a violence, in this case racist violence. The relativistic argument that is presented here (as the 'simple truth') is that there is nothing political or violent about designating other peoples as inhuman or inferior.

There was nothing particularly violent about the British settlement/invasion of Australia, so the argument goes. If there were problems, they were mostly due to the failure of Aboriginal peoples in coming 'to terms with the impact on them of European civilisation and religion' (paragraph 16). Notice the important shift in meaning here: we are dealing not with British violence but with the 'failure' of Aboriginal cultures and societies. Indeed, it was 'extremely lucky' for the Aboriginal peoples that they were 'invaded' by the British; after all, 'the history of Australia is not nearly so bloody or so brutal as that of the Americas, particularly those parts of the Americas which were faced with Spanish, Portuguese, and French imperialism' (paragraph 16).

Finally, the author admits, after carefully editing out or de-emphasising the violence done to Aboriginal peoples, that 'many things which were done . . . by the Europeans to the Aborigines were, and are in retrospect, horrifying' (paragraph 19). But this admission turns out to be another form of relativisation, another version of 'if you think this is bad, you should see South America'. The important phrase here is 'in retrospect'. From the privileged, and presumably more civilised, position we now occupy we can agree that mass slaughter was not a good thing, but at the time perceptions—at least the perceptions of the whites, which is all that matters here—were quite different. What happened was not 'genocide or racism', but rather 'the social policy orthodoxies of their day' (paragraph 20).

What this article is 'about' is the meaning of the word 'violence', and the legitimacy of deciding what constitutes violence and what doesn't. Aboriginal peoples would hardly be likely to accept this meaning of British violence; they could point out, for instance, that it wasn't the social orthodoxy of Aboriginal peoples. Nor would many Jewish or Gypsy or Slavic peoples, or homosexuals or communists who were persecuted during the Nazi period, nod sagely and say 'Ah yes, those German social policy orthodoxies of the day'.

Aboriginal perspectives and meanings are absent from this article, as are the arguments of the historians who favour the 'invasion' line. What we have here is a site in the print media which purports to be 'discussing' meanings, but which ensure, through various strategies, that only one set of meanings will appear to be 'balanced', 'sensible' and 'truthful'. This newspaper article is only one of a number of sites within a culture where the conflict over meanings—what Volosinov called the conflict of ideologies—is played out. Like the various discussions of meaning and gender, these conflicts produce realities rather than mirroring them.

SUMMARY

We can summarise the relationship between signs and meanings in three main points. First, meanings are relational. That is, meanings are produced through the relations between signs. Signs do not possess meanings in and of themselves.

Second, the interpretation of a signifier is always made through another signifier.

Third, the production of meaning is an area of ideological contestation.

FURTHER READING

Innis, R. (ed.) 1985, *Semiotics: an Introductory Anthology*, Indiana University Press, Bloomington

Volosinov, V.N. 1986, *Marxism and the Philosophy of Language*, trans. L. Matejka and I. Titunik, Harvard University Press, Cambridge, Massachusetts

Chapter 3

Cultural literacies and practices

In this chapter we are going to look at the notion of cultural practice in terms of three contextualising factors:

1. cultural rules, conventions and structures;
2. individual communication and meaning making activities of everyday life; and
3. the notion of cultural literacy.

COMMUNICATION AS PRACTICE

In previous chapters we have emphasised the point that communication is concerned with making meanings, and that the kinds of meanings that are made depend very much on the specific cultural contexts and literacies involved; that is to say, we have suggested that communication is first and foremost a cultural practice.

Communication can't be confined to those situations where people talk, write, or overtly signal to one another. Most people, for example, would accept that two people talking to one another constitutes communication; and they would probably also accept such diverse activities as sports fans shouting abuse at an opposing team, members of an audience laughing at a scene in a film, or even a student yawning and then falling asleep during a university lecture, as examples of communication.

Communication practices are not, of course, exhausted by these examples. Much of the work that has been produced in cultural studies in the last twenty years has been concerned to demonstrate the communicative aspect of all cultural activities, including attending a concert, playing a video game, reading a magazine, wearing different styles or combinations of clothes, praying in a church or temple, or tattooing a picture of Daffy Duck on your chest. These can be understood as communication practices. The questions that need to be asked are:

- How can we read these activities as forms of communication?
- What precisely do they communicate?
- To whom?
- How are specific meanings produced in communication practices?
- How do these meanings influence or regulate the kinds of activities that people engage in or perform?

Communication takes place when someone 'makes a meaning' out of a thing or an activity, even when there was no attempt to signal anything to or by anyone. Let's return to C.S. Peirce's definition of a sign that we introduced in Chapter 2: it is 'something which stands to somebody for something in some respect or capacity' (quoted in Hawkes 1977:126). This definition moves the emphasis away from the notion of communication as an exclusively intentional form of signalling, to the idea of communication as an exercise in the production and negotiation of signs.

Peirce's definition of a sign is important for three main reasons:

1. meaning making (and therefore communication) is something that occurs all the time;
2. the production of meaning often occurs outside overt forms of communication; and
3. everything we do can be produced as a sign, as meaningful—that is to say, can communicate something to someone.

Because of the preceding three points, communication must be understood as necessarily tied up with, and in a sense indistinguishable from, the notion of *cultural literacy*.

CULTURAL LITERACY

When the term literacy is used in, say, the media, the reference is usually to reading and writing skills. The notion of literacy doesn't have to be confined to this narrow meaning, however; it can be understood in a more general sense. We use the concept to refer to a working familiarity with:

- the rules, both official and unofficial, by which various **cultural fields** operate;
- the genres and discourses that characterise different cultural fields; and

■ the relationship, within a culture, between economic and **cultural capital.**

An example of cultural literacy can be seen in the Japanese film *Tampopo*. Some Japanese businessmen are having a meal at an exclusive French restaurant in Tokyo. In keeping with the 'rules' of Japanese business culture, group behaviour is strictly hierarchical. The exact nature of the pecking order is quite easy to read because each person waits for his superior to speak or act first.

Things change once the group members have to 'perform' in the French restaurant; that is, as soon as they are required to be literate in the cultural field of French food and wine. The leader of the group is obviously illiterate in this area: he can't make any sense of the food menu, and doesn't know which wines go with different meals. All of his colleagues, except for the last and lowliest, are similarly illiterate—they order what their boss ordered.

The last to order, a young businessman who has been treated with disdain by the rest of the group, turns out to be extremely literate in French food and wine. He recognises, reads and analyses the menu, and employs this skill and information in his practices. He chats confidently and intelligently with the head waiter, asks knowledgeable questions, and makes extremely 'tasteful' decisions. All his colleagues are very impressed, and this obviously augurs well for his promotion up the corporate pecking order.

The point made by the film is that he has displayed two forms of literacy:

1. he has demonstrated that he is literate inside a French restaurant; and
2. he is literate inside his own business culture, since he has understood how to use this first literacy to impress his colleagues.

There are two aspects of this kind of literacy that set it apart from the more conventional version, which relates to reading and writing skills:

1. literacy is understood as potentially referring to all fields, genres, discourses and mediums within a culture, and even across cultures; and
2. literacy is not simply understood as a kind of retrieval of rules (for instance, the grammatical rules of a language); instead, it refers to a connection between the recognition, production and retrieval of what is constituted as information, on the one hand, and its use or deployment as a communication practice, on the other.

There is, of course, a politics, and considerable cultural capital, tied up with defining what constitutes literacy. Even when definitions of literacy are broadened to take into account wider fields, they usually confine themselves to the reproduction of what we can call 'high' cultural material or information. Think of the newspaper articles that appear every few months complaining that eighteen-year-olds don't know what the Gettysburg address was, or how many plays Shakespeare wrote, or the fruit that prompted Newton to work out his theory of gravity.

There are, of course, very few articles complaining that most fifty-year-olds don't know anything about using a computer.

How does the notion of cultural literacy 'get translated' into people's practices? In order to explain this, we need to add three important concepts—cultural field, **habitus** and cultural capital—taken from the work of the French sociologist Pierre Bourdieu. We'll use these new concepts to demonstrate how cultural practices 'come about'.

Cultural fields and cultural capital

A cultural field can be be defined as:

- a series of specific institutions, rules, categories, designations, appointments and titles which constitute an objective hierarchy, and produce and authorise certain discourses and activities, on the one hand; and
- the conflict which is involved when groups or individuals attempt to determine what constitutes capital within that field, and how that capital is to be distributed, on the other.

Bourdieu understands the concept of cultural field to refer to fluid and dynamic, rather than static, entities. Cultural fields are made up not simply of institutions and rules, but of the interactions between institutions, rules and practices.

What do we understand by the term 'capital'? Richard Harker, Cheleen Mahar and Chris Wilkes, in their book *An Introduction to the Work of Pierre Bourdieu*, describe Bourdieu's use of capital in these terms:

> the definition of capital is very wide for Bourdieu and includes material things (which can have symbolic value), as well as 'untouchable' but culturally significant attributes such as prestige, status and authority (referred to as symbolic capital), along with cultural capital (defined as culturally-valued taste and consumption patterns) . . . For Bourdieu, capital acts as a social relation within a system of exchange, and the term is extended 'to all the goods, material and symbolic, without distinction, that present themselves as rare and worthy of being sought after in a particular social formation'.

Harker, Mahar and Wilkes 1990:13

is power capital?

The amount of power a person has within a field depends on that person's position within the field, which in turn is based, to a large extent, on the amount of capital the person possesses. At the same time, one of the advantages of being in a position of power is that it enables groups or agents to designate what is 'authentic' capital. Further, cultural capital is sometimes difficult to identify because it is bound up, among other things, with a person's ability to effectively read what can and cannot be done, and what is and isn't valued, within a cultural field.

Perhaps the most important thing to understand about the relationship between cultural fields and cultural capital is that capital value is largely determined within, and often confined to, a particular field—although overlapping does occur. In contemporary western youth culture—say in a nightclub—a familiarity with current dance music, an ability to gyrate for hours without collapsing, a certain dress sense, an ability to hold your alcohol, an ability to carry on a conversation when you can't hear what the other person is saying—as well as a firm butt—would probably all qualify as capital. These abilities might not, however, constitute capital in, say, the diplomatic service; then again, they just might.

There are obviously strong connections between the kinds of social, political, economic and cultural details that characterise groups of people, and the kinds of practices (from eating habits to movie-watching preferences). How do **cultural trajectories** (maps of people's cultural history, if you like) tie in with specific practices?

Let's look at a few examples. The first is the film *The Flintstones*. At the beginning of the film there are two couples—Fred and Wilma, and Barney and Betty—who are very close friends and share attitudes, tastes and values. By the middle stages of the film, however, serious tensions have arisen between the two couples, who now tend to accentuate certain important differences that divide them. There is a crucial scene in which Fred, the newly rich executive, is having dinner at an expensive restaurant with Wilma. When Betty and Barney turn up, Fred patronises and eventually insults them to the extent that their friendship is apparently destroyed.

When we try to make sense of what has happened here, the only major points of difference we can identify are that Fred now earns more money and has a better job. That might explain why Barney is resentful, except that Barney only becomes resentful after Fred changes his behaviour. How can we 'make sense' of Fred's behaviour, Barney's responses, and the breakdown of their friendship? Something happens to Fred Flintstone which changes his attitudes, values and practices and therefore changes the way he 'reads' people (the Rubbles, for instance).

Fred and Barney are both working-class men. However, once Fred has become an executive and acquired a far greater income, the close relationship between the two families breaks down. The main reason for this is that Fred (and to a lesser extent Wilma) now has access to a whole range of possible goods and services (high-tech gadgets, expensive restaurants) which, at the same time, produce and demand new dispositions and literacies (Fred would eventually have had to learn to appreciate, and talk about, fine wines, for instance, rather than beer).

Within the field of 'quarry workers', Fred's values more or less matched the economic realities of his life. (Fred wouldn't have enjoyed high society, and wouldn't have been allowed in, anyway.) Once Fred moved into a different field, he was forced to transpose and develop his values to take into account the possibilities and new demands opened up by his increase in economic capital.

When the economic gulf separating the Flintstones from the Rubbles becomes too great, the two families were split apart. Why? Because Fred's new position in life as a powerful and wealthy man more or less demands that he look down upon people like Barney and Betty, whose economic situation is so inferior to his. In other words, once Fred becomes powerful and wealthy, he has to start acting as if he has always been powerful and wealthy, which involves naturalising both his own prosperity (intelligent people, the best people, 'winners', end up wealthy) and the poverty of others (poor people are stupid, are losers).

Cultural fields themselves are not autonomous, or uninfluenced by other fields. We made the point that fields are fluid and dynamic, mainly because they are always being changed by internal practices. Other executives at Slate's Quarry Company, for instance, might read Fred's promotion in terms of certain Flintstone 'qualities' being admired by senior management, and seek to copy them (being brash and loud would become significant cultural capital). At the same time, fields are influenced and changed by what happens in adjoining fields (Flintstone's success in accidentally inventing cement might prompt other companies in other fields to start looking for Flintstone types).

One of the ways in which Fred would be changed by his admission into this new field is that his ideas, values and practices would be influenced by high cultural taste and notions of *distinction*. Bourdieu explains distinction as a kind of habitus which is associated with the upper classes, but which has spread throughout various class groups and positions to the extent that it has been naturalised as good and valuable. We really don't have the space to explain distinction in detail here; it is sufficient to say, by way of example, that certain texts get 'canonised'. Fred might end up reading *Hamlet*, staring at and appreciating the *Mona Lisa*, and drinking and collecting vintage French wines. Why? Because these (and many other) cultural texts get taught in educational systems, reviewed in newspapers, performed in theatres and exhibited in galleries and museums. The more cultural institutions tell us how valuable these products are, the more people come to accept the 'truth' of their value.

During the second half of the twentieth century the advent of so-called mass culture challenged this culture of distinction; for example, cultural institutions such as universities started including popular and mass culture texts in their subjects. Eventually, the automatic assumption that high culture (ballet, opera, poetry) was good and valuable, and popular culture (film, television, rock music) was rubbish, largely gave way to a consideration (at least in some cultural fields and institutions) of how people used all kinds of cultural products.

From this perspective, a Pearl Jam song or a 'Far Side' cartoon is just as interesting as opera or ballet; more interesting to many, because they are being used by greater numbers of people. And academics writing textbooks are likely to explain the theories of Pierre Bourdieu through reference to films like *The Flintstones*.

The Flintstones film narrative provides plenty of examples of the way the relationship between field and capital influences people's practices. A second example is the cartoon, television and film character 'Batman'. Imagine we are at the stately mansion of millionaire playboy Bruce Wayne, also known to viewers (but not identified by the residents of Gotham City) as Batman. Bruce is sitting in his plush lounge chair when the Penguin, the Joker, the Riddler and several of their lackeys intrude. They threaten him, but Wayne remains calm, cool and decidedly detached. He eventually instructs Alfred, his butler, to see these 'gentlemen' (he uses the term facetiously) to the door. The next day the trio return, but this time they are met by the Caped Crusader, who is anything ('krunch'! 'blonk'! 'flam'!) but polite. Bruce Wayne and Batman might be 'different' people, but they share the same body. Why are they associated with such radically different practices?

Similarly, put Bruce Wayne into a dinner suit and have him sipping champagne at the ballet, and you have a particular kind of person whose behaviour owes something to his material context and background. Have the same Bruce Wayne change his dinner suit for a leotard, tight shorts, a cape, a mask and the Batmobile, throw in a gang of psychopathic criminals, and all that refined behaviour goes out the window.

How does the relationship between field and capital determine or influence the cultural practices that characterise Wayne and Batman? The most obvious example is the way the two personas interact within the two different fields. Bruce Wayne is in his element at cocktail parties and society balls precisely because he knows the rules of the field, and is able to reproduce them 'naturally'. He has the kind of cultural literacy that makes him feel—and look—'at home' in high society.

If a male guest walked into a black-tie function wearing ragged shorts and an 'I Love Bambi' t-shirt, Bruce Wayne would not punch him (zock!), kick him (clunk!) or throw him over the balcony (kerplunk!). Wayne would know that the fellow was obviously a little eccentric, but probably harmless. Anyway, it would be virtually unthinkable—that is to say, not within the values of the field—to zock! clunk! or kerplunk! anyone. He would walk up to the fellow, make a few patronising enquiries about his general wellbeing, and then instruct Alfred the butler to take him to the kitchen, feed him, give him a few dollars and see him (discreetly) out the servants' entrance.

Wayne would probably try and do the same thing if the Penguin turned up to gatecrash the private concert given by Madame LeFarge at stately Wayne Manor. Sadly, things would not work out quite so well, because the Penguin would probably shoot Alfred, set fire to the kitchen, and steal Wayne's van Gogh painting.

If Bruce Wayne were Batman, however, things would be different, because Batman's cultural literacy would enable him to read the Penguin's intentions. And while as Bruce Wayne he abhorred violence, and lived to patronise people, as Batman he'd know how to respond effectively to a criminal (zock! clunk! kerplunk!).

Bruce Wayne and Batman employ practices which are effective within the specific fields they inhabit, precisely because they both demonstrate an ability to understand, successfully negotiate, and demonstrate a 'feel for', the rules of the different games they are playing in. Wayne could have thrown the lower class intruder in the t-shirt out the front door. The dispositions and values associated with field, however, place a great deal of stress on paternalism, shouldering the rich person's burden, and displaying the kind of tolerance and social sophistication associated with 'good breeding'. It is in Wayne's interest that he carefully negotiate the rules, values and dispositions of high society so as to produce practices that are not necessarily written down or objectified, but which 'everyone' in the field 'accepts'.

It is important to understand that cultural literacy involves not just negotiating rules and values, but also 'performing' them 'in the right spirit'. An example is the sport of cricket, which is supposed to pride itself on its high standard of behaviour and its commitment to sporting ethics and ideals: this is where the expression 'it's not cricket' (meaning its not the 'done thing') comes from. The worst thing a cricketer can do is 'to be seen' cheating: a former Australian cricketer was more or less ostracised, and never played for his country or state again, after he claimed to have caught a ball which, replays showed, clearly bounced.

And yet cricketers frequently 'appeal' when they know the batsman isn't out, in order to intimidate the umpire. If you're 'culturally literate' you can 'cheat' in cricket, as long is it doesn't look like you're cheating.

Another example of this point can be found in the John Carpenter film *Starman*, and it is a particularly good example because it demonstrates that the difference between, say, laws (what people are supposed to do) and practices (what they really do) is forgotten even by practitioners. In *Starman* an alien, played by Jeff Bridges, is travelling across America by car with a woman played by Karen Allen. The woman does all the driving until Bridges points out that he has been closely observing her driving the car, has analysed and taken in all the rules and skills involved, and would like to drive himself. Allen reluctantly agrees, but almost immediately Bridges runs a red light and only narrowly avoids an accident. Allen abuses him, but Bridges replies that, after watching her drive, he had concluded that the rules about road lights were as follows: green means go fast, orange means go slightly faster, and red means go very fast.

Habitus *— Cultural upbringing & values associated*

Bourdieu refers to this partly unconscious 'taking in' of rules, values and dispositions as 'the habitus', which he defines as 'the durably installed generative principle of regulated improvisations . . . [which produce] practices' (Bourdieu 1991b:78). In other words, habitus can be understood as the set of values and dispositions gained from our cultural history that stay with us across contexts (they are durable and transposable). These values and dispositions allow us to respond to cultural rules and contexts in a variety of ways (they allow for improvisations), but those responses are always largely determined—regulated—by where we have been in a culture.

The following list describes the main points Bourdieu associates with habitus (1990b:52–3):

- Knowledge (the way we understand the world, our beliefs and values) is always constructed through habitus, and not passively recorded.
- We are disposed towards certain attitudes and values, disposed to act in specific ways, because of the influence exerted by our cultural trajectories. These dispositions are transposable.
- Habitus is always constituted in moments of practice. It is always 'of the moment', brought out when a set of dispositions meets a particular problem, choice or context. Habitus can be understood as a 'feel for the game' that is everyday life.
- Habitus operates at a level that is at least partly unconscious. Why?

Because habitus is, in a sense, entirely arbitrary; there is nothing natural or essential about the values we hold, the desires we pursue, or the practices we engage in.

This is not to say that these arbitrary practices are unmotivated, and that we act out of disinterestedness. On the contrary, all practices are informed by notions of power, politics and self-interest. But in order for a particular habitus to function smoothly and effectively, each person or agent must normally think that the possibilities from which s/he chooses are in fact necessities, common sense, natural or inevitable. Other possibilities are ruled out precisely because they are unthinkable.

The rules and structures of perception that pertain to a particular habitus are inscribed on, and in, individuals as if they were 'human nature' or civilised behaviour. Everything outside those rules and structures is usually understood, when it is forced upon us, as anything from horrific and barbaric to absurd and comic.

An example of how arbitrary structures and rules are produced as a naturalised habitus can be seen in Western meat-eating patterns; cows, pigs, chickens, ducks, turkeys and sheep are all slaughtered, packaged and consumed as staple components of a Western diet, while domestic animals such as cats, dogs and hamsters are (unconsciously) excluded from this category. When stories circulate about 'foreigners' eating cats or dogs, the usual response is one of disgust and incomprehension.

What is implicit in this reaction is the notion that it is proper to eat some animals because they are 'depersonalised' (herds of cattle, flocks of sheep, but not hordes of hamsters); and we often reinforce this act of depersonalisation by naming the meat differently from the animal (we eat beef, not cow; mutton, not sheep). Animals which we personalise and regard as pets, on the other hand, are almost impossible to think of as food. Imagine, if you can, a camper starving in the Australian outback, faced with the possibility of having to eat a koala to survive! Cannibalism would probably be an easier alternative.

This dilemma occurs in *The Restaurant at the End of the Universe* (Adams 1980), the sequel to *The Hitchhiker's Guide to the Galaxy*:

> A large dairy animal approached Zaphod Beeblebrox's table, a large, fat meaty quadruped of the bovine type with large watery eyes, small horns and what might almost have been an ingratiating smile on its lips.
>
> 'Good evening,' it lowed and sat back heavily on its haunches, 'I am the main dish of the day. May I interest you in parts of my body?' It . . . gazed peacefully at them.
>
> Its gaze was met by looks of startled bewilderment from Arthur and Trillian, a resigned shrug from Ford Prefect and naked hunger from Zaphod Beeblebrox.

'Something off the shoulder perhaps?' suggested the animal, 'Braised in a white wine sauce.'

'Er, your shoulder?' said Arthur in a horrified whisper . . . 'You mean this animal wants us to eat it?' whispered Trillian to Ford . . . 'That's absolutely horrible', exclaimed Arthur, 'the most revolting thing I've ever heard . . . I think I'll just have a green salad,' he muttered.

'May I urge you to consider my liver?' asked the animal. 'It must be very rich and tender by now, I've been force-feeding myself for months.'

'A green salad,' said Arthur emphatically . . . 'Are you going to tell me . . . that I shouldn't have green salad?'

'Well', said the animal, 'I know many vegetables that are very clear on this point.'

Adams 1980:92–3

Zaphod Beeblebrox is completely unconcerned at the prospect of eating the animal, but most of the party find it difficult to eat something that has been personalised to the extent that they have been talking with it. Arthur switches his attention to something that is about as depersonalised as you could find, for him (a green salad), only for the animal to make the point that green salads can be personalised, too ('I know many vegetables . . .').

Systems, rules, laws, structures and categories of meaning and perception can only function effectively as habitus if we don't think about the sociocultural conditions of their production and existence; what Bourdieu calls 'the forgetting of history which history itself produces' (1990b:56). Most Western cultures accept, for instance, that life forms are divided into categories, such as mammals, reptiles, amphibians, birds, insects and fish. These categories—which have their own specific characteristics—are used in producing stories about life on Earth, stories which start with primitive life forms (such as fish) that evolve, inevitably, into the highest form (mammals). There is usually a logic to these stories which explains, for instance, why dinosaurs died out and were replaced by mammals, and why human beings became the dominant mammals. Recently, however, evidence has come to light suggesting that dinosaurs sometimes behaved like reptiles and sometimes like mammals, and that their extinction, rather than being part of an inevitable replacement of reptiles by mammals, may have been accidentally caused by meteor falls or volcanic eruptions.

Those new details challenge the rigidity of the system used in the West to classify life forms, but still leave it more or less intact. Consider, however, the following excerpt from a short story by the Argentinian writer Jorge Luis Borges, quoted by Michel Foucault at the beginning of his book on Western taxonomies of knowledge, *The Order of Things*. 'This book first arose,' Foucault writes:

> out of a passage in Borges, out of the laughter that shattered, as I read the passage, all the familiar landmarks of my thoughts—our thoughts, the thoughts that bear the stamp of our age and our geography— breaking up all the ordered surfaces of existing things . . . This passage quotes a 'certain Chinese encyclopaedia' in which it is written that 'animals are divided into: (a) belonging to the Emperor, (b) embalmed, (c) tame, (d) suckling pigs, (e) sirens, (f) fabulous, (g) stray dogs, (h) included in the present classification, (i) frenzied, (j) innumerable, (k) drawn with a very fine camelhair brush, (l) et cetera, (m) having just broken the water pitcher, (n) that from a long way off look like flies.' In the wonderment of this taxonomy, the thing we apprehend in one great leap . . . is the . . . stark impossibility of thinking that.
>
> Foucault 1973:xv

Foucault's reaction to this extract helps us understand how arbitrary rules and categories of thought are, at the same time, both motivated and tied up with questions of power and politics. Two of the main binaries used, in the last two hundred years, to distinguish Western cultures from non-Western cultures were 'scientific/primitive' and 'civilised/barbaric'. Western explanations and narratives of the world corresponded to something called science, and possession of 'authentic' scientific systems for producing knowledge was a central marker, perhaps the most important marker, of whether a culture was civilised, like the West, or primitive and barbaric.

Moreover, it was only a short step from designating a culture as uncivilised to categorising its people as non-human or subhuman, and therefore without the rights accorded to civilised peoples. Most of the colonialism that occurred in the past two hundred years—and still goes on today, in different forms—was rationalised in terms of particular categories or systems of Western thought being privileged over those of so-called primitive cultures.

Perhaps the most crucial aspect of habitus, then, is that it naturalises itself and the cultural rules, agendas and values that make it possible. But there are also a number of other important points that can be identified in Bourdieu's definition.

First, conditioning associated with a particular type of existence, based on shared cultural trajectories, produces the habitus. Now this can seem a difficult notion, because we are not talking about something as straightforward as, say, the Marxist idea of class categories based on positions occupied within the economic sphere. Habitus is certainly informed by the idea of class, but members of a group share a particular habitus because of general cultural contexts and trajectories. A rather unusual example of this point is the John Carpenter film *Big Trouble in Little China*, which concerns the adventures of a swaggering, over-the-top American truck driver, played by Kurt Russell, in the demonised underworld of San Francisco's 'Little China'.

We refer to this as an unusual example because the film seems to be quite overtly concerned with denaturalising what we might call a macho American habitus (as exemplified by the practices of the Kurt Russell character) by demonstrating how that habitus does not take into account, nor cope with, 'oriental' experiences (involving magic and demons). All the while this is going on, however, it is evident that the American and Chinese communities share, to no small extent, a common habitus. How? One of the most important aspects of habitus is that it regulates the overall set of possibilities that a person can take up and negotiate; that is to say, it regulates what meanings, values and narratives—practices—are thinkable.

Kurt Russell and the Chinese characters in this film are separated by certain dispositions and trajectories (such as experiences of, and a belief in, magic and demons, on the Chinese side, and scepticism on Russell's side), but at the same time they have a great deal in common:

- the macho banter shared by nearly all the men;
- the acceptance by both American and Chinese characters of narratives and values associated with bravery, chivalry and romance; and
- the high degree of cultural literacy displayed by the Chinese characters in reading and making sense of Russell's overblown rhetoric and posturing.

These all provide evidence of a shared American/Chinese world view, a shared habitus, even as the film tries to suggest that America and 'Little China' are worlds apart. What largely produces this shared habitus, of course, is the pervasiveness of American cultural institutions and products (coming out of film and television, for instance) and their ideologies. Chinese families interact like families in American sitcoms, elders come out with sage, homespun wisdom, and gender relations are dominated by the narrative of romance. Habitus is constituted, as Bourdieu suggests, out of 'durable, transposable dispositions'. *Big Trouble in Little China* suggests that even in the apparently diverse cultural mix of the US, those cultures (whether based on race, ethnicity, or economic capital) can still be understood, to some extent, as sharing a habitus.

Moreover, because a habitus is transposable, persons from different cultures can still adjust their practices to fit in with different contexts. Kurt Russell's character, on finding himself taking part in an underworld expedition against Chinese demons, faces a challenge to the validity and practicality of his habitus. However, he is able to transpose that habitus, and the dispositions and values that characterise it (machismo, individuality, anti-sentimentality, cynicism, aggression, self-confidence, an obsession with individual honour, a sexist attitude towards women), for two main reasons:

1. because the rules of the two different games are not all that different (for instance, the villain is both an American capitalist and a Chinese demon, which suggests some kind of analogy between capitalist America and demonised China); and
2. because Russell is able to pick up, in a self-consciously clumsy and comic way, the knowledges and skills (involving ritualised combat, for instance) which allow his habitus to remain useful.

Habitus, as we mentioned earlier, is always 'oriented towards the practical': dispositions, knowledges and values are constructed, not passively consumed or reinscribed, by persons who use their understanding and feel for the rules of the game as a means of furthering and improving their own standing and capital within a cultural field. It must be stressed that at the same time as agents pursue their own practical ends through a manipulation of the rules of the game, what they construct as their 'interests' are themselves produced by and through habitus.

Let's return to Kurt Russell and *Big Trouble in Little China*. Russell is concerned to aggressively promote his macho reputation in order to attract the sexual interest of the heroine (played by Kim Cattrall), earn as much money as he can as quickly as possible (by gambling, for instance), and repay any slight or damage done to his honour. When Russell simply reproduces the postures, discourses and actions—the practices—of this 'tough-guy adventurer', he is comically ineffective (his rhetoric or pose, for instance, is often not attuned 'to the moment', not appropriate to the overwhelming odds he finds himself up against). He is far more effective when he isn't constrained to act as a fearless adventurer; when he acts and makes use of his skills 'of the moment' (for instance, by instinctively catching a knife and throwing it straight back at the villain).

Russell is most practical in his practices, and most furthers his interests, when he 'feels' his way through the game rather than deciding what to do before it is required. However, as we pointed out, those interests (maintaining his masculine reputation and honour, for instance) do not come out of a vacuum: Russell pursues them precisely because they have been constituted as interests for him. At various times in the film it makes more sense (in terms of personal safety, for instance) for Russell to drop out of the adventure; but that would mean, of course, rethinking what constituted his interests and thus the most crucial, personalised, and therefore unconscious part of his habitus.

Habitus always makes a 'virtue out of necessity'. This means that just because there is a close relationship between 'objective probabilities (for example, the chances of access to a particular good)' (Bourdieu 1990b:54) and 'agent's subjective aspirations ('motivations' and 'needs')' (54), people don't necessarily make those kinds of calculations and decisions freely, uninfluenced by habitus. On the contrary, Bourdieu makes the point that those decisions are always already made:

> The most improbable practices are therefore excluded, as unthinkable, by a kind of immediate submission to order that inclines agents to make a virtue of necessity, that is, to refuse what is anyway denied and to will the inevitable.
>
> Bourdieu 1990b:54

The Kurt Russell character's ultimate decision to reject the possibility of a relationship with the heroine, which would probably involve some form of domesticity, and take to the open road alone is an excellent example of making a virtue of necessity. The romance narrative that runs through the film insists that the chance of a relationship between the two be played out right to the end, but Russell's final, and seemingly disinterested, rejection of a relationship is an example of the way in which what will inevitably be denied is denied in a disinterested way, as if a choice were possible. The heroine is middle class, professional, and a feminist. Marrying Russell (a loud-mouthed, sexist truck driver) would be unthinkable, if only because the benefits of having Russell as a partner (his sexual attractiveness) would be outweighed by the negatives (What would her friends and colleagues say? How long before she became bored with his macho rhetoric and posturing?). Russell knows this, which is why he rides off into the night.

CULTURAL PRACTICES AND POWER

Bourdieu's notions of cultural field, capital and habitus help us to understand how cultural practices are simultaneously free and regulated, conscious and unconscious. But what part does power play in the regulation and negotiation of those practices? Bourdieu's theory of practice is based on a notion of power as both restrictive and productive; a notion he takes, implicitly, from Michel Foucault.

Foucault makes a number of general points about how power functions. First, power isn't a thing that is held by, or belongs to, anybody. Kings or queens were able to exercise power because it belonged to them—they received power from God. But for Foucault, power now functions in terms of the relations between different fields, institutions, bureaucracies, and other groups (such as the private media and other businesses) within the state.

There is a notion that, in democracies, power 'belongs to the people'. But for Foucault, not only are the people, as an organic group, 'invented' by politicians and others, people are themselves produced by, and subjected to, what he calls the forces of **bio-power**. Bio-power refer to the technologies, knowledges and discourses that are used to bring about the regulation and management of populations. Bio-power analyses, controls and defines the human subject, its body, and behaviour. In many ways it is analogous to what Bourdieu calls the habitus; bio-power, like the habitus, is a kind of 'writing of the body and the soul' which starts soon after birth, and continues throughout the subject's life. Every institution and field (school, church, sport, university, workplace, prison, pubs, club) leaves its 'mark' on subjects, shapes their taste (to love reading Jane Austen novels, to despise trashy romances), and orients and disposes their trajectories (to university, then to a law firm servicing the underprivileged), values and behaviour.

The way people come to understand the world, the values they hold, and how they treat themselves and others, are largely brought about, for Foucault, when people are subject to the apparatuses of bio-power. But bio-power, like the habitus, doesn't 'stop working' when people move on (say, from school to work). Once our ideas, values and bodies have been formed, part of the 'duty' associated with bio-power (and the habitus) is that we make sure that we remain good, healthy subjects; that is, we become 'self-regulating'.

There is a good example of this in the comedy series *Blackadder*, when the title character, played by Rowan Atkinson, finds himself attracted to what he thinks is a young man—it's actually a woman in disguise. Blackadder reacts to his feelings by interrogating his recent and long-term behaviour, desperately looking for some clue as to 'where he went wrong' and stopped being 'normal'. He finds evidence for his 'deviancy' in the most trivial matters (for instance, his fashion sense), and seeks out advice from people about 'what he's really like'. Of course when it's revealed that the 'he' is really a 'she', he feels immense relief—he's a 'normal and healthy' man after all.

Foucault's notion of power operating as a form of self-interrogation closely informs Bourdieu's notion of the regulatory dimensions of the habitus. In Bourdieu's terms, Blackadder's habitus precludes him from thinking of himself as anything but heterosexual, and when experience (seems to) proves otherwise, the habitus automatically 'kicks in' to defend itself (its values, dispositions, limitations) by branding the self as 'outsider'—in this case, as pervert or deviant.

Foucault would seem to be suggesting that there is very little escape from power, and that bio-power and its technologies and apparatuses completely regulate and control human ideas, bodies and behaviour. This is not the case. In contemporary culture there are countless 'authorities', such as cultural fields and institutions, producing discourses and knowledge.

People are often quite sceptical about attempts, on the part of institutions and their discourses, to control what they think and do: even 'official knowledge' has lost its status and credibility. Many people are perfectly willing to believe any number of rumours, originating from the Internet, about conspiracies to murder Princess Diana, or cover-ups of alien landings. On the other hand, just as many people take no notice of the latest scientific research which finds, say, that drinking red wine is bad for you, simply because there was probably a study a few months earlier suggesting that drinking red wine helped prevent heart disease. Because of this, it is becoming increasingly difficult to verify or authenticate much of what enters into the public domain, especially when it comes from sources such as the Internet.

Foucault not only demonstrates that power doesn't completely dominate people's lives and thinking; he also suggests that power is, first and foremost, productive. Bio-power and its technologies, institutions and discourses, produce a variety of categories of people and behaviour. But of course as soon as you produce categories of what is normal, healthy and good, you produce other categories—the pervert, the deviant, the troublemaker, the problem child, the homosexual, the hysteric, the kleptomaniac, the pyromaniac, the psychotic. In some ways, forms of social-scientific knowledge and research 'make these people up' as they go along. So power, for Foucault, literally 'produces its own opposition'—which means that, as well as dominating and regulating people's lives, it also automatically creates spaces where people work and think against it.

SUMMARY

In this chapter we have looked at the specific ways in which communication practices are produced within cultures. We pointed out that:

- practice is always something decided and negotiated 'of the moment', and therefore cannot be reduced to the level of a simple reproduction of the laws, rules and systems of a culture; and
- at the same time, practices are not produced 'in a vacuum': there are strong connections between a person's cultural trajectories, the

kinds of attitudes, values, and agendas they have, and their activities and behaviour.

Pierre Bourdieu's notions of habitus, symbolic and cultural capital, and cultural field enable us to understand how the attitudes, values, ideologies and dispositions which shape and determine practices need to be naturalised before they can become effective. In other words, we have to forget or edit out a whole range of other views and possibilities in order to produce our practices comfortably and 'naturally'. That there seems to be a perfect match between the attitudes, values, agendas and desires we have, and what is more or less objectively available to us, occurs not because each group in a culture has a 'natural' habitus, but rather because the habitus functions by making a virtue of necessity and by ruling out what would be difficult to achieve as 'already impossible' because it is unthinkable.

Bourdieu's ideas are complemented by Foucault's theory of the way bio-power functions to regulate and 'normalise' subjects. But just as the habitus is challenged and transformed as subjects move across different cultural fields, so with Foucault the many different competing 'authorities' and discourses engender a sense of scepticism in people, which helps to distance them from the control of bio-power. Further, bio-power, by creating categories of unnatural and unhealthy subjectivities, produces subjects ('the criminal', for instance) who are 'naturally' inclined to think and act against it.

FURTHER READING

Bourdieu, P. 1990, *The Logic of Practice* trans. R. Nice, Polity Press, Cambridge

Bourdieu, P. 1998, *Practical Reason* Polity Press, Cambridge

Certeau, M. de 1988, *The Practice of Everyday Life*, trans. S. Rendell, University of California Press, Berkeley, California

Chapter 4

Framing contexts

This chapter examines the ways in which we read and make sense of texts in terms of their cultural contexts or frames. Contexts function as cultural frames within which to make sense of texts, frames which operate through our knowledge of, and literacy in, a variety of other contexts.

Texts circulate widely within a variety of contexts and situation types. They last for a time and then disappear from circulation, perhaps to reappear later in a different form. Riddles, jokes, fashions, limericks, songs, advertising slogans and jingles, memorable lines from movies, characteristic sayings of public figures, whole texts and fragments of texts of all kinds are used and re-used within cultures in ways which take them away from any definitive original context.

For any text to be recognisable and readable it needs to draw upon already established and shared sets of meanings. It must be repeatable beyond its context of production, or what the French theorist Jacques Derrida calls *iterable*. That is, it must be capable of functioning repeatedly in the absence of an 'original' sender, an 'original' receiver and an 'original' context. Jokes and riddles are particularly good examples of texts which are iterable; for them to be meaningful, it is not necessary that we know who first told the joke, to whom, in what immediate situation. We laugh upon hearing the punchline to a joke, and so strong is this expectation that many people will laugh even if they don't 'get the joke', simply because it is the expected social behaviour in the context.

All texts carry elements, or traces, of context with them. Mikhail Bakhtin, the Russian critic and theorist, coined the term **dialogism** to refer to the way in which texts, through their relationships with other texts and other contexts, become charged with these traces. Any text resonates with the meanings of other texts, and other contexts or places in which that text has been. Thus a text does not mean in isolation, but exists in a dialogue with other texts.

Consider the following riddle:

Question: What were the two dingoes arguing about outside a tent?

Answer: Eat in or take-away?

How can we make sense of the dingo riddle without reading it in the context of a number of other texts and contexts? People throughout the world were aware of the mysterious disappearance in 1980 of baby Azaria Chamberlain from her parents' camp site near Uluru/Ayers Rock in the Australian desert, and of her mother Lindy's controversial claim that 'a dingo has taken my baby' (see Sanders 1993). The extensive media coverage and high level of informal debate about the event and the subsequent trials provide a huge body of intertexts (related texts), among them riddles and jokes such as this one. The riddle makes sense as part of an ongoing dialogue with other texts such as news reports, headlines, media interviews, legal trials, and conversations. Did Lindy Chamberlain kill Azaria, or was she taken by a dingo? The riddle is a chunk of dialogue that functions as part of a much wider-ranging intertextual dialogue which debates this and other questions, and in which many different voices take part.

As literate members of a culture, we employ our knowledge of other texts to make sense of what we see, read and hear, and when speaking, writing or communicating through visual or other media, we expect others to draw on **intertextuality** to make sense of our communication practices. But how does this intertextuality work? We won't necessarily have a shared set of specific texts with those we are communicating with, as happened to a large extent with the almost blanket media coverage of the Chamberlain case, where a body of texts was made very public on a mass scale.

INTERTEXTUALITY

In a given context, members of a culture can predict, to an extent, what kinds of meanings will be made. That is, we can 'unpack' texts by analysing their functional relation with a context (this will be discussed in more detail in Chapter 7). Intertextuality provides another dimension to this process of making sense of what is going on; we do this by reference both to the immediate context of situation and to the wider context of culture, through intertextuality.

Intertextuality refers to the process of making sense of texts in reference to their relations with other texts. It involves the circulation and exchange of meanings, not as atomised bits (words/signs) but as packages of meaning. Let's look at intertextuality from the perspective of the individual language user. As individuals, we each have different literacies which arise out of the histories of the texts and meaning making practices we've experienced—produced, viewed, read or witnessed. For each event or process of meaning making in which we are involved (and we are involved in these from birth to death), we draw upon our knowledge/embodiment of other texts—their similarities and differences—in relation to the event or process in which we are taking part. Our embodied knowledge of other texts allows us to produce intertextual frames which can be used to read still more texts. In order to understand how this works, we'll look at three of the main 'frames' through which cultural meanings are produced and 'packaged'—narratives, genres and discourses.

Narratives

Narrative refers to a way of structuring meanings in the form of a story. Narratives involve the telling of a tale, with a sense of a sequence of events in some kind of temporal order, as in the nursery rhyme:

> Jack and Jill went up the hill to fetch a pail of water.
> Jack fell down and broke his crown
> And Jill came tumbling after.

While we could read these sentences as unrelated events, there is a strong convention which says they should be read as linked events that follow one another in time, although the story lacks explicit markers of time (such as 'one day', 'then', 'next' etc.). Instead, we read the order in which they are presented as the order in which they happened.

What is more, we frequently also read in a *causal* connection between the narrated events; that is, a prior event is read as the cause and a subsequent event as the effect. Why is this convention about narratives significant? Consider the following narrative:

> A storekeeper had just turned off the lights in the shop when a man appeared and demanded money. The owner opened a cash register. The contents of the till were placed in a bag, and the man left hurriedly. The police were notified of the incident immediately.

Note how we make a number of assumptions or inferences based on a reading of this text as a narrative. We assume, for example, a 'cause-and-effect' relation between sentence 1 (a man appearing and demanding money), sentence 2 (the owner opening a cash register) and sentence 3 (the contents of the till being placed in a bag). We also assume that within sentence 3, there is a causal connection between the contents of the till going into a bag and the man leaving (although we are not explicitly told this). In order to maintain these inferences, we also need to assume certain things about the identity of the participants; for example, that the storekeeper is also the owner, and that the man who demands money is the same person who leaves hurriedly. In other words, we read this text as meaningful in part because of a number of textual clues (the mention of a store owner, a till being emptied, an incident being reported to the police), and in part because we make sense of it as a narrative composed of events in a causal relation with one another. Nowhere is it actually stated that a robbery has taken place, yet most readers of this text will argue that that is what the text is about. The text fits a recognisable story type—a narrative of a robbery.

This brings us to a related use of the term narrative: to refer to the way in which particular generalised stories circulate widely within a culture and are seen as valid and predictable. Another term for such culturally ratified stories is **ideology**. An example of such an ideological narrative is 'heterosexual romance':

> Boy meets girl. Boy falls in love with girl. They get married and live happily ever after.

or 'capitalist success story':

> Working-class boy studies diligently. Leaves school. Gets a job. Works hard. Is promoted/starts own business. Becomes rich and successful.

Such 'story types' are to be found not just in novels, films and TV soap operas, but also in news and documentaries, not to mention gossip, folklore and oral history. The heterosexual romance narrative has provided the format for countless movies and novels. Many variations of such narratives are possible, but cultures tend to validate some stories over others. To test this claim, try rewriting the heterosexual romance as a homosexual romance. How does replacing the term 'girl' with 'boy', or 'boy' with 'girl' affect the cultural values attached to this narrative? Which cultural groups would such a narrative be acceptable to, and which would not accept it?

Another variation is exploited to comic effect in the TV science fiction comedy *Red Dwarf*, when the android character, Kryten, sums up the plot of one episode as follows:

> Ah, it's the old, old story. Droid meets droid. Droid turns into chameleon. Droid loses chameleon. Chameleon turns into blob. Droid gets blob back again.

Red Dwarf IV, Byte One, 'Camille'

Narratives are used as ways of interpreting and structuring everyday life, and can take on a very powerful function in validating the events in people's lives. An example of the validating power of narratives is the way in which the heterosexual romance myth is used within some cultural groups as a measure of a woman's 'success' in life; those women whose lives don't match this narrative may be judged, or even judge themselves (in some sense), 'failures'.

Genres

Genres are types of communication practices which help us to organise and make sense of texts. Examples of genres are:

- sermons;
- rental leases;
- conversations;
- poems;
- flirtations;
- newspaper articles;
- jar labels;
- bus tickets;
- arguments;
- science fiction.

Genres are text types or forms of communication associated with a social purpose and occasion. Becoming literate within a culture thus involves learning which genres are appropriate to specific social contexts and occasions. This may range from quite clear-cut rules for highly structured and ritualised occasions (such as religious ceremonies), to less formalised occasions in which the range of generic choices may be wide. For example, a genre such as a committee meeting follows a conventional format with a set structure and a number of obligatory elements:

- recording of the names of those present;
- apologies;
- confirmation of previous meeting's minutes;
- business arising from minutes; and
- other items of business.

Such an occasion is also structured in terms of rules about who may speak and when.

In contrast, a spontaneous meeting of friends may provide the occasion for a range of genres, such as gossip, casual conversation, jokes, appointment making, narratives of various kinds, and perhaps also argument or insults. Who speaks and when is not structured formally, and everyone involved is likely to compete for turns at talking. At the same time, however, these less formalised events are structured by certain more or less unconscious rules or conventions, and not everyone is likely to succeed in gaining equal 'air time'. Some speakers are likely to dominate informal conversations because they possess what Bourdieu refers to as *cultural capital* (a set of resources or literacies which are culturally valued).

How are supposedly informal social events and conversations structured by unconscious rules? A group of people at a cafe can be expected to behave, and talk, in certain ways about certain subjects which correspond to that social genre (the genre of a 'cafe gathering'). Now, as Bourdieu points out, their behaviour and conversation (no matter how apparently eccentric or spontaneous) are already predetermined to some extent by their literacy in the genre (Bourdieu 1991a). Different 'positions' can be taken up (one person might intentionally 'bait' another, that person might retaliate, the rest of the company might urge them on, but all in 'fun'), and different subjects can be used to drive this interaction (sporting team allegiances, romantic entanglements, a person's sense of fashion). What is important is that this conversational behaviour, despite appearances to the contrary, always takes place within the framework of a shared cultural literacy and set of generic rules. However, these rules can never really be acknowledged, because if they were acknowledged, the spontaneity would disappear.

What would happen if a member of the group refused to abide by these unconscious rules? The genre would fall to pieces, and so would the social occasion, in all probability. If, for instance, one of the members insisted on bringing their highly detailed company financial figures into the conversation, or someone actually started to mock another person's fashion sense in a way that was obviously not 'in fun', these 'intrusions' would have to be quickly rejected. The 'rules of the game' of a cafe gathering could be almost as difficult to defy or challenge as the (formal) rules of chess.

How are speaking rights determined within such informal social genres? Some people may be (unofficially) 'assigned' the role of dominance or centrality, precisely because they possess a literacy which helps keep the conversations, and the interactions that make up the genre, going. A person who is seemingly able to pluck interesting or funny observations 'out of the air', or to successfully redirect a fading conversation, might be expected to occupy a central place in the genre regardless of that person's cultural capital; or rather, they might occupy a central position because of the capital associated with helping to keep the genre running smoothly.

While genres provide frames for social interaction, and constrain the ways in which this proceeds, they can never entirely control or predict how meanings will be made in a context. This is because genres are never entirely single or pure. As long as we retain the perspective of communication as a dynamic process, we must recognise that the performance of genre can involve one genre giving way to or interrupting or blending with another. This is a defining characteristic of the medium of television; Raymond Williams has referred to it as 'televisual flow' (Williams 1990). Not only are programs continually interrupted by advertising, but a parade of different genres passes across the TV screen (game shows, cartoons, soap operas, news, current affairs, crime dramas, movies).

Moreover, elements of one television genre may occur in another; for example, footage of a police car chase is a generic element from crime dramas which may also occur in television news. One of the things that usually distinguishes the different uses of generic elements (say, a car chase in a crime drama from the same thing on the news) is the type of discourse which narrates, describes and explains 'the action'. In the crime drama the discourse used is likely to be highly emotive, personalised and colloquial, something along the lines of 'Those thugs have pushed their luck once too often—they're dead meat'. It would be (reasonably) unusual to find a news reader or on-the-scene reporter employing the same kind of discourse.

Discourses

Discourse is a term which is frequently used in the general sense of text as a social process. More specifically, the concept of discourse can be used to distinguish discourse types, or different ways of speaking or meaning associated with particular institutions. For example, associated with institutions such as the law, religion, the education system and the family are discourses or ways of speaking which are characteristic of those institutions and their practices.

Michel Foucault was responsible for developing the concept of discourse as we are using it here. Foucault's concern with discourse is with its power to structure, classify and normalise the social world (Foucault 1972). Discourses, he argued, owe their control over their material and subjects—their portion of the social world—to their ability to seem natural and self-effacing. By identifying the ways in which discourses operate, we are able to make them 'visible' and to reduce their degree of control.

An important function of discourse is to express the meanings and values of the institution. Kress says of discourses that they are:

> systematically organised sets of statements which give expression to the meanings and values of an institution. Beyond that, they define,

describe and delimit what it is possible to say (and—by extension—what it is possible to do or not to do) with respect to the area of concern of that institution . . .

Kress 1985:7

For example, the discourse of education (or more specifically, western compulsory public education) is likely to encode a set of common values, to be found across a number of institutional sites and occasions, such as teachers' discourse in the classroom, the policy documents of education bureaucrats, or principals' addresses at school assemblies and 'speech nights'. Lemke outlines some of these values:

> We believe that education and all its rules are constructed for the good of students and in their interests. We justify and rationalize every restriction on students' rights and freedoms as being 'necessary' in their own interests. We believe that the use of power and even force to compel students to do as we wish is justified by their natural irresponsibility and the good we are doing them.

Lemke 1990:84

Values such as these (and others) are likely to be implicit rather than explicit, but govern in a powerful way which practices and meanings are likely to be acceptable within the institution. Discourses thus produce power relations; they specify what relations are possible and valued in specific institutional contexts. They classify and assign value not only to objects and practices, but to social relations. In the case of educational discourse, what it means to be a student is defined and classified, as well as what rights and what social relations are possible or desirable for students.

Discourses never exist in isolation. So while a discourse may attempt to impose its values within its sphere of influence, and even beyond—as Kress puts it, 'a discourse colonises the social world imperialistically, from the point of view of one institution' (1985:7)—other discourses may challenge it, check it, coexist with it either peaceably or otherwise. Students, for instance, don't have access to, nor are they usually literate in, the official discourse of education; however, they have their own set of discourses (less easily labelled, because less obviously institutionalised), which again usually go unrecognised by those occupying official positions of power within the institution (teachers, bureaucrats). Student discourses (which might be specifically derogatory about teachers, for example) are normally denied any official value within the institution (for the obvious reason that teachers and bureaucrats make those decisions). When students do come forward to speak 'officially' (at school functions, for instance), they are normally expected to make use of discourses closely associated with the institution (they might talk about the community of the school, the much-loved and hard-working teachers).

Some discourses are more strongly institutionalised than others; for example, legal and religious discourses are strongly regulated through their respective institutions. Other discourses, such as feminist discourse, environmentalist discourse, or the discourse of indigenous rights, may fight to be heard against more established discourses, and are produced by those groups whose (repressed or oppressed) status within a culture is subject to struggle or contestation.

Although some discourses may be regarded as less institutionalised than others, this does not mean that they are somehow more open, or less complex or structured, than overtly institutionalised discourses. For example, student discourses within the education system have their own rules and characteristics, which, although susceptible to change, are likely to be relatively homogeneous and enjoy widespread (unconscious) acceptance. In this context it is worth recalling Frank Zappa's rebuke to members of the crowd at a concert who were abusing the 'boys in uniform' (police who were attending the concert): 'Everyone's in uniform here.' Of course, there is no official body or figure in rock concert crowds or in school yards to oversee or scrutinise discursive practices (as there is in a law court, for instance, where a judge might disallow certain discourses as illegitimate), but the amount of capital involved in using student discourses appropriately and effectively, and the loss of capital involved in not 'performing' adequately, ensures that rock concert crowd or student discourses are likely to be 'reproduced' through the weight of that social pressure.

It is also important to note that even (and perhaps, particularly) discourses which appear to be strongly institutional in character are not necessarily attached to one group or institution, or to one function within a culture. Graeme Turner makes this point when he defines discourse as:

> socially produced groups of ideas or ways of thinking that can be tracked to individual texts or groups of texts, but that also demand to be located within wider historical and social structures or relations.
>
> Turner 1990:32–3

Discourses travel through and across cultures, and there is really no limit as to the uses that can be made of them. As an example of this, look at the way technological discourses are deployed in advertising genres, regardless of the audience's potential literacy in such discourses. Advertisements for cars and stereo equipment routinely make use of quite technical discourse in order to carry across the values associated with the institution of science and technology (values such as progress, excellence, 'proven reliability') and to reinscribe these upon the product being promoted.

As another example, look at the way in which medical discourses have been picked up by New Age culture. On the surface, official medical culture and New Age culture are involved in a kind of antagonistic relationship: medicine tends to equate New Age alternative remedies with 'quackery', and New Age culture tends to characterise official medicine as arrogant, inflexible and inhuman. At the same time, advertisements for alternative medicine products often make use of medical or scientific discourses precisely because such discourses ('scientific tests demonstrate') still carry a significant amount of cultural capital—even with New Age audiences.

Discourses thus range from those which are widely regarded within a culture as prestigious and authoritative, to those whose power and authority is limited to certain social groups. Some discourses have the institutional power to enact the realities and values they represent (such as a judge pronouncing someone 'guilty', or a priest pronouncing two people to be married). The authority of others may be limited to certain contexts; as we have suggested, the discourses of 'New Age' or alternative medicine, which may have credibility and acceptance within certain communities and groups, are largely excluded from the discursive realms of institutionalised medicine. Articles on iridology and healing by touch are likely to be excluded from traditional medical journals, and research by practitioners in these areas is unlikely to be funded by wealthy medical foundations.

Let's summarise what we have dealt with so far.

- Narratives are ways of structuring experience into a sequence of events, or story. These are often culturally predictable to some degree.
- Genres are types of texts used for social purposes in specific contexts.
- Discourses are ways of speaking associated with particular institutions and the conventions and values of those institutions.
- Genres and discourses can combine so that the values of a discourse are embedded in the genre in order to achieve a particular social purpose.

All of these concepts—narrative, genre and discourse—function as framing devices which link the texts in which they operate to the wider context of culture. Cultural patternings of texts—the frames by which we recognise, classify and make sense of texts—are not fixed but are all the time being produced by us as members of a culture. Terry Threadgold expresses this as follows:

These intertextual frames are never part of an abstract 'system' (in the Saussurean sense). They are always and only constructed and reproduced in texts as social processes, that is, as events, performances. They 'pre-exist' any particular 'use' only as 'chunks'—familiar, taken-for-granted 'ways of speaking'—in other texts.

Threadgold 1989:117

To see in more detail how these concepts can be applied to texts, we will use a case study, involving a comparison between two genres and the discourses and narratives involved.

DISCOURSE, GENRE AND NARRATIVE: THE REPRESENTATION OF TWO ABORIGINAL WOMEN

In this case study we will look at two texts, one in a women's magazine and one in a newspaper magazine, in order to examine in detail how narrative, genre and discourse can function to frame meanings. These texts are about two Australian Aboriginal women, both 'successful' in the public eye: the first (see Figure 9, page 68) is an article on former tennis player Evonne Cawley in the *Australian Women's Weekly* (July 1992:12–13), and the second (see Figure 10, page 70) is an article on magistrate Pat O'Shane which appeared in the *Australian Magazine*, the magazine supplement to the *Weekend Australian* newspaper (31 July–1 August, 1993:8–12). The values which are given to these two women and their lives are rather different. We will examine the ways in which narrative, discourse and genre shape the ways these two women are represented.

Let's start by looking at the genres of the two texts. Both share the genre of magazine article, but there are also generic differences between them. The *Women's Weekly* article, 'Evonne goes back to the beginning', fits within the women's magazine mass market formula which focuses on celebrities as well as cooking, fashion and domestic issues. As a celebrity and sportsperson, Cawley has had recurring coverage in the *Weekly* throughout her career. She is also constructed (visually and verbally) within a traditional paradigm of femininity as the gentle wife and mother. At the top of the double-page article is a photograph of Evonne with her smiling family clustered around her. She has her arms around her young son, and her daughter is resting her arms on Evonne's shoulder. She is framed within discourses of conventional femininity and the family, discourses closely associated with the traditional women's magazine. The discourse of Aboriginality also provides an intertextual frame for reading this text, and one which can potentially emphasise her difference from the dominant white culture of the magazine and its readership. But the article frames this discourse in terms of a search for personal identity, through phrases such as 'I can remember, I can remember' and 'One of our tennis greats is staging a personal comeback'. In this way, Cawley's story fits within the consensual values of the *Weekly*.

By contrast, the article 'In the case of Pat O'Shane', appears in a magazine inserted within a 'serious' broadsheet newspaper aimed at business people and professionals. The article is produced in terms of the generically constrained news values of conflict and controversy, and is concerned with O'Shane's somewhat controversial career as a magistrate who believes in speaking out on social issues. As in the Cawley article, O'Shane's Aboriginality is brought forward as an issue, but unlike Cawley's, O'Shane's identity is not produced through discourses of femininity which render her less problematic. She is presented not as a wife and mother (although she is both of these) but as a 'career woman', a vocal feminist and an Aboriginal activist. Where Cawley's narrative is framed through discourses of femininity and personal self-fulfilment, O'Shane's story is framed by the discourses of Aboriginal rights and feminism, discourses which are overtly political.

It could be argued that these two articles are different because the women they purport to be about are different, and have very different personal styles or politics. But can this be the only reason for the different meanings and values constructed around their stories? We need also to ask why each magazine has chosen to do an article on Cawley or on O'Shane. Is it only random choice that has Evonne Cawley's story in the *Women's Weekly* and Pat O'Shane's in the *Australian*? Our answer to this question is that the selection of these particular women is motivated. That is, the choice of subject/interviewee is generically and ideologically constrained—Evonne Cawley is selected because her narrative can be framed within the consensual values of the *Women's Weekly*, while Pat O'Shane can be framed in terms of political debates about feminism and Aboriginal rights in the *Australian* and other newspapers. These two texts, then, construct meanings around gender and ethnicity in ways which are constrained quite broadly by the ideological values of the particular mass medium (news magazine versus women's magazine).

We'll move now to a consideration of the narratives each text deploys. Each article is structured around discourses of Aboriginality involving narratives of the subjects' lives. Although these are both stories of Aboriginal women who grew up in humble circumstances in country towns, and went on to achieve success in their chosen fields, the two narratives differ significantly.

Evonne Cawley's narrative is highly personalised and recounts a search for increased knowledge and awareness of her Aboriginality as a narrative of personal growth (see Figure 6). No causal connections are established between the events of her childhood and her current

Figure 6 Narrative of Cawley's life (awareness of her Aboriginality)

- idyllic rural childhood—a period of innocence
- schooling—when she learned of shooting of Aboriginal people—felt 'strange, bewildered', not knowing more of her own culture was 'frightening'
- during her tennis career, Cawley 'resisted pressure from Aboriginal groups to take a stand'
- after returning to Australia from the US, she goes through a process of self-discovery through learning about Aboriginal culture ('angry I didn't learn at an earlier age')
- involvement in Aboriginal issues—presented as passive? ('her return to Australia dovetailed neatly with the establishment . . . of the . . . Council for Aboriginal Reconciliation . . . with which Evonne has become involved')

'awareness'. In her narrative, Aboriginal oppression and racism are not named (but Cawley refers to these issues vaguely as 'what happened', 'all these things'). According to Cawley, 'It was something I've always wanted to do, to make people realise that all these things happened in the past purely through ignorance.' By making racism a historical 'hiccup', which can be cured through education, Cawley's narrative edits out the political elements of an understanding of racism.

In contrast, Pat O'Shane's life narrative is an overtly political one, in which issues of race and gender are foregrounded and direct causal connections are made between her political beliefs and her personal experiences of poverty and racism. However, unlike that of the Cawley article, this narrative is not constructed as uncontested (see Figure 7). (At least) two fairly polarised readings of O'Shane's life are put forward— in which not only evaluations of O'Shane but categories and events pertaining to her life are contested as part of an ideological battleground. O'Shane's words and opinions are cited and form one version of her story but alongside this narrative is one produced by the journalist (Legge), who reframes O'Shane's story to construct a different narrative.

So a single 'happy-ever-after' type of narrative is produced in the *Women's Weekly* story, while two narratives at political odds with one another are produced in the *Australian Magazine* article. The differences between the narrative treatment in each article can not only be related to the broad generic features of the magazine type and audience noted above, but are also produced through the specific genres employed by each article. The Cawley text functions as a 'personal problem' or confessional—a type of article generic to women's magazines (Muller 1991:82). In keeping with this, the discourse is personalised and emotional, and the narrative is one of personal development. Cawley is

Figure 7 Narratives of O'Shane's life

O'Shane's narrative of her life	Legge's narrative of O'Shane's life
• rural childhood: conflict, racism, sexism, poverty, unemployment	• ? 'difficult' childhood (narrative casts doubt on this claim)
• political awareness and commitment	• a 'fighter', 'rabble rouser', 'stirrer', 'boat rocker', 'Always the victim'
• achievement despite the system	• succeeded among many others less 'noisy about [their] success'
• holds a position which enables her to speak out, to critique social/judicial systems	• has achieved a privileged position, and is exploiting it and her status as female/Aboriginal ('she's something of a protected species—Our Lady of the Politically Correct')

quoted talking about her feelings, family moments and personal experience in an intimate way.

The *Australian Magazine* article enacts the genre indicated by its apparently playful title, 'In the case of Pat O'Shane'. There is a generic slippage between the genre of feature article and the judicial genre of court case. Terms such as 'case' and 'doubt' seem to slide between non-technical discourse and technical legal discourse, and the structure of the article incorporates the testimony of various 'witnesses', with prosecution alternating with defence. The writer of the article seems to set herself up not only as a reporter writing about an interview but also as a judge interpreting the witnesses' testimony for the readers (jury).

Another significant feature in these two texts is the use of **citation**, the quoting or reporting of the speech of another. Citation is a technique for introducing other voices into a text. These two texts both make use of citation. The ways in which the journalist/narrator frames the voices of others in each article relates directly to the specific genre. The combative, legal genre of the O'Shane article is characterised by its writer's use of a controlling narrative voice. The narrator does not allow the voices she cites to stand in an open dialogue with one another. Despite the pseudo-dialogic mode, with the semblance of journalistic 'balance' through quoting voices both in support and in criticism of O'Shane, the writer continually interrupts this apparent dialogue to frame, interpret and redefine. Her narrative voice-over frequently functions to undercut O'Shane's voice and O'Shane's narrative in order to impose her own (see Figure 8).

The confessional genre of the Cawley article calls for rather different narrational politics. The narrative voice here is unobtrusive, supportive, non-judgmental, implicitly endorsing Cawley's values and actions. The

Figure 8 Citation (underlining identifies the reporter's voice)

Reporting O'Shane's speech:
O'Shane vehemently denies that she is the beneficiary of largess. <u>Always the victim.</u>
Plus, she points out, you battle your way through preselection, then you have to
cop the party line. <u>Not O'Shane. No fear.</u>

Quoting O'Shane's speech:
'. . . I haven't been allowed any latitude at all and I'm not going to be stopped by
any adherence to unstated or unwritten rule.' <u>That is for sure.</u>

Reporting and quoting O'Shane's father (to challenge her account of her childhood):
<u>He does not think his children suffered racial abuse at school</u>: 'Nothing very
serious.' <u>He denies the poverty.</u> 'There was plenty like us and some worse off.'

Quoting a newspaper:
'If she takes up the appointment,' reported a newspaper before Pat O'Shane's
acceptance of a job as a magistrate in NSW, 'it would not be the first time she
has broken new ground. She was the first Aborigine to graduate at law at an
Australian university, the first Aboriginal barrister and the first Aborigine to head a
government department—not that she enjoys this categorisation.' <u>Not much.</u>

---

mode is one of monologue rather than dialogue, with Cawley's the only
cited voice. The narrator's identification with the subject is constructed
through her indirect reporting of Cawley's speech/thought. This sets up
a patronising relationship which involves speaking for the other, as a
mother might answer for a child in the child's presence ('Evonne is
hoping . . .', 'Evonne said it was interesting . . .', 'Evonne is now
looking forward to going bush'). The use of first name in the Cawley
article constructs an intimacy between the writer/narrator and Cawley,
and draws the reader into this intimacy also. Compare this to the use
of O'Shane's surname to refer to her in the *Australian Magazine* article.
This functions to construct the more distant tone appropriate to its
'combative' genre.

   In both stories, narratives of Aboriginal women's lives are constructed; narratives which could be contextualised in terms of a wider
debate about social justice and the workings of oppression. In both
stories, there is an attempt to depoliticise these narratives by reducing
them to the level of the personal and the individual. In the *Women's
Weekly* text this is achieved apparently as a joint construction by
writer and interviewee, while in the *Australian Magazine* there is contestation over the narrative.

   This case study demonstrated the ways in which genres, narratives
and discourses interact in quite complex ways in texts, and are selected

and coded into texts as ways of framing meanings, and, particularly, ways of assigning ideological value.

SUMMARY

This chapter has suggested that in making sense of context we draw on the immediate context of situation and intertextual frames, in particular:

- narrative;
- genre; and
- discourse.

Narrative, genre and discourse always carry the traces of other contexts, and any text can be read in terms of such traces, which constrain its meanings along with the constraints of its immediate context. As readers of texts and makers of texts, we bring these frames to bear on our understanding of 'what is going on' in any process of making meanings.

FURTHER READING

Fairclough, N. 1989, *Language and Power*, Longman, London, Chapter 2

Kress, G. 1985, *Linguistic Processes in Sociocultural Practice*, Deakin University Press, Geelong, Victoria, Chapter 1

Kress, G. and T. Threadgold 1988, 'Towards a social theory of genre', *Southern Review*, vol. 21, no. 3, pp. 215–43

Figure 9 'Evonne goes back to the beginning'

'I CAN REMEMBER,
I CAN REMEMBER'

ONE OF OUR
TENNIS GREATS IS
STAGING
A PERSONAL
COMEBACK

Right: Evonne Cawley with her husband Roger and children Morgan and Kelly. The family is looking forward to 'going bush'.

To Evonne Cawley, the sweet smell of home is that of dust on earth floors when water is laid on it in the heat of the day.

This and fishing in the inland rivers and creeks of NSW with her grandmother and aunts are cherished memories of a childhood which ended when she was 11 and left home eventually to become one of the world's greatest tennis players.

Now she is about to take a new direction, to seek out her Aboriginal heritage, of which she says she knows very little.

'All I remember of growing up is living part of the time in the Aboriginal mission in Griffith,' she told The Weekly. 'We left there when I was about two, when my father found work at Barellan. But we spent a lot of time at the mission and they were probably the happiest times of growing up.

'Everybody was having fun. There were plenty of kids to play with, and I learned to swim in the irrigation canals. I remember playing rounders and dancing around fires at night. I even remember the smell of the dirt floor when it was brushed over in the heat of the day, and then water put on it, and there was this beautiful fresh smell.'

Evonne is one of four Australian athletes chosen to represent Australia as

Olympic torch-bearers at Barcelona, an honour which thrills her.

She and her husband, Roger, moved back to Australia from the US last December to live in Noosa with their children, Morgan, 10, and Kelly, 14. They made the decision to return for good after taking a long holiday here.

'I was quite happy in America—I just didn't realise how much I missed Australia until I got back to it,' Evonne said. 'I've done pretty well everything I set out to do, I'm satisfied with my life. But there has always been something missing, a gap.'

Evonne is hoping that gap can be filled by writing a book and making a television documentary about her attempts to understand and know her Aboriginality.

'I realised after Mum died last year that making the documentary would be a great opportunity to learn about my heritage, not only for my sake, but for my kids', too.'

Last year for the first time, the family saw a performance by Aboriginal and Island dancers in Cairns. 'After that, we had to get Morgan a didgeridoo,' she said. 'He's putting out little calls and sounds, but he can't keep it going.'

Evonne began her education about her people by reading a book about the killing of Aborigines by white settlers. Among the tribes to suffer were her own Wiradjuri people.

'It made me sad, but more than that, it made me angry that I didn't know this before,' she said.

In school, Evonne's only lesson about the Aboriginal role in white settlement of the country involved writing an essay.

'We were asked to pretend to be an early settler and give an account of everything that happened during our day. One of the things we had to include was shooting the Aborigines,' she said.

'I felt quite strange at the time, a little bewildered. But that was what we learned about.

'Many different emotions are coming out as I read now about what happened. Mainly, I think I am angry I didn't learn at an earlier age. That's why I think it's so important that they teach this in the schools, so they can appreciate their heritage and feel proud, so that they can do a lot of other things with confidence. I know just from my experience that not to know was frightening.'

Evonne said it was interesting to see Aboriginal beliefs being adopted by the modern world. 'Now, everybody is looking after the environment—Aborigines lived in harmony with themselves and the land for so many years.

'And now you hear psychics say you were somebody else in another life. Aborigines weren't really afraid to die, because they believed their spirit would come back through another child, or an animal.'

After months of reading about her people, Evonne is now looking forward to going bush with the family to find out first-hand about their traditions. 'I am really keen to see the Aboriginal lands. I've always had dreams about living off the land,' she said. 'I love nature, I love roughing it.'

The documentary, also featuring Morgan and Kelly, will be produced for an international audience, according to Roger.

In the past, Evonne has resisted pressure from Aboriginal groups to take a political stand. But her return to Australia has dovetailed neatly with the establishment, last year, of the Federal Government's Council for Aboriginal Reconciliation. The council, with which Evonne has become involved, aims to foster better understanding between Kooris and non-Aborigines.

'It was right up my alley,' Evonne said. 'It was something I've always wanted to do, to make people realise that education is the most important thing, that all these things happened in the past purely through ignorance.'

Elizabeth Johnston is a Brisbane-based freelance journalist. Johnston 1992: 12–13

Figure 10 'In the case of Pat O'Shane'

MANY ADMIRE HER, MANY FEAR HER.
EVEN SOME FELLOW BLACKS WISH SHE
WOULD SHUT UP. BUT UNPREDICTABLE
PAT O'SHANE, AUSTRALIA'S MOST
OUTSPOKEN MAGISTRATE, ISN'T
ABOUT TO ZIP HER LIP WHILE
MISOGYNY AND RACISM PLAGUE THE
JUDICIAL SYSTEM.

'If she takes up the appointment,' reported a newspaper before Pat O'Shane's acceptance of a job as a magistrate in NSW, 'it would not be the first time she has broken new ground. She was the first Aborigine to graduate in law at an Australian university, the first Aboriginal barrister and first Aborigine to head a government department—not that she enjoys this categorisation.' Not much.

. . .

She's a fighter. A rabblerouser. A stirrer. Always has been. As a schoolgirl she used her fists, as a teacher she used her tongue. It has stood her in good stead. As a young lawyer in the Alice Springs Aboriginal Legal Aid office she told the white advisers to make their own coffee. As a political activist in Sydney she got angry when her black male comrades tried to steal the limelight after the hard yakka had been done. As a senior bureaucrat during the Wran Labor government she spoke out often and vehemently, attacking the Liberals, the federal Labor leadership and her Aboriginal critics. As a magistrate she has stated publicly that male judges are misogynists and women are more intelligent than men.

In January, she dismissed charges against four women who defaced a Berlei Bra billboard, insisting the real crime was committed by the advertisers for promoting pictures of a woman scantily dressed being sawn in half. She has rubbished the self-governing Aboriginal body, the Aboriginal and Torres Strait Islander Commission (ATSIC), and denounced the reconciliation process initiated by the Keating Government. Recently a federal Labor MP nominated O'Shane as his choice for Australia's next and possibly last governor-general. No way, mutter those a little closer to the action. Not because she's black or a woman. Indeed Lois O'Donoghue, the Aboriginal woman heading ATSIC, is the favourite.

Boat rockers make people nervous. That is the risk they run. At the height of the Berlei Bra fracas O'Shane said she was the victim of a sexist and racist campaign. 'I receive the kind of inordinate public attention I get because I am an Aboriginal woman, for no other reason.' It is a very effective shield. Racism still rules in the suburban heartlands and far reaches of rural Australia but rich veins of white guilt run deep through the educated elite. In a postscript to O'Shane's biographical contribution to *Tall Poppies* the book's editor, Susan Mitchell, described her subject as tough. 'Nobody or nothing would ever destroy her belief in herself. She was a tall poppy who had been cut down to the roots and, having bloomed again, God help anyone who ever tried to cut her down.' Staunch conservatives and Aboriginal leaders are least afraid to challenge her views. Others who disagree with her shy away from taking a shot because she's something of a protected species—Our Lady of the Politically Correct.

. . .

If the pluck is Irish, the anger is not. Talk to O'Shane about her childhood and she tells about poverty. About tents and dirt floors. About going without meals. She seethes over the racism. Over the sexism. She claims her father was ostracised by his workmates and found it difficult to get accommodation for his family. She remembers the taunts of 'black gin' at school.

Talk to Patrick O'Shane about the past and he puts a different spin on it. Maybe old age has mellowed him. Maybe it's because he's a white male. But he challenges the grim tenor of her account. He denies he had trouble from his workmates. He says the family's sporting prowess helped community relations. He does not think his children suffered racial abuse at school: 'Nothing very serious.' He denies the poverty. 'There was plenty like us and some worse off.' He denies he had any trouble renting places to live. As for the tent, well, he takes exception to that. The tent was temporary, he says, lasting only until he had built a home on land at the northern end of Holloway's Beach. And the dirt floor? That riles him most. 'That's bloody nonsense,' he says of his daughter's description. They have had this argument before. 'I remonstrated with her about this,' he harrumphed. 'I carried kerosene tins of beach sand to put on the earth floor. I was right, and she realised there was a vast difference between clean yellow sand and earth. Even earth's not dirt.'

Pat O'Shane shakes with rage at having to account for the discrepancy. 'I mean he must have forgotten the stories that he told me,' she spits. 'We did have a f...ing dirt floor and we did carry water for a mile and a half . . . the fact of the matter is that we were bloody poor . . . I mean I kept that

family from age fifteen to seventeen. I was the only one in that family who had a regular income. Why my father would say that I don't know, I can only say that he's a very old man and we've had this out before with other members of the family and their recollection certainly accords with mine.'

. . .

O'Donoghue suggests O'Shane is very capable, 'so long as she sticks to her field'. No chance of that. Reticence is not her speciality. But she must learn to take what she gives without screaming foul play. 'When you're in public life you've got to expect a bit of that,' says O'Donoghue. 'I don't think it's because you're a woman and you're black. I've never found it to be so. I think it's because of your actions.' O'Donoghue is a quiet achiever. A conformist who plays by the rules. 'You can't get away with speaking out so much on the bench or as a bureaucrat. If you want controversy . . . go into politics.'

This is not an option which appeals to O'Shane although it has been put to her time and time again. 'People write to me, they ring me up, they talk to me at parties, they stop me in the street, but I've never been interested in politics.' It's the system, she complains, 'So undemocratic.' Plus, she points out, you battle your way through preselection, then you have to cop the party line. Not O'Shane. No fear.

© *Australian Magazine*. Legge 1993: 8–12

Chapter 5

Ideology

In our chapter on communication and practice (Chapter 3), we described Bourdieu's notions of cultural field, habitus and cultural capital, and showed how and why practices come about. We made the point that cultural field 'writes itself' into existence, in a sense, because each field produces and deploys discourses and narratives that determine what can and can't be thought, without appearing to be doing anything of the sort. These discourses and narratives, which operate as if they were as natural to us as breathing, are usually termed ideologies.

Ideology functions to convince its audiences that the ideas it offers up are timeless and ahistorical; that is to say, they have always been, and always will be. Different aspects of our everyday culture—our eating habits, religious beliefs and material goods, for instance—are usually experienced in this way. We see ourselves as 'civilised', for instance, because we celebrate Christmas, have the scientific and technological capacity to mass-produce sophisticated goods, and eat with a knife and fork. These aspects are all produced, within Western cultures, as natural and valuable. A culture which didn't celebrate Christmas, didn't have access to science and technology, and favoured eating with the fingers would not only be perceived as different and exotic; generally speaking, it would also be understood as inferior and less valuable, perhaps even less human.

Why is this the case? How does the material context of a culture come to be naturalised and valued to the extent that it can be used to differentiate the human and the non-human? After all, our material and cultural contexts are anything but natural. Take Christmas, for instance. The celebration of Christmas is generally presumed to date back to early Christian times, but in its present form dates to nineteenth-century Britain. And eating with forks was considered bad manners by Louis XIV,

King of France, in the seventeenth century; well-mannered people used a knife and their fingers. As for the Western claim to scientific and technological mastery, this again is only a recent phenomenon, dating from about the Renaissance (in the fifteenth century). For the three and a half thousand years before the Renaissance, Asian cultures (such as China and India) led the world in the development of technology.

HOW IDEOLOGY FUNCTIONS

We can define ideologies as discourses and narratives that circulate in a culture and determine, to a large extent, what can and can't be thought, and what can and can't be done. In order for ideologies to be effective— in order, for instance, that Christmas, or eating implements, or access to science and technology be understood as having a natural value that extends across cultures and across history—ideologies have to decontextualise their own culture, their own material conditions, their politics, laws, pleasures and values. Ideologies try to hide the *contingent* nature of thoughts and activities within a culture; that is to say, they try to convince their audiences that certain values, ideas and activities are more or less natural, and that things have always been this way, or should remain this way. To sum up: ideologies function in an attempt to make the specific or the particular seem generally applicable, and to *naturalise* meanings.

Ideologies have some kind of *group basis* within a culture; in other words, ideologies construct and promote meanings which privilege one culture, or one section of a culture (which can be based on class, occupation, race, skin colour, gender, age, sexual preference, religious affiliation, nationality or general physicality) over another. For example:

- until the last thirty years, woman were excluded from many occupations and most of the professions because they were not considered (mainly by men) to be capable of carrying out the required work; and
- until the last ten years in American professional football, non-white athletes were very rarely considered for the role of 'quarterback'. The supposed reason for this was that quarterback was a 'leadership' position which required a level of intelligence beyond the capabilities of non-whites.

These circumstances were produced, perpetuated and naturalised through the circulation of ideologies.

We made the point that ideologies functioned predominantly to naturalise and perpetuate differences within a culture; paradoxically, however, this is usually done through the attempted erasure of differences. Ideologies are often deployed, for instance, to convince other groups that their interests are the same as those of the group producing the ideology.

One obvious example is those television commercials for kitchen or cooking products which usually feature a male voice telling women what wonderful cooks they are (because they use the right brand of margarine or butter or pasta), how important they are to their family (who presumably would all starve without the mother's cooking), and what a wonderfully harmonious group the family is, with the father having an outside (therefore 'real') job, the children going to school, and the mother at home devoting her life to the others.

One function of ideology, then, is to create a notion of *community* where everything is harmonious, just and workable as long as different groups stick to their 'natural' place. Even though it is obviously in the interest of men that women don't compete with them in the workplace (that is to say, it is in the interests of certain groups of men that women stay in the home), the ideology of many kitchen and cooking advertisements pushes the idea that this arrangement is in the interest of everyone; it is best for women that things stay this way, and women would suffer if other arrangements held sway (if the woman wasn't at home, the family would be unhappy, and consequently the woman would be unhappy).

This kind of ideological narrative isn't just played out in commercials. A considerable number of contemporary Hollywood films—*Fatal Attraction* and *Cape Fear* are two obvious examples—are pre-eminently concerned with two closely interrelated themes:

1. the movement of women into the workforce; and
2. the decline, within the family, of the authority of the father.

Another factor is the threat posed to the family by sexually active and assertive women who aren't 'maintained' within the confines of the family unit. In both *Fatal Attraction* and *Cape Fear*, the father's infidelities threaten to destroy the family, and in the end it is only the loyalty and courage of women—the mother and/or the daughter—that saves the father and the family, and restores the father to his position of 'rightful' authority as head of the household. *Fatal Attraction* and *Cape Fear* are examples of ideological narratives demonstrating what things would be, or are, like in a 'post-margarine-commercial' community where some men and women have refused to fulfil their (natural) duties.

Ideologies try to convince groups in a culture that the value that is assigned to certain signs or markers of difference (gender, skin colour) is natural. This allows the members of privileged groups to behave as if they were naturally superior to other groups. We previously referred to the important role played by science and technology as a marker of civilised, and therefore human, behaviour. Michael Adas, in his book *Machines as the Measure of Men* (1992) points out that from the eighteenth to the middle of the twentieth century Western colonialist activities—in Asia, Africa, America and Australia—were largely justified and rationalised in terms of the West's scientific and technological superiority. Markers of science and technology came to mean that one group was human and superior, and other groups, which didn't possess those markers, were inhuman and inferior.

Ideological narratives are produced by groups within a culture in order to privilege their own position, and to 'naturalise' the inferiority of other groups. One of the ways this happens is through *repetition*. Ideas are repeated, with variations, in as many mediums, genres and fields as possible, so that the ideology comes to pervade the culture. In the end the ideological position or value becomes so familiar that most members of the culture no longer question the assumptions on which it is based. Every part of the culture repeats the ideology, everybody accepts it, so it must be true. In other words, the repetition of ideology across the culture, as Bourdieu suggests, helps to ensure that we forget that ideology . . . is ideology.

Ideology doesn't usually criticise alternative ideas—they are normally treated as if such alternatives were unthinkable. And if, for some reason, they are thought or suggested, they are usually disqualified from consideration by being branded as . . . ideology.

We might refer back to that visit to Gallipoli by an Australian delegation headed by the then prime minister, Bob Hawke, to commemorate the 75th anniversary of the ANZAC landing. You will recall that the Australian journalists covering the event discovered to their horror that Turkish journalists were writing that the Australians had come to Turkey to apologise for their unprovoked invasion during the First World War.

The ANZAC landing at Gallipoli had become a cornerstone of Australian national identity and value; that is to say, it had been produced as an ideological narrative which had edited out numerous possible contexts of the landing. Gallipoli, for those Australian journalists, meant the bravery of Australian troops, and the mateship and selflessness of those involved; but they could only maintain that ideological position by conveniently forgetting the people the ANZACs were fighting against, and by forgetting that the ANZACs were invading another country which had its own version of events.

Doubtless there were Turkish versions of the Gallipoli story, and they probably bore little or no relation to the ANZAC legend. This was unthinkable to most Australian journalists, and presumably to most

> **Karl Marx** was a German political economist and philosopher who is usually considered, along with Freud, Darwin and Nietzsche, as one of the founders of modern Western thought. Marx was the most influential of the group. His theories inspired the Bolsheviks in Russia, the communists in China, and countless revolutionary groups throughout the twentieth century. Marx's main works, all of which emphasise the importance of the economic sphere in human activity, include the three volumes of *Capital, Grundrisse, The Communist Manifesto, The Eighteenth Brumaire* and (with Engels), *The German Ideology*. All of the theorists we refer to in this chapter are responding, to a large extent, to Marx's work.

Australians. Ideology had succeeded in decontextualising Gallipoli to the extent that the only role for the Turks was as 'bit players' in an Australian narrative.

IDEOLOGY AND MATERIAL CONTEXTS

What we have presented, up to this stage, is a very general conceptualisation of the notion of ideology and the way it functions. Our next step is to explain how ideology influences and determines communication practices, and the way people come to think of their identity, or subjectivity. The most prominent theorist of ideology, and its influence on people's thoughts and actions, was the German philosopher Karl Marx. Marx did not coin the term ideology, but he was largely responsible for giving the term everyday currency. Marx did not have a single theory of ideology—his notion of ideology changed across his writings—but we will discuss the version that has come through as being representative. Consider this quotation from Marx:

> The mode of production of material life conditions the social, political and intellectual life processes in general. It is not the consciousness of men that determines their being, but, on the contrary, their social being that determines their consciousness.

> Quoted in O'Sullivan *et al.* 1991:108

Marx's main point was that relations of production, and social being, determine consciousness. This means that social conditions and material contexts *(over)determine* our understanding of the world. To think otherwise is, for Marx, to see the world ideologically, or upside down. Ideology is a kind of false consciousness, a duplicitous and abstracted version of the world put out by the ruling classes in order to maintain the subordination of the lower classes. Ideology would include all those narratives and explanations of events, practices and activities which attempt to draw attention away from the material contexts and conditions in which people live, and the political and economic realities that define and determine people's existences.

For Marx, what was important in capitalist cultures was the relation between the owners of the means of production (capitalists) and those who sold their labour for wages (workers). Explanations about the realities of everyday life had to take this as their point of departure. Within this context, ideology could be understood as attempting to do two important things:

1. to construct that relation as something other than exploitative and oppressive and historical; that is to say, ideology idealised and naturalised the relations between capitalists and workers ('capitalists and workers were part of a team or community helping to create wealth for everyone, and helping the nation to prosper'); and
2. to draw attention away from the inequalities and oppressiveness of everyday life, and the politics of the material contexts which controlled people's lives.

In Marx's version of ideology, 'something else' is substituted for 'reality' so as to provide a false meaning of life. This something else could be a story about romance, religion, patriotism, or the family. There is an excellent example of this practice in the Nicholas Roeg section of the film *Aria*, which is made up of a series of short films based on the music and themes of famous opera arias. In Roeg's film, a group of obviously desperate and impoverished revolutionaries is going to attempt to assassinate a nobleman. A considerable part of the film is taken up with emphasising the desperation of the plotters, who are badly clothed, hungry and cold, and not really adequately equipped or prepared for the assassination attempt. The nobleman, on the other hand, is confident, well dressed, and undisturbed by material needs. He lives 'on a higher level' of existence. The pathetic assassination attempt fails, the plotters are killed, and the nobleman is united at the end of the film with his lover. The operatic aria, which comes on at this point, is rich, lush and romantic, and celebrates the highly romantic ending to the story.

Roeg's point, in this film, is that aspects of high culture, such as opera, produce stories of life that concentrate on, emphasise and value so-called high feelings and sensitivities, and promote these as being the most significant aspects of life. Moreover, these high feelings and values have generally been associated, in high culture, with the nobility or the upper classes. The idea of a (genuine) peasant or low-class worker being a high romantic figure is unthinkable in, say, a Shakespearean play or a Wagnerian opera.

Roeg's short film demonstrates how false consciousness works. The romantic love between the nobleman and his lover is produced as 'the' meaning of life. Everything else—the suffering of the workers, for instance—is edited out, unless it can be shown to fit in with this romantic narrative. In the film, the plotters are presented as a threat to the romance, and they are quickly edited out—killed—so that 'love can triumph'.

Conventional Marxist notions of ideology are characterised, then, by two points:

1. the overdetermining role of the relations of production and the economic sphere as an explanation for the realities of life; and
2. the use of stories, narratives and explanations to create a false consciousness which edits out those political and economic realities.

Ideology, in this sense, can be understood as the means by which the dominant class disguises the true nature of its relation with subordinate classes and thus helps perpetuate inequality and oppression.

IDEOLOGY AND SIGNS

Marx's pioneering work on ideology was developed by the Russian Marxist V.N. Volosinov, a philosopher and linguist who wrote a very influential text titled *Marxism and the Philosophy of Language* (1986) (see Chapter 2). We are not going to deal with this text in any broad way (it is largely concerned with critiquing various linguistic traditions from a Marxist perspective), but instead will concentrate on some ideas Volosinov posited about the connection between ideology and language, or signs.

For Volosinov, ideology is produced at the same time that signs are produced as meaningful. Without signs, he argues, there would be no ideology. All cultural meanings—which is to say all meanings because there can be no meaning outside culture and language—are produced by signs such as words, clothes, posters, films and photographs.

Volosinov's text is particularly important because it alerts us to the point that since all meanings are produced within cultures, there can be no natural meanings, or pre-cultural meanings. Ideologies work, of course, to naturalise their meanings and perspectives; but if there are no natural meanings, then a culture can be understood as a kind of ideological battlefield in which various groups strive to impose their meanings at the expense of other groups.

One example of culture as an ideological battlefield is the 1960s television comedy *Gilligan's Island*. In this series, a group of people are marooned on a previously uninhabited Pacific island. The group is composed of a selection of 'types' from American society: the skipper, the millionaire couple, the scientist, the country girl, the movie star/sex goddess and Gilligan, a lowly sailor. All the characters act entirely in keeping with their type: for instance, the scientist (the 'professor') is technically minded but also often impractical and nerdy, and the millionaire male (Mr Howell) reduces everything to a matter of money.

The interesting thing about this series is that the island serves as a microcosm for (certain areas of) American culture, in that each type tries to explain every problem, address every crisis, and most importantly run the island in terms of their own 'world view'. The professor wants things to work in an orderly, sensible, intellectual, rational and scientific fashion; which means, of course, that as he is (in his opinion, and in terms of his cultural capital) the person most closely associated with those characteristics, he should be in charge. Every sign (the trace of a native presence, the material conditions providing them with food and clothing) is ideologised by 'the professor'; that is to say, it is produced as meaningful in terms of the values of a particular field and ideology (in this case, scientific rationality).

For Ginger, the movie star, what overdetermines life on the island is the culture of Hollywood: she must be admired, she must be seen as sexy, she must be able to present herself as glamorous. Whereas the professor might see the island as a material context that had to be researched and catalogued, for Ginger it is an exotic setting perfect for a movie (with her as star). Whereas a sign of native life might be treated as an anthropological opportunity by the professor, Ginger would see it as the opportunity to meet somebody tall, dark and handsome (and presumably male).

In Mr Howell's view, of course, they are both wrong: the island is a place to make money, every decision can be read in terms of financial considerations, and the indication of a native presence would be read as an opportunity to buy their canoe and get home to the stock exchange, or maybe trade with (that is, exploit) them for goods.

Marx's version of ideology argues that consciousness is produced through an understanding of the reality of material contexts, in particular an understanding of economic contexts and relations (the relation between workers and capitalists, the importance of the ownership of the means of production). From a Marxist perspective, everything that happens on the island can (more or less) be explained in terms of the actions of Mr Howell, and his capitalist operations. But as we have seen, there are many competing identities and ideologies on Gilligan's Island.

How can we make sense of this? Volosinov makes the point that economics is just one of a number of spheres we have to take into account. If we go back to Gilligan's Island and fantasise a little, we might be able to clarify things.

Let's presume that Mr Howell has set up a factory on the island. The factory produces coconut products (coconut milk, ice creams, shampoos). Work is overseen by the skipper, the professor runs the technical side of things, and Gilligan (a blunderer) and Maryanne (a simple country girl) do the labouring. Obviously ownership of the means of production is crucial here. Mr Howell is the wealthiest and most powerful person on the island. Moreover, he increases his wealth by creaming off the surplus value created by the labour of Gilligan and Maryanne.

Can we presume, then, that this economic power will automatically translate into an ability to control the meanings and practices on the island? The answer Volosinov—and Bourdieu—would give (if they were viewers of *Gilligan's Island*) is 'not necessarily'. Why? Remember the professor has a considerable amount of cultural capital: his intellectualism, his supposed rationality and problem-solving skills, and his air of scientific detachment would all count for a great deal in certain circumstances.

Let us presume Mr Howell wants to cut down all the guava plants on the island because they compete with the coconut trees for space and nutrients. The professor, however, is extremely interested in doing research on guava trees. He tells the others that his research is extremely important because it will tell them more about the environment in which they live, and could help them to survive when they start running out of food. The professor has the cultural capital here that Mr Howell lacks. Mr Howell can talk about profits and higher wages, but the professor can ideologise this struggle in terms of long-term environmental damage, the pursuit of important knowledge, and his ability to decide—given his supposedly detached, objective background—what is in the best interests of the group.

We made the point in Chapter 3 that habitus—roughly translated as the set of dispositions an individual or group acquires according to its particular path through a culture—largely determines thoughts, practices and values. The professor and Mr Howell, in our *Gilligan's Island* fantasy, are taking part in an ideological struggle involving different types of habitus, and therefore different values, goals and agendas. For Mr Howell the only important consideration is to make as much money in as short a time as possible; the professor's references to research, scientific value and long-term ecological damage are simply nonsense standing in the way of his profits. The professor, on the other hand, thinks Mr Howell's values crass and philistine; he cannot have some loud-mouthed, uneducated millionaire jeopardising the search for knowledge.

Mr Howell has an advantage over the professor in that he is a wealthy capitalist and can largely control the media on the island—he owns the newspaper that Ginger puts together once a week. The professor, on the other hand, has a considerable amount of cultural capital—associated with his profession—that is likely to influence people as much as Mr Howell's wealth. If Gilligan were to enter the conflict—suggesting, for instance, that the dispute could be resolved by getting rid of all the vegetation on the island—his position would have little or no chance of success because he has neither financial nor cultural capital.

What this demonstrates is that some groups within a culture—normally those with the greatest economic or cultural capital—have a greater opportunity to promote their ideologies to wider audiences, and to convince those audiences to accept their claim to power. The term we use to describe this process, developed by the Marxist theorist Antonio Gramsci (1986), is **hegemony**.

HEGEMONY

The central point to Gramsci's notion of hegemony is that people are not usually forced to concede power or control to another group or groups; rather they are convinced that their interests are best served by that other group being in power, or that one group is 'naturally' superior. They become convinced that:

- the dominant group's interests are the same as their interests; or
- it is in their interest for the dominant group to be in power; or
- the dominant group deserves to rule. (American capitalists of the 1890s supposedly dominated American politics because of Darwin's notion of 'natural selection', and European kings and queens supposedly ruled through the 'grace of God'.)

Ideology, and hence hegemony, is produced, according to Gramsci, through various cultural institutions, some of which are more powerful than others. This point was taken up by the French Marxist Louis Althusser (1977), who was interested in the way in which cultural institutions (such as the school system, religious groups and the family) help the spread of ideology, and the construction of hegemony, by producing 'cultural identities' for people. Althusser called this process **interpellation**. Identity, for Althusser, was bound up with the way institutions produce (interpellate) individuals and groups. These identities are characterised by certain supposedly natural values, goals, desires and affiliations.

How is interpellation tied up with ideology and hegemony? In the Brian de Palma film *The Untouchables*, the Elliot Ness character (played by Kevin Costner) chases and apprehends a member of the Mafia on the roof of a tall building. The gangster, who has just helped murder one of Ness's men, gives himself up, but taunts Ness by suggesting that the justice system won't convict him and that he will go free or serve a short sentence. At this moment the audience has been 'set up', if you like, to take on a particular identity. The audience has seen one of the good guys (a member of the Untouchables) murdered by a ruthless criminal (from the Mafia), who is about to get away with his crime (because the justice system doesn't work properly). At the same time the gangster is standing close to the edge of the roof and Ness has him in his power.

If you were to ask members of the film's audience—away from the film—if they were in favour of police officers executing criminals rather than turning them over to the courts, presumably most of them would answer in the negative; that is to say, they wouldn't be in favour of the police murdering people they suspected of committing a crime. However, in this film, at this moment, the audience is positioned, is interpellated, through the following questions being implied in the action of the film:

- Do you think the Untouchables are brave men doing a necessary and valuable job?
- Do you think the Mafia gangsters are despicable, ruthless killers not worthy of human status?
- Do you think it fair that this particular gangster should be able to murder a police officer and get away with it?
- Do you think justice would be done if Elliot Ness were to force him off the roof (which is what he does)?

The individual members of the film's audience are 'given' identities through this action, identities in keeping with the ideology of the film (which is that the justice system protects criminals, who should be disposed of).

The connection between hegemony and the interpellation of identity has been explored by Ernesto Laclau (1990), who argues that cultural identities or subject positions are perhaps the most important sites of ideological conflict within a culture. This means there are no essential identities or subjectivities; rather, subject positions (student, woman, feminist, worker) are:

- empty, and then filled up, or made to mean, as they are ideologised;
- always undergoing changes of meaning; and
- able to carry a variety of meanings.

An example of subject positions being exchanged and then being filled up by different ideologies can be found in the film *Europa, Europa*, which is set in Germany at the beginning of the Second World War. The main character in the film is a male teenager who has a mixed identity: he is Jewish but lives in a part of Eastern Europe where German is spoken, along with a number of other languages. Because of the radically different contexts in which he finds himself, he is continually forced to (ex)change identities:

- when the Nazis start sending Jews to the concentration camps, he escapes and passes himself off as a German;
- then he is captured by the Soviet communists, and becomes a good communist, fighting for the Soviet army;
- when his company is wiped out by the Germans, he starts talking German, and convinces the Nazis that he is a fellow German who has been separated from his people;
- he is so good at being a German and a Nazi that he becomes one of the leading lights in the Hitler Youth and is formally adopted by a high-ranking German officer;
- at the end of the war, he is captured by the Soviets, who prepare to execute him; then
- desperate, he changes identity once again, telling them that he is Jewish. The Soviets refuse to believe him: they point out that if he were Jewish, he would have ended up in a concentration camp.

The identity switching in this film exemplifies Laclau's point that subject positions are taken up and filled in, and change in meaning, rather than being essential or tied up with substances. The teenager was Jewish as long as that was the role required of him. Being Jewish was fine—in a Jewish community—but the Nazis brought a new series of meanings to that subjectivity: Jews were worthless, less than human, and had to be eliminated. The subject position of a German was fine—among Germans. For the Soviets, who were being invaded by Germany, a German had only negative meanings—negative enough to get you shot. A communist was a good subject position—among Soviet communists, but not among Nazis, who tended to kill communists without question. A Nazi was a good subject position—among Nazis, but not among Soviet troops at the end of the war, who were killing most German soldiers they came across, but were liberating Jews, which is why it became useful to be Jewish—again.

What this example demonstrates is that people have the ability to 'negotiate' ideology: the teenager doesn't just go along blindly with each interpellation; he 'fits in' so as to look after his own interests. And the same applies to the audience watching *The Untouchables*. Obviously not all members of the film's audience are going to be successfully interpellated. People who have a habitus similar to the Mafia character's, for instance, will simply refuse the identity that is offered to them. At this point it is important to refer back to Bourdieu's ideas: many members of the audience will be not be successfully interpellated, because the ideology and subjectivity 'offered to them' is in conflict with their habitus, or the values of the field(s) in which they are located. And as we pointed out in Chapter 3, the contemporary world has so many sources of information and texts all competing to tell us 'the truth' about things. In an age of the Internet and globalisation, and of information flows that cross national boundaries in a few seconds, it is difficult for one ideology to completely dominate a culture.

GLOBALISATION AND IDEOLOGY

Claude Lefort, who writes from a position very close to Laclau's, has theorised about changes to ideology in an age of mass media and globalisation (Lefort 1986). Lefort distinguishes between 'bourgeois ideology' and 'new ideology'. Bourgeois ideology makes use of 'capitalised ideas'—the Family, Humanity, Nation, Science, Property—which are posited as being original and sacred truths. Dominant groups within a culture ideologise these terms just as subject positions are ideologised, so that the Family might be read, for instance, only as a certain type of family (father, mother, two children), and as operating in specific ways (the father is the breadwinner, the mother takes care of the domestic scene).

This sets an example, and operates as a model, which all other 'families' are measured against and have to copy.

Lefort argues, however, that bourgeois ideology is dying out and being replaced by what he calls 'new ideology'. New ideology is a product of mass media, globalisation and general advances in communications technology. This new technology is able to reach mass audiences, and appears to be able to erase time and distance; after all, at any time satellite-based communication systems can 'bring together' people from all over the world. New ideology uses this apparent erasure of time and space to pretend to have effected a general erasure of all differences. For Lefort, dominant groups within a culture *perform* communication by bringing every possible group—no matter how weird, exploited, disaffected, marginalised or fringe—into the communication network. The message is, 'If your group has a problem, come on a television current affairs show, along with a representative of business, someone from the government, a women's representative, a greenie, an ex-serial killer, and someone from the migrants' association, and we'll talk about it.'

Dominant groups take people's minds away from differences, oppression, exploitation and wrongdoings by making it seem as if everyone's views are taken into account and everyone is consulted. According to Lefort, this performance of communication doesn't actually change anything; what it does do is make it look as if things could change.

The new ideology, for Lefort, can be defined as the use of globalising and mass communication technology to talk away differences. This ties in closely with Gramsci's notion of hegemony; after all, nothing naturalises one group's domination as much as the apparent erasure of all hierarchies. Are there racial problems in the US? Is the American police force full of racists? Do you want to do something to change things? Fine: go on *Donahue* or *Oprah* and have a debate/discussion with the mayor and a representative of the police force. Chances are you can have a perfectly reasonable discussion, get to know and appreciate and understand one another, and feel a whole lot better about things. Of course nothing will have changed, which is, Lefort argues, exactly the point.

SUMMARY

In this chapter we suggested that ideology can be understood as the result of a particular kind of reading practice, a practice which naturalises the relationship between signs and meanings in an attempt to constrain and determine what can and can't be thought.

We described the Marxist arguments that social relations are based on economic relations, and that ideology works to conceal the economic overdetermination of social life and the class exploitation that accompanies it.

We also explained that Volosinov modified Marx's theories by suggesting that ideology is produced at the same time that signs are read as meaningful, and that cultures are ideological 'battlefields' in which different groups compete in order to impose their meanings on others, a process Gramsci designated 'hegemony'.

We then described how Althusser and Laclau both emphasised the production or interpellation of identities as the most significant site of ideological conflict

Lastly we introduced Lefort's notion of a new form of ideology that is specific to the globalised world.

FURTHER READING

Laclau, E. 1987, *Politics and Ideology in Marxist Theory*, Verso, London
Lefort, C. 1986, *The Political Forms of Modern Society*, MIT Press, Cambridge Massachusetts
Marx, K. 1981, *Surveys from Exile*, Penguin, Harmondsworth
Zizek, S. (ed.) 1994, *Mapping Ideology* Verso, New York

Chapter 6

Subjectivity

In the chapter on ideology we examined how identities—what we refer to as subjectivities—could be understood as sites of ideological conflict; that is to say, we followed the suggestions made by Althusser and Laclau in arguing that identities/subjectivities:

- are not essential or permanent; but
- are produced and made meaningful within a culture.

In this chapter we'll look more closely at the way subjectivity has been theorised within contemporary cultural theory, with particular reference to two questions:

1. If subjectivity is produced within cultures, how does this process occur? In other words, how do subjectivities become ideologised?
2. What part does the body play in the production of subjectivity? What are the ramifications of treating human bodies as ideologised signs?

The best starting point for a consideration of how subjects are 'produced' is the work of Sigmund Freud. His theories have been picked up and used in a variety of ways, and have passed into everyday culture in many popularised forms. Prior to Freud, ideas about subjectivity had been strongly influenced by the work of the philosopher René Descartes, who argued that the human subject was a rational, reasoned and (self)-conscious entity whose identity was made certain, was proven, by his self-consciousness: 'I think, therefore I am.' Descartes presumed that the 'I' that was spoken or written was the same as the entity that spoke the word, and that this 'I' was a stable and knowable entity. Humans, for Descartes, were reasonable and rational beings who were in full possession, at least potentially, of themselves; that is to say, their minds were masters of their (bodily) castles.

Marx, Nietzsche and Darwin, in their different ways, had already cast increasing doubt on Descartes' theory of subjectivity. Marx argued that, rather than being conscious subjects, people live in false consciousness under capitalism. For Nietzsche, consciousness was the result of a forgetting of the ways in which the body had been produced, formed and manipulated, and reason was simply an ideology (in other words, the notion of reason was not natural, but was produced historically). Darwin's notion of evolution tied this Cartesian godlike human subject rather too closely to amphibians, reptiles and monkeys.

These three theorists had already chipped away at Descartes's rational and self-knowing human subject: Freud finished off what was left. Generally speaking, Freud argued that the human subject was not in control of itself because its activities—its actions and practices—were influenced by desires that necessarily emanated from the subject's unconscious. More specifically, Freud suggested that human subjectivity was bound up with:

- sexual drives;
- the Oedipus complex; and
- the unconscious.

For Freud, our biological drives—such as the desire for food—are 'taken over', in a sense, by sexual drives, which attach themselves to some part of the body that was the site of biologically driven pleasure, such as sucking milk from the mother's nipple(s). In early (pre-Oedipal) childhood, these drives move across and around the body, attaching themselves to any biological drive, and (potentially) sexualising the whole body.

The second stage in this process of the production of (sexualised) subjectivity is the Oedipus complex. Broadly speaking, the child's first and, in a sense, only love object is the mother, but the child (who is, for Freud, more or less naturalised as a male) learns that it cannot desire its own mother (this is socially taboo), so these desires are repressed and rendered unconscious. The child is accepted into a culture and is given, and learns to take on, specific subjectivities, mainly through the process of transferring its previously unconstrained sexual drives into 'appropriate' activities (say, heterosexual activity).

The final stage in this process of becoming a subject is the production of the unconscious. Those repressed desires (repressed because they defy or scandalise conventional cultural notions of what is appropriate and natural) 'return' in a variety of ways: through slips of the tongue, in sublimation (where sexual desire is transferred onto 'higher' activities, such as writing a text book on communication and literacy), in fetish-ising certain objects (you can't have the person you desire, so you collect her/his clothes, and make do with those), and in dreams.

Dreams are the best known site of 'the return of the repressed', perhaps because Freud wrote a book on interpreting them (Freud 1986b). Repressed desires attempt to be articulated within consciousness, but consciousness refuses to have anything to do with them. Those repressed desires may intrude into consciousness through dreams. Sometimes this may take place in an obvious way (I dream I want to have sex with X), but more often than not the repressed desire attaches itself in a less obvious way to the dream narrative. The point here is not so much that dreams can be read, but rather that the human subject is a split subject, split between conscious and unconscious desires, which means that we can never really know ourselves, simply because there is a part of us which can never be acknowledged, and can only appear in dreams.

Let's look at an example of these Freudian concepts as they are played out in popular culture. In David Lynch's film *Blue Velvet*, the narrative is concerned with two innocent teenagers (played by Kyle McLachlan and Laura Dern) who live in a sleepy, respectable American town. One day McLachlan finds a human ear in a field: his subsequent attempt to get to the bottom of the mystery pushes the couple into an underworld of violence and murder controlled by a psychopath named Frank (played by Dennis Hopper).

Now, dreams are often thought of in positive terms; the 'American dream', for instance, refers to the achievement of, among other things, an economically successful life. In pop songs, references to dreams and 'dreaming about you' are again usually highly positive; they suggest the achievement of some important part of our life and identity, the desire to have something or someone that will make our lives complete.

Blue Velvet is interested in exploring the other side of dreams, the side where what is repressed is given expression. The psychopath Frank is almost a walking 'return of the repressed': in one scene, which is secretly watched by Kyle McLachlan, Dennis Hopper as Frank sexually abuses a woman called Dorothy (Isabella Rossellini) while openly playing out his desires for his mother. In one of the more ironic, and disturbing, scenes in the film, Hopper and his gang viciously beat up McLachlan while in the background Roy Orbison's 'In Dreams' is being played. The film is too complex to reduce to a few general points, but we can suggest that:

■ Frank is more or less a representative of everybody's (or at least every male's) repressed desires, and the violence that accompanies those desires; and

- every dream (the American dream, romantic dreams) is informed by desire, and therefore by violence of some kind.

What the film makes clear, then, is the very Freudian point that our cultural identities are dreamed up, if you like, and that any notion of rational and knowable identity is always a dream that has an unstable and violent side to it. At the end of the film Kyle McLachlan and Laura Dern end up together and everything seems fine . . . in dreams.

SUBJECTIVITY, DESIRE AND LACKS

Freud's theories of subjectivity were picked up and elaborated upon by the French psychoanalyst Jacques Lacan. Perhaps Lacan's most interesting contribution was the notion of the 'mirror stage' (Lacan 1977). Lacan suggested that a child understands itself as a series of disconnected, atomised parts until the advent of what he called the **mirror stage**. When the child sees its reflection (in a mirror, for instance), it recognises itself as a whole, a unity. This is the departure point for the child's assumption of subjectivity, but it is not without its problems. Although the child

Sigmund Freud was an Austrian physiologist who more or less 'invented' the discipline of psychoanalysis. During the first two decades of the twentieth century, Freud published a number of ground-breaking works dealing with such issues as the **unconscious**, *repression*, dreams, perversion and the central role of sexuality in human cultural life. His most influential texts include *The Interpretation of Dreams*, *The Psychopathology of Everyday Life*, *Civilisation and Its Discontents*, *Beyond the Pleasure Principle*, *The Ego and the Id*, *On Narcissism*, *Totem and Taboo*, *Moses and Monotheism,* and several famous 'case studies' ('The Rat Man', 'Schreber', 'The Wolf Man', 'Dora', 'Little Hans').

Jacques Lacan was a French psychoanalyst who is perhaps best known for his rather radical 'return' to Freud's theories, which he felt had been 'domesticated' by American ego psychology. Lacan's work has exerted a considerable influence on cultural theorists over the last forty years, particularly in the areas of subjectivity, desire and the workings of the unconscious. Lacan's most influential works include his published seminars, *Ecrits* (a selection of his writings) and *The Four Fundamental Concepts of Psychoanalysis*. For a very accessible introduction to Lacan's theories, we suggest Elizabeth Grosz's *Jacques Lacan: A Feminist Introduction.*

recognises itself, at the moment of recognition 'itself' is . . . 'over there'. In other words, at the moment subjectivity is given, it is also taken away: 'I am here, but I am also over there . . . am I here or there?'

As the child moves from a relationship based on its close connection with its mother (what Lacan calls the **imaginary**) to a full integration into society and culture, its identity will always be defined in terms of some other; something or someone is desired in order that the *lack* in the person's identity be filled in. Like Freud, Lacan identifies Oedipus as the crucial moment for the production of specific, subject identities, and like Freud he understands this process as being necessarily gendered (for instance, any identity in a culture is based on what Lacan calls the 'Law of the Father', which means that women are produced as non-male, as lack, as being castrated compared with men).

Our identity, for Lacan, is always changing and being transformed as we search for something or someone that will 'complete us', whether it be another person (love, romance), religion or the achievement of wealth or distinction. Further, this completion can never take place, of course, because our identity is caught up in a circle of desire that never meets itself.

Lacan's notion of subjectivity is often exemplified in Hollywood romance narratives where the (inevitable) male hero desires a particular woman who is usually described as being 'part of me', 'my fulfilment', 'my salvation' or 'the real meaning of my life'. A more Lacanian version of this narrative is to be found in the Hitchcock film *Vertigo*. The hero, played by Jimmy Stewart, falls in love with a woman, played by Kim Novak, who appears to commit suicide. Stewart is obsessed with the woman, and can't function once she has been removed from his life. In Lacanian terms, she was the 'other' who would have completed him, and her death seriously threatens to undermine the possibility of his social and cultural identity.

Stewart comes across another woman (who is actually the original woman, but she doesn't tell him that). He attempts to re-create what he thinks is a look-alike of the first woman, so he can recreate his 'original'. His obsessiveness eventually results in the woman being killed (for real this time), but her death provides a liberation (for Stewart!), because he now knows that the woman who was his 'fulfilment' was a fake. Stewart becomes a normal, well-adjusted member of society because his desire is no longer attached too closely (too obsessively!) to one person, but can now move from one object to another without his ever having to face the truth that there is nothing to his desire (no woman can ever 'complete' his identity). Stewart almost loses his identity, because he gambles that identity on, and commits his whole life and being to, an illusion . . . which he comes face to face with. The fact that the woman ends up dead isn't a major issue in *Vertigo*, which, like most Hitchcock films, is primarily concerned with the ramifications of male desire and subjectivity. In other words, women are predominantly understood, in this and other Hitchcock films, as commodities to be exchanged by men.

Psychoanalytical theories of subjectivity are far more complex than we have suggested here, but perhaps we could sum up their contributions in the following, very generalised terms:

- Subjectivity is not essential or unchanging, but is tied up with the way cultures order and constrain our bodies and desires.
- Our identities are always based on something that is not conventionally understood as part of ourselves; for instance, repressed desires or an other who is both us and not us.
- Cultural identity is largely determined by the way bodies are gendered.
- Cultural identities are illusions which must be maintained if we are to continue to function within that culture.

One of the criticisms made of psychoanalytical theories is that they are too generalised, even universalist and ahistorical, and don't give any account of the specific ways in which different identities are produced within and across cultures. Michel Foucault is one theorist who more or less rejects psychoanalytical accounts and focuses instead on the way in which cultures produce subject positions through institutionally sanctioned and legitimated discourses.

SUBJECTIVITY, DISCOURSE AND SEXUALITY

Perhaps Foucault's most useful and accessible analysis of the *discursive production* of subjectivity is to be found in *The History of Sexuality Volume*

Michel Foucault was a French cultural theorist who between the 1960s and the early 1980s wrote a number of important texts which enquired into the relationship between cultural institutions (the prison, schools, hospitals, the family) and the production of subjectivities. Foucault's most influential contribution was to theorise about and describe the way bodies and identities are regulated through various mechanisms and discourses (medical, psychological, pedagogical, legal). His major works include *Madness and Civilization*, *The Birth of the Clinic*, *Discipline and Punish* and his three-part *The History of Sexuality*.

One: An Introduction (Foucault 1980) where he focuses on the ways in which the notion of sexuality came to be seen as the key issue in understanding and evaluating self and identity. Foucault starts by rejecting the conventional idea that during the nineteenth century, and particularly in the Victorian period, sexuality was repressed and censored, whereas in the twentieth century a kind of sexual liberation occurred. Foucault makes the point that, on the contrary, during the Victorian period an extraordinary amount of material was produced about sexuality. He writes:

> At the level of discourses and their domains . . . There was a steady proliferation of discourses concerned with sex-specific discourses . . . from the eighteenth century onward . . . [there was a] multiplication of discourses concerning sex in the field of exercise of power itself: an institutional incitement to speak about it, and to do so more and more; a determination on the part of the agencies of power to hear it spoken about, and to cause it to speak through explicit articulation and endlessly accumulated detail.
>
> Foucault 1980:18

Foucault refers here to the disciplining of sexuality; that is to say, sexuality is taken as an object of study by various authorities and institutions, and subjected to the gaze and analysis of medical and other sciences. Sexuality is identified, according to Foucault, as the site that would give up the truth about each person; and scientific instruments, theories and techniques were called on to help in this deliverance. The term Foucault uses to describe this process, whereby scientific knowledge of the subject is employed as a means of disciplining, evaluating, categorising, regulating, developing and reforming the subject, is bio-power, which we introduced in Chapter 3.

As we pointed out in Chapter 3, the advent of bio-power replaced, for Foucault, old-fashioned exercising of power (by the king, for instance) as naked violence, punishment or threat, with the notion of scientific normality. From this time on, subjectivity was understood as a form of normality which had to be adhered to. People's subjectivities came to be regulated through being written about. From the moment a child comes into contact with institutional authorities (which these days is the day of its birth), those institutions produce discourses which define normal identity and carry the seal of scientific credibility and authority.

Sexuality is only one of the areas, of course, that have been targeted by discursive regulation, but it is an extremely important one. To quote Foucault again:

> sex . . . was at the pivot of the two axes along which developed the entire political technology of life. On the one hand it was tied to the

disciplines of the body: the harnessing, intensification and distribution of forces, the adjustment and economy of energies. On the other hand, it was applied to the regulation of populations, through all the far-reaching effects of its activity. It fitted in both categories at once, giving rise to infinitesimal surveillances, permanent controls, extremely meticulous orderings of space, indeterminate medical or psychological examinations, to an entire micro-power concerned with the body. But it gave rise as well to comprehensive measures, statistical assessments, and intervention aimed at the entire social body or at groups taken as a whole. Sex was a means of access to the life of the body and the life of the species. It was employed as a standard for the disciplines and as a basis for regulations.

Foucault 1980:145

Let's look at the main points in this passage. First, sex is used to normalise and regulate individual behaviour and practices, and to create hierarchies of subjectivity based on the approximation to a sexual norm or set of norms. Heterosexuality, for instance, is normal and valuable, while homosexual activity is perverse and should be eliminated.

Second, both the micro and macro processes of normalisation and regulation involve increased surveillance by the state and its institutions and practitioners (educational, medical, psychological, legal). Throughout our lives, institutional agents (teachers, doctors) direct us towards normal behaviour.

Third, there is a presumption that not only is sex the 'answer' to individual and mass identity, but that sex is to be found in every aspect and corner of existence. Foucault is particularly critical of psychoanalytical claims that sex informs all our actions.

Fourth, sex becomes both the marker of individuality ('your sexuality is what you really are, and what distinguishes you from others') and the key to reshaping that individuality ('this is what we want you to become, and it is through the manipulation and regulation of your sexuality that you can be normalised').

Finally, the institutional surveillances, descriptions and analyses of these 'sexualised' human bodies produce knowledge which underpins regulation and normalisation. What this means is that scientific knowledge is closely linked to the exercising of power. The knowledge produced and used by institutions (by teachers and doctors, for instance) is not neutral or disinterested. There is a politics to it.

What kind of evidence is there for these claims? Think of the way in which western cultures and their institutions and discourses have made the notion of the *deviant* and deviance (as opposed to normality) so central to the notion of identity. For instance, we can refer to a whole series of so-called deviant subject positions—involving, for instance, 'male' homosexuality, lesbianism, nymphomania, frigidity, masturbation, paedophilia, exhibitionism, infertility, impotence, masochism, sadism, bondage—all of which have been 'identified' by scientific or quasi-scientific discourse and institutions and used to categorise and 'explain' people.

Moreover, none of these categories 'existed' until the last 200 years or so; that is to say, there were homosexual practices (in ancient Greece, for instance, such practices probably constituted a relatively large proportion of all sexual practice), but there wasn't the subject category 'the homosexual', nor the 'illness' of homosexuality.

Another example of Foucault's thesis can be found in the way sexuality functions in popular institutions and discourses. Any reading of lifestyle magazines demonstrates that sexuality and sexual practices have become virtually the principal criterion for determining social normality, identity and value. What these magazines simultaneously presume and reproduce is the notion that people understand themselves in terms of, and are completely dominated by, an interest in sexuality (theirs and everybody else's). Consider, for example, the contents lists, taken from an issue of *Dolly* magazine (see Figure 11).

Dolly is a magazine generally aimed at teenage girls, and its contents are divided into the following sections:

- Features;
- Health & Beauty;
- Make-up Manual;
- It's Special;
- Rock;
- Fashion;
- Fiction;
- Real Life; and
- a collection of columns listed under 'Every Month'.

In the first section, 'Features', only two articles are specifically about sexuality and identity ('Is it cool to lose your virginity?' and 'Why he thinks you're desperate'), but at least half of the other feature articles produce sexuality, or at the very least body image, as an important marker of identity and worth. The 'Are you insecure?' quiz (81), for example, uses the following scenarios as the basis for its questions:

- Your boyfriend dumps you, without giving you a reason.
- You're in a cafe, and you see an absolutely beautiful guy with a killer smile sitting at the other end of the room.
- When you look in the mirror, you see . . .

Figure 11 Contents page of *Dolly* magazine, September 1993

FEATURES

62 Is It Cool To Lose Your Virginity? So you're scared about being the only virgin in your group. Does this mean you should have sex just for the sake of getting the first time over and done with?

70 The Daintree Is In Danger How we can save the Daintree Rainforest from being destroyed

72 The Price of Acting Dumb We take a look at which celebs have made stupid career decisions

78 The Mouth That Roared Billy Baldwin bags just about everyone in Hollywood, from Tom Cruise to Julia Roberts

80 Are You Insecure? Do our quiz to find out if your confidence rates

99 Daring To Make A Difference Check out why these six girls are the coolest in the country

108 Why He Thinks You're Desperate We find out why guys don't want the girls they think they can easily get

116 Read Poppy's Lips Lipstick queen Poppy King tells us why megastars want to wear her make-up

HEALTH & BEAUTY

46 Sport Report Snooker

48 Body Rap

126 Make Me Up

MAKE-UP MANUAL

83 The Ultimate Make-up Manual

84 Two Weeks to Great Skin The amazing 14-day diet that will clear up your complexion

88 Colour Coded Find out which make-up shades suit your skin tone

92 A Bundle Of Beauty Tanya Arpadi lets you in on what life as a model is really like

96 Best Buys For Under $20 Forget the beauty hype and suss out these sensational bargains

IT'S SPECIAL

17 Win 1,000 Rock Books You can score the exclusive Michael Jackson photo album, and stacks of other must-reads

19 Win 200 Revlon Packs Get your hands on Cindy Crawford's favourite moisturisers

74 Subscribe To *Dolly* And Win The massive Pert Shampoo giveaway

76 Dolly Club Natural knits and the most awesome freebies

127 Fun Foto Win a wild Summertime bikini

ROCK

38 Spin Out Music reviews

60 Diesel Lobbies For A Different Direction Why Diesel has had enough of his old rock'n'roll routine

106 Lenny's Comin' Our Way As he prepares to tour Down Under, we try to find out what makes Lenny Kravitz so sexy

FASHION

24 Tropical Tie-dye Once you take a look at this hip gear, you'll be dyeing to get into the tropics

52 The Best On The Beach We've found the sexiest swimsuits that will suit every body

Courtesy of *Dolly* magazine

Moreover, a number of questions which don't appear to be connected with sexuality provide options/answers that work to sexualise the question. For instance, one option regarding 'the biggest worry you might have in giving a speech in front of the whole school' is that 'All the boys in the front row will fall in love with you'. And in the article 'Which TV character do you most relate to?', one of the options is '*Melrose Place*'s Jo—she's dating the most gorgeous guy around'.

It's not just these specific articles that conflate sexuality with identity, interest and value; other sections, whether they refer to fashion, beauty hints, fiction, medical advice, rock or media stars, share this tendency:

■ the fiction 'Beverly Hillbillies 0810' asks, 'What's made the libidos of the male ranchers go through the roof?';

■ the regular column 'What matters' (listed on the contents page under 'Every Month') is about not 'blaming rape victims';

- in Fashion, there are references to 'the sexiest swimsuits that will suit every body' and 'Baring your midriff'; and
- in Rock, the magazine asks 'what makes Lenny Kravitz so sexy?'.

This preoccupation with sexualised identities is not confined to the written pieces; if anything it is more accentuated in the photographs used in the magazine, most of which define their subjects (both male and female) as sexually attractive, alluring, available or assertive. This goes for both the pin-up (of a semi-clad male), and the fashion, celebrity and advertising shots. Most of these photos share the following characteristics. The emphasis is on bare flesh, or on clothes that accentuate curves, such as swimsuits or tight-fitting outfits. Shots are often centred on breasts, thighs or buttocks. A large proportion of the photos of women have the woman staring, lips pursed, at the camera. Many of the photographs are sexualised through the choice of pose, with women coyly half covering themselves, or sticking out their breasts, or appearing to be undressing. Much of the clothing that is worn in these shots is 'tantalisingly' half-revealing (half open or partly see-through). Finally, the camera angles used in some of the shots again accentuate and work to help reveal conventionally sexualised areas (by being directed down a dress top, or up legs).

This magazine, which we think is not unrepresentative of magazines targeting the Western youth market, strongly sexualises most of its written and visual material. How does this tie in with Foucault's notion that sexuality is used to produce, regulate, normalise and evaluate social identities? Let's consider the following extract from the article 'Why he thinks you're desperate' (Unreich 1993:109), and make use of Foucault's insights to analyse the way the article deals with the question of social identity (see Figure 12).

The first two paragraphs set up a romantic narrative which positions both subjects (Naomi and David) as potentially fulfilled and happy precisely because they had been integrated into 'normal' sexualised subject positions: 'they were perfect for each other . . . David spent the evening holding Naomi's hand (while) . . . she spent the night gazing into his eyes'. What we have here is a normalising narrative (they are more or less promised perfection through being perfect for the other) which is based on their both assuming gendered roles that are simultaneously valuing and valued. The man values the woman by holding her hand; and by letting him hold her hand she legitimates him as a desirable man. The woman values the man by gazing into his eyes, and by offering himself up as her temple, he transfers some of his value to her.

So far, so good: 'It was all going to work out fine'—but it didn't. Why not? What follows doesn't read like the kind of scientific or

Figure 12 'Why he thinks you're desperate'

YOU WANT HIM BAD, AND YOU'RE SURE IF YOU FOLLOW HIM AROUND LONG ENOUGH, HE'LL WANT YOU TOO, RIGHT? WRONG. ACTING LIKE THIS WILL PROBABLY SCARE HIM AWAY. RACHELLE UNREICH LOOKS AT WHAT MAKES GUYS THINK YOU'RE DESPERATE FOR A DATE.

When I introduced Naomi to David, I was sure they were perfect for each other. They shared a weird sense of humour, and were the only people I knew who loved both Stephen King novels and country music.

Sure enough, they went out on a date and really hit it off. David spent the evening holding Naomi's hand and speaking about Dwight Yoakam; she spent the night gazing into his eyes. I told her it was all going to work out fine.

What I didn't anticipate was Naomi's determination to make David hers. The following Monday, she bought two tickets to the theatre, and sent them to him. That Wednesday, because he'd said that he loved Pearl Jam, she sent him all the CDs they'd ever recorded.

On Thursday, she called him for a chat, and on Friday she dropped over to his house, unannounced, after work, in a gorgeous black dress. His eyes lit up when he saw her, but, three hours of conversation later, they had a glazed look. After that, he didn't return her calls, and went out of his way to avoid her.

Naomi couldn't believe it. What had she done wrong? She'd laughed at his jokes, agreed with everything he said, and acted loving and sweet and good-humoured all the time. Couldn't he see that she'd make a perfect girlfriend?

But, the fact she didn't realise was that if you're the slightest bit desperate to be with a boy, he'll sense it. Most males have a commitment phobia, so you can imagine how turned off he gets if it's obvious you're trying to hook him.

You may think you're being subtle, but believe me, a guy knows when you're walking the long way between your science and maths classes just so you can bump into him.

Courtesy of *Dolly* magazine. Unreich 1993:109

quasi-scientific discourses produced by a major social institution (psychology or medicine, for instance), but there are quite extraordinary similarities at work here. The article is scientific, to a certain extent, in that it:

- describes and analyses, in an almost anthropological way, Naomi's practices;
- writes out of a position of presumed knowledge, which allows analysis and diagnosis to take place; and
- identifies the 'problem' (the deviance, if you like) in Naomi's behaviour.

Naomi's deviance is based on her inability to produce herself as a normal sexualised person; that is to say, her practices mark her out as 'desperate'. She has produced herself 'as a commodity', as something that can be exchanged (for male company, approval, sexual interest), but her commodity value is destroyed by her 'deviant' behaviour. The excesses

Judith Butler is an American feminist and gender theorist who very usefully employs and combines both psychoanalytical theories and the work of Foucault to address issues of the production and reproduction of subjectivities. Her ability to move across and combine complex and seemingly antithetical theoretical positions makes her one of the most interesting and important cultural theorists writing today. Her most recent books are *Gender Trouble* and *Bodies that Matter*.

of her behaviour (sending David the tickets and the CDs) are diagnosed as an abnormality which, at the very least, puts her into the 'uncool' category.

Not exactly scientific, you think? But it does have some functions in common with medical or psychological discourses. That is, this story is produced as a narrative of normality, as a description and diagnosis of deviancy, and as a warning about the consequences of that deviancy (a version of 'stop it, or you'll go blind!').

We referred to Foucault's theories of the relationship between institutions, discourses and knowledge, on the one hand, and the production and regulation of normalised subjectivities, on the other. If there is one major shortcoming with Foucault's theories, however, it is his disinclination to theorise about these moves at the level of practice. In other words, Foucault's work helps us to understand what happens, but he is less helpful with how it happens. To address this, we'll stay with the 'Desperate' article but consider it in terms of the theories of gender and subjectivity offered by Judith Butler.

SUBJECTIVITY AS PERFORMANCE

Butler specifically addresses this question of the relationship between subjectivity and practice in her book *Bodies that Matter* (1993). She suggests that the sexualising of the body, and as a result the production of identity, occurs through what she calls 'the reiteration of norms' (10). This means that bodies don't come to mean naturally; rather they are produced as meaningful by discourses which divide them up and evaluate them (female breasts are sexualised in a particular way, as are men's stomach muscles, for instance). At the same time, people respond to these discourses by 'performing' their bodies 'in time' with these discourses. The effect of the combination of discursive evaluations and imperatives ('this is what bodies mean, therefore do this') produces what we might call performances of subjectivity.

Let's return to Naomi and David. Naomi is performing 'appropriately' as a young woman at the beginning of the narrative: remember, she does all the right things, such as allowing her hand to be held and gazing into David's eyes. What we have here is a romance genre, and in this genre, at least according to *Dolly*, the appropriate performances involve:

- David being in control ('holding her hand'); and
- Naomi doing the worshipping ('gazing into his eyes').

Everything was 'going to work out fine' as long as they remembered their lines and moves and didn't 'misperform'. But as *Dolly* makes clear, Naomi's performance fell to pieces. It is interesting that the *Dolly* article, which seemingly deals with supposedly deep and meaningful feelings and topics like romance and love, should so unashamedly and unambiguously diagnose the failure of the relationship in terms of misperformance. Naomi fails to perform like a young woman. She gives up her passivity in favour of a performance which is much too close to what is expected of the man.

This doesn't mean that Foucault is wrong when he suggests that identity is sexualised in terms of notions of normality, and that deviance is treated as a kind of medical or psychological disorder. All it means is that we have to extend Foucault's ideas about normality and regulation to include Butler's insight that repeated and appropriate performance is the means by which normality is reproduced—as a practice.

Moreover, Butler points out that certain gender genres, and the successful performance of those genres, have been used to construct hierarchies within cultures. The broad genre of 'masculine performance' has generally been valued over that of 'female performance', for instance. Similarly, a successful male performance—this will vary from one context to another—will be valued over unsuccessful male performances.

If we accept that masculinity and femininity are performed, we need to consider such questions as, what kinds of performances are normally legitimated, and what constitutes a successful performance? The answer to these questions will of course vary from culture to culture, and even within cultures. Cultures usually ensure that there are very serious political, social and economic consequences involved in the non-performance or misperformance of gender genres. We will now provide three examples of what we might call the 'politics of gender misperformance': the first involves the misperformance of masculinity, the second the misperformance of femininity, and the third the 'overperformance' of masculinity.

GENDER (MIS)PERFORMANCES

Example 1: A misperformance of masculinity

When the then US president, George Bush, went to Tokyo in 1992, he did so with the express purpose of convincing the Japanese to further open their domestic markets to American goods and services, thereby cutting the huge trade surplus Japan was running with the US.

Before Bush left the US the discourses he and his advisers used could be described as aggressive and masculinist: the US was sick of being fobbed off by the Japanese, the US was the superpower, and the Japanese would listen and act accordingly, or else.

Unfortunately, at a state dinner in Tokyo, Bush became ill, threw up on the trousers of then Japanese prime minister Kiichi Miyazawa, and fell under the table. Finally he was assisted to his feet, and needed help to leave the room.

Nothing was ever officially made of the incident (the Japanese expressed sympathy, and Bush said he was fine), but American newspapers lambasted Bush as a 'wimp'—a charge that had been made on other occasions. Indeed, to a certain extent, the subsequent US invasion of Panama, and the war with Iraq, could be understood in terms of the United States's—and particularly Bush's—attempts to successfully perform its much-questioned 'masculinity'.

Example 2: A misperformance of femininity

In the Professor Anita Hill/Judge Clarence Thomas affair, Hill accused Thomas, who had been nominated to the US Supreme Court, of sexual harassment (for a different discussion of this event, see Chapter 1). During the Senate questioning of Hill, she remained cool and in control, and did not offer anything like the kind of performance the all-male inquiry panel expected.

After Thomas's appointment was confirmed, a number of senators said they didn't believe Hill because she hadn't responded to questions in an emotional manner, and it was also suggested in the press that Hill's performances weren't 'warm enough'.

Nobody would have complained if a male general or diplomat or lawyer had performed in a calm and composed manner in this settting— in fact, it would have been expected. Anita Hill, on the other hand, was expected (by men) to perform as a woman who had been sexually harassed: that is to say, emotionally.

Example 3: An 'overperformance' of masculinity

In 1991 the then world heavyweight boxing champion, Mike Tyson, was convicted of raping seventeen-year-old Desiree Washington. At his trial, Tyson made no attempt to play down his 'masculinity'. He boasted that he found it difficult to keep his hands off attractive women and usually tried to have sex with them as soon as possible.

Tyson's performance was a good example of how a normally acceptable masculine performance could become illegitimate (Judge Thomas recognised this and played down his masculinity). Tyson's performance became illegitimate because it clashed too obviously with, or devalued, aspects of other legitimate gender performances: the victim was a woman, but she was also a seventeen-year-old girl and another man's daughter.

These examples all demonstrate that gender performances are at the same time political performances, with serious consequences. And yet despite the strong influence these genres, narratives and performances undoubtedly exercise over people, they don't entirely control practices associated with gender. One reason for this is that while each performance must be like previous performances, no two performances are ever exactly alike—if only because no two contexts are exactly alike. Time and repetition produce normality and regulation, but they also produce deviation and change. That there are so many gender genres and performances testifies to Freud's point that deviance is more or less the norm in Western culture.

COMMODITISING SUBJECTIVITY

As we pointed out in our previous chapter on ideology, people don't just conform to the ideas and imperatives coming out of the media, advertising and governments. The notion of cultural literacy implies that, to a certain extent, people are aware of the different kinds of pressures and influences that are placed upon them to be 'healthy' or 'normal', and can find ways to negotiate them. People can 'get away with' all kinds of performances of subjectivity if they know how to 'play the field'. A good example of this is the way the financial success of the 'Gay and Lesbian Mardi Gras' in Sydney (it brings in thousands of tourists every year, and attracts large crowds) has put a large number of different (supposedly deviant) subjectivities 'on show' to the public. Now this activity is a 'one-off', and it doesn't mean that gays and lesbians aren't still subjected to (official and unofficial) communal violence. But once these subjectivities and their performances are given official and public 'exposure', even for economic reasons, then it becomes more difficult to (officially) define them as 'deviant' and 'non-human'.

In fact, in some cultural spheres so-called 'deviant' subjectivities, or their characteristics, can come to constitute cultural capital. People pick out different hairstyles, character types, clothing, ways of walking and talking, body shapes and styles in order to 'commoditise' themselves; and many of these 'subject fashions' they choose are taken from the influential world of popular audio/visual culture, which sometimes puts 'deviant' subjectivities 'on display'. Once these subjectivities circulate within a culture, they have the chance of becoming 'legal tender'—that is, accepted as (more or less) 'normal' or even fashionable—and can be taken up by people wishing to 'commoditise' themselves.

What do we mean by the term **commoditisation**? Within contemporary western culture, it is important to note that many texts, whether written, spoken or visual, are produced as commodities to a certain extent. In addition to the idea of **commodity** as a thing that is produced by a commercial enterprise for sale to a target market (the commodity of the video game, for instance, is likely to be designed for a youngish, computer literate audience), 'non-commercial' texts may undergo commoditisation to some extent. As Arjun Appadurai writes:

> I propose that the commodity situation in the social life of any 'thing' be defined as the situation in which its exchangeability (past, present, or future) for some other thing is its socially relevant feature.
>
> Appadurai 1988:13

If a company produces a video game, it does so in order to exchange that commodity—that text—for capital, both financial (sales figures, profits) and cultural (the prestige involved in having the biggest-selling, or an award-winning, video game). The same process applies to subjectivities. When a person dresses up before going to a disco, or cuts away the body section of a shirt to reveal incredibly tight stomach muscles, or goes to the gym to help produce those stomach muscles, we can say that the text's—that is, the subject's—most 'socially relevant feature' (at least for the owner/author) is its 'exchangeability' (those stomach muscles can be exchanged for social popularity, sexual responses, admiring glances). Moreover, there is nothing to stop what we might call the 're-commoditisation' of a text—almost to infinity. A male who uses his 'gym-built body' to attract a partner (long or short term) can be used by the new partner to commoditise her or himself (the logic being 'I'm valuable because I have an attractive partner').

SUMMARY

In this chapter we have argued that subjectivities are culturally produced, and that the identities we take on and use are closely connected to our communication practices. We suggested that subjects are:

- always split because they are partly constituted out of repressed or unconscious desires;
- produced, regulated and normalised through the mechanisms and discourses of cultural institutions;
- connected to communication practices through the notion of appropriate gender (and other generic) performances; and
- able to pick and choose, and incorporate, different aspects of subjectivity in order to commoditise themselves.

FURTHER READING

Appadurai, A. ed. 1988, *The Social Life of Things*, Cambridge University Press, New York

Butler, J. 1993, *Bodies that Matter*, Routledge, New York

Butler, J. 1997, *The Psychic Life of Power*, Stanford University Press, Stanford, California

Foucault, M. 1997, *Michel Foucault: Ethics The Essential Works 1*, edited by P. Rabinow, Penguin, London

Laplanche, J. 1999, *Essays on Otherness*, Routledge, London

Chapter 7

Texts and contexts

In Chapter 4 we looked at the ways we make sense of communication practices in terms of contextual frames such as discourse, narrative and genre. In this chapter we extend this work on contexts by examining the interdependent relationship between contexts and communication practices (or texts). We introduce techniques for analysing text/context relations, and use these to develop a more detailed understanding of the effects of contexts on communication practices, and vice versa. In order to do this, we will draw on concepts from the broad field of social semiotics.

SOCIAL MEANING MAKING

Social semiotics talks about meaning making as a social practice, carried out by social agents in a social (and cultural) context. It is concerned with questions such as:

- How do acts of meaning making get negotiated in particular contexts?
- What wider social and cultural frames (narratives, genres, discourses) do communication practices relate to?
- What social relations, power relations and ideological values are implicated?
- How does a particular communicative act (text) operate to reproduce or to change these relations and values?

Social semiotics draws on the semiotic notion of communication or language as a system of signs, which provides a range of potential meanings to its users. Cultures make meanings from an enormous variety

Who does social semiotics?

The term 'social semiotics' comes from the work of the linguist M.A.K. (Michael) Halliday, who published his book *Language as Social Semiotic* in 1978. Halliday was born in the United Kingdom and moved to Australia in 1976 to become Professor of Linguistics at the University of Sydney. Most people who call themselves social semioticians or who do social semiotics would acknowledge Halliday's work as foundational. Among his writings are a functional grammar of English (1985) and a very accessible short account of his theories, co-authored by Ruqaiya Hasan (1985). Hasan and Halliday have also written together on cohesion in texts (1976).

Work in this area began by focusing on language. J.L. (Jim) Martin has developed Halliday's theory, particularly in relation to register, genre, ideology and discourse (1985, 1986, 1992).

In 1988 Bob Hodge and Gunther Kress published their book *Social Semiotics*. This presented social semiotics as an analytical approach to a wide range of cultural texts and issues. It also linked with work which related social semiotics to other contemporary critical theories (Kress 1985, Kress and Threadgold 1988, Threadgold 1986).

of sign systems: bodily, verbal, visual, ornamental, architectural, musical etc. Recall that Saussure argued that meaning, or signs, were produced through a system of relations and of difference—that is, meanings were defined in terms of what they were not. However, unlike Saussure, social semiotics does not maintain a fixed distinction between the code or *langue* (some sort of idealised grammar or set of rules) and performance or use (*parole*).

Instead, like Bourdieu, social semiotics sees social meaning making as about behaviour or practice. Meaning systems are never closed or finite, but always open, dynamic and changing, as we recreate the system of possible meanings continuously through our communication practices.

Sign systems are sets of potential meanings, and the output of these systems is actual choices, what people say or do. We need to qualify and explain what is meant by 'choice'. Choices within semiotic systems are not made freely by individuals. They are 'choices' in the sense of one option among many potential options available within the system (meaning potential). In the actual performance or practice of meaning making, people don't make free choices as to how or what they will mean. There are always constraints on meaning making. Meaning potentials are just that—potential meanings. The actual meanings made are limited by two important conditions, the conditions of *access* and of *context*.

First, not everyone within a culture or community has access to all the possible ways of speaking, writing or meaning that culture potentially allows. The cultural trajectories of individuals and groups endows them with different dispositions and literacies. Not everyone has access to the same educational opportunities. Not everyone has grown up able to speak more than one language or dialect. Others have had to learn the national language as a second language when they were adults. What is more, the lack of educational, economic or even social capital tends to work against some groups accessing contexts (such as going to university) where they could acquire that capital and literacy.

Second, acts of meaning making always take place within a context, and contexts constrain and limit the range of meanings that can be made. People cannot break into song in the middle of a formal written examination. (Or at least, if they did, the consequences would be unfortunate; they would probably be ejected, and fail the exam.) Contexts are markets or fields, in Bourdieu's terms, in which certain practices are appropriate and carry capital within that field, and others do not. Contexts are always already shaped and framed by the cultural patterns we use to make sense of them (narratives, genres, discourses etc.).

TEXT

At this point, we need to introduce another element of the theory—the concept of text. While this is a familiar and widely used term in semiotics, literature and educational contexts generally, the way in which it is used (and thus what it can mean) within a social semiotic approach is distinctive and important.

Texts are produced through the choices made within systems of meaning making (semiotic systems). A text is a unit of meaning which operates within a context. We can view texts from two perspectives:

1. as product (synoptic perspective); and
2. as process (dynamic perspective).

Like communication in general, texts can be thought of as things/objects, or as actions. The synoptic perspective, or the view of text as product, is the one most people are familiar with—when we talk about texts we think of a book, a poem, possibly a TV program. However, texts exist not so much as objects which can be picked up and carried around (a paperback, a video cassette) but as events which unfold in time and space. A conversation is a type of text we can readily think of in these terms. It is a fluid, interactive process in which all participants take turns to contribute, shaping the direction and structure of the text jointly as they go along.

Other texts do not show their processes of production so clearly; for example, printed texts, such as books and newspapers, are presented to readers as completed objects. Nevertheless, they too go through stages of production, during which their 'final' form is cumulatively constructed, negotiated, and altered in different ways. And even this so-called final form is still subjected to ongoing cultural change and negotiation. One obvious example is the different versions of popular texts, such as films (there is the original black and white *Casablanca* and the 'colourised' text; the first release of *Blade Runner* and the more recently released 'director's cut') and music (the tape, record or CD version, the original recording or the remastered tapes), which makes it difficult to talk about any 'final' version of a text.

Perhaps less obvious, but even more important in some ways, is the way in which texts are changed through undergoing different kinds of commoditisation within a culture. A song might be written for a band and appear on their CD; but it also might then be picked up by advertisers and used in a television commercial. This change of context completely changes the text: it now (potentially) means a number of very different things. One interesting example of this kind of re-commoditisation is the character Patsy Stone in the television series *Absolutely Fabulous*. The chain-smoking, hard drinking and sexually aggressive and active character became a cult figure for the gay community; during the Sydney Gay and Lesbian Mardi Gras in 1995 there was a float full of Patsy Stones. Take a text to another place and use it in different ways, and you have a 'new' text.

One of the reasons why we are able to communicate with others, despite the problem of 'difference' discussed above, is that there is a degree of probability or expectedness in the way texts unfold within contexts (Halliday & Hasan 1985:9–10). Thus, while texts and contexts can never fully determine one another, as members of a culture we are able to anticipate broadly the types of communication practices which will take place within a context. We are able to understand and respond to texts actively and appropriately to the extent that we are familiar with their contexts. That is, literacy about *texts* is inextricably tied up with the possession of literacy about *contexts*. Both constitute forms of cultural literacy.

CONTEXT

Contexts can be understood as the particular environments in which communication, texts and meaning making occur, and in which they function as meaningful. The context is the situation in which we make sense of a text or meaningful practice. For example:

- a crowd of supporters yelling 'Go, go, go!' as a swimmer representing their country is about to win the 400 metres freestyle in the 2000 Olympics; or
- a parent shouting 'Go, go, go!' as her dawdling children are about to miss the school bus.

The same words are uttered in each context, but can we say that they mean 'the same' in both contexts? Certainly, what those words mean to the swimmer (excitement, support, encouragement) is likely to be very different from their meaning to the reluctant school children (parental nagging and over-anxiety).

In each case, the interaction between text and context produces more meanings than the dictionary definition of the word 'go' can possibly encompass:

> *v.i.* Start, depart, move, continue moving, with self-originated or imparted motion, from some place, position, time, etc., specified or obvious.
>
> *Concise Oxford Dictionary*

There is a temptation to discuss contexts as if they are 'out there' in plain view, as part of 'reality'. But the view that contexts are non-semiotic, unlike texts, which are made of meanings, has a catch. Like texts, contexts are semiotic constructs. They are ways of making sense of the world. Context is a conceptual dimension, a way of reading what is going on 'out there'. There are as many potential contexts available to a person as there are meanings of a text, and these contexts may continue to inform or determine meanings, or may quickly give way to other contexts. Moreover, it is not as if we are aware of all the contexts that are influencing our actions or the meanings we make. One of the more interesting points about Freudian psychoanalysis, for example, is that it posits an unconscious aspect to our 'selves' which obviously can influence our actions, yet which we can never fully comprehend.

Why are contexts so unstable and difficult to explain? An Olympic swimming final appears to be a stable and clearly defined context. How can this context be read in different ways? First, the way the swimmer reads this context will be different from the way the supporters read it. For a start, the context in which the swimmer hears the crowd's chant is probably one which includes the swimmer's own physical and psychological state, the number of supporters, how close the other competitors are, and whether the swimmer is about to break a new world record. Other less immediate elements of this context could include the country's medal tally in the Olympics thus far, and the swimmer's own recent performances, as well as that of the competitors. The swimmer's supporters will read the context differently from the other swimmers' supporters, as will the media commentators who, a few days earlier, suggested that the swimmer was a 'has-been'.

In making sense of contexts, we take into account a number of aspects, including both the immediate situation, and the wider context, such as:

- what is going on, and where;
- those involved;
- the role of the text in the situation;
- the other texts (intertexts), which are related to this one; and
- the wider social and cultural context (framed in terms of narratives, genres, discourses).

By acknowledging that contexts are semiotic and can be read differently, we acknowledge that contexts are subject to negotiation. Defining contexts is a political issue, since establishing the meaning of a context is a way of establishing the meaning of a text.

An example is the way the terms 'rape' and 'sexual harassment' can be applied to particular contexts within Australian culture. Recently, a judge stated that the penalty for a man found guilty of rape should be lessened because the woman he raped was a prostitute. The judge decided that in determining the degree of seriousness of this rape, the woman's profession was a relevant aspect of the context. Others in the community, particularly women's groups and prostitutes, strongly disagreed with the judge's definition of the relevant context in this matter.

As another example, consider sexual harassment. What one person sees as a playful joke may be seen by another as unwanted and threatening behaviour. This has a great deal to do with gendered power differences in contexts such as the workplace. A power inequity, as we saw in Chapter 1, means that the same context is effectively not 'the same' for the more powerful participant as it is for the less powerful.

The relationship between texts and contexts is thus an interdependent one. Each affects the other, although it cannot be said either that contexts determine texts, nor that texts determine contexts. As Halliday and Hasan express it, 'the text creates the context as much as the context creates the text' (1985:47).

It might be useful to reiterate, however, that while everyone can bring different contexts to bear on texts, there is a considerable political dimension to the way in which some contexts are privileged over others. There are a number of contexts in which the various colonial activities in Africa, America, Australia and New Zealand might have been 'understood'; indeed, the context we bring to bear on this issue will determine, for instance, whether we use the word 'invasion' or 'settlement' when we refer, say, to Australian history in the eighteenth century. Australian Aboriginal peoples brought their contexts to bear on understanding and explaining British actions in 1788, but the British decided that those contexts didn't count.

Similarly, the various forms of discrimination and exploitation that have been practised against women in western cultures over the centuries have been perpetuated, to no small extent, because it was argued that women could only understand things in terms of 'private' contexts, whereas men could bring wider, public contexts to bear on issues; or, to put it another way, women could only understand things emotionally, while men were supposedly capable of bringing reason to bear on their thoughts and actions.

ANALYSING CONTEXTS

In this section we combine Foucault's and Bourdieu's ideas about field and power (discussed in Chapter 3) with a social semiotic approach to analysing context. The social semiotic framework we are drawing on here comes from the linguist M.A.K. Halliday. Halliday proposes a model for analysing text/context relations which accounts for the interpendent relationship between particular social contexts and the kinds of textual practice that take place in these contexts. He suggests that we can separate context into three aspects or dimensions:

1. Field—what is happening? What is the communication about?
2. Tenor—who is taking part? What is their part in the interaction? What positions are they taking up?
3. Mode—how is the text structured? What part is the code or language playing?

When contexts are analysed in this way, it becomes clear that the range of field, tenor and mode options cannot freely combine with one another. That is, some combinations are more likely than others. For example, we would not expect a context in which an executive listens patiently while a cleaner plays a guitar and sings a ballad about how to balance the budget (although it is possible to imagine a context for this—a TV comedy). The social action (giving advice about the budget) does not match the tenor (an executive whose job it is to know how to balance budgets being advised by a cleaner whose tasks do not include being expert at this). Nor does the mode (guitar ballad) match either the field or the tenor. Our sense of these kinds of incongruity constitutes a form of cultural literacy about communication and contexts.

Field

We have already introduced the concept of cultural field (see Chapter 3). We'll re-examine this and show how it can be applied to the analysis of texts or practices in relation to their immediate and wider contexts.

For Halliday, the field refers specifically to the social action of the text, what the language (or other semiotic resource) is being used to do:

> The **field** of discourse refers to what is happening, to the nature of the social action that is taking place: what is it that the participants are engaged in . . . ?
>
> Halliday 1985:12

In identifying the field, or social action, we recognise that it is an activity which is meaningful within a social system. 'What's going on' may be wholly 'language-in-action' or it may be an activity structured through other semiotic resources (visual, non-verbal).

But fields are characterised not only by certain types of subject matter, or social activity; according to Foucault, they also: lay down rules and procedures, assign roles and positions, regulate behaviours, movements and what can be said, and produce hierarchies.

Fields are 'the discursive and institutional domains where cultural and textual practice occur' (Luke 1996:327). In order to analyse the context of these practices, then, we need to ask:

- What is the social activity performed by the text, or the social occasion in which the text is embedded?
- What is the subject matter of the text?
- What discourses are involved, and what institutions?
- What rules and procedures associated with the field are implicated through the text? How are these being negotiated?
- What institutional values and hierarchies are implicated through the text?

Typically, the kind of social action going on also influences the subject matter, or what the interaction is about. While these two aspects of field, the social action and the subject matter, are linked, they do not necessarily determine one another. If the social action is 'doing the washing up', the participants may be discussing whether the washer has cleaned a plate adequately, or the quality of the detergent, but are just as likely to be discussing topics unrelated to what they are doing, such as the state of the economy or the neighbours' divorce. As a relatively relaxed social occasion, the textual activity is not strongly tied to particular discourses, rules and values.

Other fields do regulate their associated social action, behaviours, subject matter, discourse and values more strongly, in particular those fields which are under the overt control of a central institution. Obvious examples can be found in the fields of religion, law and education. For example, within the field of education, and the social occasion of a school science lesson, the subject matter is expected to be, and largely will be, science, although the participants will probably also be talking about various other (unofficial) topics.

Teacher: Yesterday we were talking about, uh, *wave* motion. And we said that *sound* was a particular *kind* of wave motion. Can anybody remember what kind of wave motion sound *is*? [To student with hand raised.] D'you remember? [Student indicates she only wants the pass to the bathroom.] Why should I give you a pass? [4 seconds, laughter] When you can't answer a question like that? [2 seconds, then to class:] What kind of wave motion is sound?

Student: It's—it's a *wave* motion.

Teacher: Sound is a *wave* motion. What *kind* of wave motion?

Student: Sound wave.

Teacher: Sound is a wave, what *kind* of wave?

Another: Vibration.

Teacher: What *kind* of vibration?

Student: Waves.

Teacher: What *kind* of waves?

Eugene: Are you asking which one of those four?

Teacher: *Mhmm.*

Eugene: Oh . . . um, uh long- long-i-tud-inal wave.

Teacher: Eugene is correct. [Others comment, whistle] [31 seconds, writing at board]

Lemke 1990:246–7

The social action is that of instruction, through a classroom lesson, and more precisely a teacher questioning students to test their recall. The associated subject matter is the discourse of science, evident in word choice ('wave', 'vibration', 'longitudinal', 'motion'). Here is a text whose field is under the official control of the teacher, in whom the authority of the institution is vested. The textual practices available to the teacher and to the students are constrained by certain rules (about who may speak, under what circumstances), a hierarchy (the teacher is 'in charge' and has more expert knowledge than the students, therefore the students are to obey and to learn from the teacher), and a set of values (education improves us as individuals, education is for the students' own good).

The social action, however, is not exclusively or purely the 'official' field. There are moments when the field escapes from the teacher's control, for example when a student raises her hand as if to respond to the teacher's question but instead performs the social action of 'seeking permission to go to the toilet'. Students often use such techniques to challenge the teacher's control of the field without appearing to do so—what we can call a *tactic*. A tactic is an attempt, by those who do not have 'official' power, to achieve their own ends (Certeau 1988), often by using the 'official' rules for their own purposes.

Tenor

Meaning making is a form not just of social action but of *interaction*. When we make meanings we address them to some other—a listener, reader, or audience, actual or implied; sometimes we simply address meanings to ourselves. Communicative acts are not just simple exchanges of information, but are about the allocation, negotiation, acceptance or rejection of a variety of social relations. **Tenor** refers to this interactive dimension of communication. Here is Halliday's definition of tenor:

> The tenor of discourse refers to who is taking part, to the nature of the participants, their statuses and roles: what kinds of role relationship obtain among the participants, including permanent and temporary relationships of one kind or another, both the types of speech role that they are taking on in the dialogue and the whole cluster of socially significant relationships in which they are involved?
>
> Halliday 1985:12

When we 'read' a text, whether it is a written text, a spoken interaction, a set of gestures, a photograph or a television program, we enter into a relation with that text and with the agent which produced it. To communicate is not merely to give and receive neutral information, but to enter into a relation with some other. This social relation is mediated in and through texts or meaning making practices. For example, a street sign: HARBOUR BRIDGE LEFT LANE sets up a relation between the motorists who read it and the sign itself. The sign addresses motorists on behalf of the social agent who installed the sign, presumably the road traffic authority. It directs the motorist; that is, it gives the motorist directions ('traffic in the left lane goes to the Harbour Bridge') and at the same time it gives the motorist an instruction ('take the left lane if you want the Harbour Bridge').

If we refer to Halliday's definition of tenor, we can make several observations about the tenor relation between the motorist and the sign. First, we can note that this is a temporary, if not momentary, relation set up between motorist and road sign. The driver notes the sign, makes a decision about which lane to take, and drives on. Second, the tenor involves one participant 'telling the other what to do' and thereby taking on the status of authority over the other (with respect to the social action or field in which both are involved).

As you can see from this example, tenor relations need not outlive or transcend the interaction which produces them. The concept of a relation does not imply a 'relationship' in the everyday sense of the word—that is, a socially identifiable, personalised connection between individuals. Instead, the concept of tenor arises from the function that language (or some other semiotic resource system) has in specific contexts, as interaction. Many of these kinds of interaction do carry with them relationships we readily recognise and name (mother–daughter, boyfriend–girlfriend, prosecution lawyer–witness). Other, more transitory and less socially stable relations such as the relation between the motorist and the road sign do not have labels. That is why we need a critical vocabulary in order to specify this dimension of context.

We can analyse tenor relations in more detail using the categories suggested by Poynton (1985). She identifies three aspects which constitute tenor:

1. social distance (contact);
2. emotion or attitude (affect); and
3. power.

Each of these aspects can be brought into play in a context through a variety of specific markers, or socially constructed attributes.

Contact, or social distance, refers to the positioning of the participants as socially intimate or distant. Is the text personal or impersonal, formal or informal, public or private in its address? Compare the impersonal and public address of the road sign example to the personal and private tone of a love letter. Is the relation one of solidarity or antagonism (us/them)? Compare the tenor relations (and verbal and non-verbal practices) of members of opposing football teams onfield during a match to their relations when grouping together to lobby the local government authorities for better sporting facilities in their town.

Affect refers to the kinds of attitudes and emotions that are being displayed as part of the interaction. The absence of overtly expressed attitudes or feelings is as significant as their presence in constructing tenor relations, and is often generically constrained. For example, three different genres dealing with 'science' in a broad sense may display different degrees and types of affect:

1. academic scientific writing strives to be emotionally neutral and 'objective';
2. popular science reporting in a magazine may try to present science as 'fun' or 'exciting'; and
3. a pro-conservationist speech will use quite emotive language (e.g. praise for the wonders of nature, indignation and contempt for organisations responsible for polluting the environment).

Power refers to the extent to which the participants are positioned as equal or unequal. In Bourdieu's terms, power can be described in terms of the amount and kinds of capital available to social agents within particular cultural fields. Capital may be acquired or negotiated on the basis of such attributes as physical strength or skill, socially institutionalised authority, social status (class-based, wealth-based, hereditary), or expertise (Poynton 1985:76–77). However, the extent to which a particular attribute or form of capital ties in with power flows is contingent on the cultural field; a black belt in Judo is not going to help you come out on top within the cultural field of an interview for a job in a creative multimedia design company (unless the position is that of security guard).

Foucault makes the point that power relations are mobile and power is multiple: that is, it is not held centrally by any institution or authority, but is always under negotiation between agents in particular local sites (Luke 1996: 325).

Power, and also contact and affect, then, are not fixed or pre-determined elements of context which then shape texts and meaning making in predictable ways. Tenor relations may evolve and shift during the interaction.

For example, consider a situation in which a student comes to see a lecturer to ask for an extension of time for an assignment. The context is already pre-structured to an extent in terms of the relative power and status of the two people concerned. Lecturers have a higher status than students because of their role within the educational institution, their qualifications and their level of relevant expertise. The lecturer has institutional authority over the student, being in a position to evaluate the student's work, allocate grades, decide course content and so on.

These tenor factors mean that the student would probably not come in and yell at the lecturer, demanding an extension, and the lecturer would be very unlikely to apologise profusely to the student for not granting one. The student would probably address the lecturer by title and surname (indicating the lecturer's higher status and also a degree of formality and distance). The lecturer might use the student's first name, or not address the student by name at all (how does this position the student?). The lecturer would remain seated and the student would stand unless invited to sit. These would all be markers of the unequal status and power relations of the two participants.

However, this relation may be negotiated and changed as part of the communication process. For example, the student may burst into tears, explaining that the recent death of a family pet has made it extremely difficult to concentrate on study. The social distance (contact) may shift from relatively formal and distant to a slightly more personal relation. The lecturer may offer the student a box of tissues. With decreased social distance and formality, the dimension of affect is likely to become more overt, with the discussion of feelings and the use of non-verbal markers of sympathy (pats on the shoulder, sympathetic looks).

The student could even turn 'the rules of the game' to the student's advantage, by paradoxically using the 'sad plight' as a way of getting what the student wants (the desired extension) by playing on the lecturer's sympathy. This tactic would make a weakness into a strength, and through a form of cultural literacy in this particular 'game', negotiate a 'win'.

As this example suggests, the relation between context and meaning making is a dynamic one, in which elements of context may shift as part of the process. Further, each element of tenor—power, contact and affect—may be taken for granted as part of the 'accepted' background or may be brought into focus as under negotiation. Here is an example where different aspects of tenor are brought to the fore as the interaction proceeds.

Mother:	Don't do that. Move it away, if you want to rock it. [The child is rocking on a chair.]
Child:	No.
Mother:	You'll go straight to your room if you bang my chair . . .
Child:	I hit you with a teddy.
Mother:	Poor teddy! Teddy's crying. You hurt his head. He's got a headache now. He wants to be my teddy.
Child:	No [taking teddy]. He hasn't got a tummyache. He's got a fat tummy. I want to see the water in there . . .

Painter cited in Poynton 1990:68

The mother begins by directly asserting her power over the child by issuing a command ('Don't do that') and then a threat ('You'll go straight to your room if you bang my chair'). The child's reaction exemplifies Foucault's insight that power always produces its own resistance!

However, the mother then changes to a different strategy, downplaying her own power in order to shift the interaction away from a conflict over the child's behaviour. She turns the child's act of aggression ('I hit you with a teddy') into the topic (field), and talks about the teddy's feelings ('Poor teddy . . .') and how the teddy will want to be hers now. In this way the mother shifts the tenor so that it is focused on affect and contact rather than on power/control. (The values embedded in the mother's narrative about the teddy convey a moral lesson for the child: if the child is angry or violent then others will not want to be close to the child.)

This example, like the previous one, demonstrates that there is no one-to-one, deterministic relation between an identifiable social relation, such as parent–child, and the ascription of power, authority and control, but that these are constantly under negotiation.

So far we have discussed field and tenor as separate dimensions of context, however, they are closely interrelated in actual practices, and cannot be regarded as separate (or 'independent variables') for a number of reasons. First, as we pointed out above, power relations are contingent on field—what is a basis for negotiating power/capital in one field may not be in another. Capital needs to be recognised as legitimate within a particular cultural field. Secondly, cultural fields are shaped by discourses which not only produce and regulate forms of social action, knowledge and 'subject matter', but also social positions, hierarchies and values (relations of contact, power, and affect).

Mode

Finally, we will briefly discuss the third element of context, mode. **Mode** concerns the formation of the communication as a text, including the code/s and the medium/s involved. Halliday offers the following definition of mode:

> The mode of discourse refers to what part the language is playing, what it is that the participants are expecting language to do for them in that situation: the symbolic organisation of the text, the status that it has, and its function in the context, including the channel (is it spoken or written or some combination of the two?)
>
> Halliday & Hasan 1985:12

While Halliday is primarily concerned here with language, mode is concerned precisely with the choice of a semiotic system or code. Within any system, more delicate (precise) mode options are available. Within language, a text may be formed through the medium of speech or of writing, just as in painting an image may be done in oils or in watercolours. Verbal texts may be dialogue or monologue, printed or handwritten, scrawled on the back of an envelope or typed on official letterhead stationery.

Together, the concepts of code and medium remind us that texts are material forms as well as meaning-making practices. The code and the medium make possible, and also limit, the range of meanings. They provide a diversity of materials (mediums) and ways of shaping these materials (codes). Technology is continually expanding the ways in which these mediums and codes can combine, as well as opening up new mediums. Prehistoric humans had a fairly limited range of mediums with which to make meanings. They had visual media, such as carvings and cave paintings, and possibly other systems such as dress, adornment and dance, and no doubt used their bodies as a medium of non-verbal communication, through gesture, touch and so on. By contrast, in the twentieth century, and heading into the twenty-first, we have not only what we can call 'simple' mediums such as speech, writing and graphic representation, but increasingly make use of multimodal texts (combinations of several mediums, often using 'new' technology). Television, film and CD-roms are prime examples of such mediums, since they can combine sound (speech, music) and a range of visual media.

The analysis of mode is critical to understanding the ways in which texts come to mean as they do, since the other two elements of context, field and tenor, need always to be read against the possibilities offered by the mode. Let's examine how this works in an advertising text (see Figure 13).

The Sony ad appears in a print medium, a magazine, and employs both verbal and visual codes. The photographic image of the compact hi-fi system is the central and dominant image in the text. Its central placement relates to the field; the social action is that of advertising a product to potential consumers. The product takes centre stage against a plain background. Another code, music, is also alluded to by the images of musical notes.

The verbal text supplements the visual text by amplifying (no pun intended) the information the image presents and extending the field of discourse. The verbal text also sets up specific tenor relations of persuasion the image alone probably could not accomplish.

Putting field, tenor and mode together

Let's now fill out our analysis of the Sony text in relation to the dimensions of field and tenor. We have noted that the social activity is promoting a product for sale, and that this is pursued in part through placing the visual image on 'centre-stage'. The ad deploys a number of

Figure 13

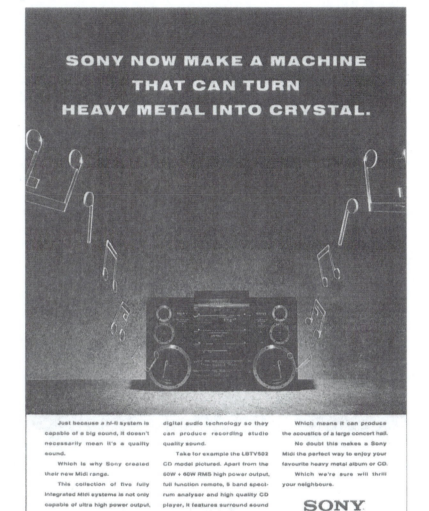

Courtesy of Sony Australia

overlapping cultural fields—music, technology and even alchemy—all in the service of the broad cultural field of advertising.

The verbal text constructs the cultural field of music equipment technology (there are references to 'digital audio technology', 'ultra high output', '5-band spectrum analyser'). The technological discourse functions to invoke values associated with technology and science in general, such as 'reliable', 'state-of-the-art' and 'progressive'; values which are also explicitly supported by the marketing discourse ('high quality', 'the perfect way to enjoy . . .'). Science here is in the service of consumer pleasure.

The text also draws on a discourse of music and music appreciation, appealing to wide tastes through references to both 'heavy metal' and 'the acoustics of the concert hall'. The term 'heavy metal' is used in the large print at the top of the text as well as in the body text underneath, and can be read as belonging to two different discourses. In the heading, SONY NOW MAKE A MACHINE THAT CAN TURN HEAVY METAL INTO CRYSTAL, the association between 'heavy metal' and 'crystal' comes from the discourse of medieval alchemy, the science of turning base metals such as lead into precious metals such as gold. The pun on 'heavy metal' comes from its double meaning, as a term from both musical and chemical discourse, at least for those readers who have the cultural knowledge of both discourses. The double meaning is also carried through, for those who have a different set of cultural literacies, in the images of crystal notes floating away from the CD player. Contrasts, or binaries, such as heavy/light, classical/popular music can be picked up on by readers of the advertisement. These all help to produce the social action of 'advertising' by suggesting the transformations this marvellous piece of equipment can perform for the buyer. That is, they are all motivated by the function of 'promoting a product to a potential consumer'.

What kind of tenor relations does this text produce? The advertisement is worded as if the *power relations* between the producer of the text and its audience were equal. The 'speaker' of the ad seems to assume that the readers have similar expertise in hi-fi, since many technical terms are used without explanation. While we, the audience, may not know this much about hi-fi, we may find it flattering to be treated as if we do possess this form of capital.

In terms of the *contact*, we might consider that it is not very close, since there is no direct contact with the speaker. The text is produced by an anonymous agent and disseminated to thousands of people through the mass media. Nevertheless, in the last two paragraphs the ad addresses us in a personalised and familiar way, and talks about 'your favourite' music, 'we' and 'your neighbours'. This interpellates the reader in a relation of implied solidarity, a community of shared values. The ad seems to say 'Trust me, I know what you like and you'll like this'.

The *affect* of the ad is very positive, with terms of praise used for the product ('studio quality', 'high quality') and suggestions about the pleasure the buyer will derive from the product ('the perfect way to enjoy your favourite . . . album or CD').

This analysis is a way of making explicit the very familiar and 'taken-for-granted' aspects this text has in common with many other advertisements. While the text addresses the reader in terms of a relation of apparent equality, pseudo-personal appeal and 'feel-good' effect, these features of tenor relate directly to the ad's selling function. This example of the ad genre has a relatively familiar and predictable set of characteristics, which relate in fairly obvious ways to its social purpose. However, as audiences' cultural literacies in reading ads (and reading ads critically) become more and more developed, advertisers are pushed to develop new and different ways of 'selling'. We only have to compare ads from, say, the 1940s and 1950s, with contemporary ads, to see how the genre has shifted in response to changing audience literacies.

SUMMARY

This chapter identified the concepts of text and context as important in analysing communication practices. The relationship between text and context was identified as a dynamic one, in which texts and contexts interact with one another.

In making sense of contexts, we take into account a number of aspects, including both the immediate situation or social occasion, and the wider context, including:

- what is going on, and where;
- those involved;
- the role of the text in the situation;
- the other texts (intertexts) which are related to this one; and
- the wider social and cultural context (framed in terms of narratives, genres, discourses).

We suggested that our awareness of the relation between text and context, as users of language and other semiotic resources systems, constitutes a form of cultural literacy.

In order to analyse contexts, we discussed a social semiotic model informed by the theories of Bourdieu and Foucault. We argued that contexts can be broadly analysed in terms of field, tenor and mode.

FURTHER READING

Bourdieu, P. 1991, *Language and Symbolic Power*, ed. and introduced by J.B. Thompson, trans. G. Raymond and M. Adamson, Polity Press, Cambridge

Halliday, M.A.K. & R. Hasan 1985, *Language, Context and Text: Aspects of Language in a Social-semiotic Perspective*, Deakin University Press, Geelong, Victoria, Part A

Poynton, C. 1985, *Language and Gender: Making the Difference*, Deakin University Press, Geelong, Victoria, Chapter 6

Chapter 8

Speech genres

In this and the following two chapters, we examine the genres, practices and literacies associated with the three primary communication mediums: spoken, written and visual. We discuss and critique the assumptions and values associated with these mediums (such as that speech is sincere and spontaneous, writing is distant and authoritative, and visual texts are objective and faithfully represent 'reality'). We show that the ways in which spoken, written and visual practices and genres occur require particular forms of literacy.

We'll begin by discussing the social life of speech—how varieties of speech are developed, their contexts of use, and associated spoken literacies. We then look at the characteristics of speech versus writing, and finally at speech as a mode of interaction (dialogue), and as a site where power relations are negotiated, challenged or enforced.

THE SOCIAL LIFE OF SPEECH

Speech is regarded as the most basic and primary means of communication. It is the one we acquire, as individuals, before many other semiotic systems. It is also regarded, in accounts of the evolution and development of human beings, as having developed earlier than writing. Speaking and listening are activities we usually perform without reflecting very much about what we are doing, and which seem to 'come naturally'. In contrast, writing is something we are very conscious of having had to learn how to do.

As children, we learn how to mean primarily by learning how to speak. Of course, babies also rely heavily on facial and gestural signs as a means of communication and interaction. Beyond behavioural symptoms such as crying when they are wet or hungry, babies develop ways of interacting symbolically with those around them. Even before they are able to demonstrate control of 'adult' language, very young children use vocal sounds to respond to and interact with those around them, apparently gaining pleasure merely from the process of 'having a conversation'.

Speech, then, is a fundamental human activity. However, we should not be fooled by the deceptively 'natural' character of speech as a phenomenon and speaking as a practice. Neither speech as a social practice, nor our capacity for speaking, develop in a social or historical vacuum. Languages and specific modes of speech develop in particular social and historical contexts.

It is impossible to talk about 'speech' without considering *what* we speak, that is, which language, and the history of that language. For many, but by no means all of the readers of this textbook, English will be your first language; that is, the language you learned to speak first. But English is not a pure phenomenon—Australian English is not the same as American English, or New Zealand English, or so-called Standard British English. To trace the history of any language, and its various inflections and dialects, is to trace the history of the colonising of some groups by other, dominant groups.

For example, Standard British English was once a *dialect* (variant language type) spoken predominantly by the merchant class in London. With their increasing social power in the late Middle Ages, the variety of language members of this class spoke gradually became associated with—indeed, colonised—not only trade and finance but other influential institutions, such as government, administration, law, religion, literature and education. It became accepted as standard, or 'correct' English, at the expense of other varieties of English, and these other dialects came to be regarded not only as incorrect but as reflecting the morality and lifestyle of their speakers, who were largely working class as opposed to merchants, who were the emerging capitalist class (see Fairclough 1989:56–8). Other types of speech, and those who spoke them, were regarded as 'vulgar', 'ignorant' and 'slovenly', and yet, but for a turn of history, one of these 'non-standard' dialects might have become established as Standard English and revered in the place of the East Midland dialect.

Thus the values attributed to a language are largely determined by the social and political status of the group which speaks that language—the language of a dominant group becomes the 'prestige' language, and the languages of the dominated are devalued.

A similar story can be seen in relation to the pidgins and creoles of colonised countries such as America and Australia. *Pidgins* and *creoles* are composite languages, a mixture of two or more languages, usually as a result of colonisation. The colonised people adapt elements of the language of their colonisers and combine it with their own language. The result is a pidgin which is used as a 'common language' for communication between the colonisers and the colonised. When a pidgin becomes the first language of a generation it becomes a creole. For example, most non-European Torres Strait Islanders speak a language called Torres Strait creole or *Broken*. It is increasingly accepted as the official language of the islands. For the indigenous inhabitants of the islands, for many years, it was regarded as 'standard English', until increasing contact with English speakers on the mainland led to the realisation that it was not the English of the mainland Australia Anglo-Celtic community. Instead, as Shnukal points out, it was (and in many cases, still is) regarded 'as a "bastardised", "fractured", "ungrammatical" form of English' (Shnukal 1983:30). This produces a form of linguistic racism, which has very real effects for Torres Strait creole speakers in terms of access to employment and access to education, in mainland society if not in island society.

Speech, whether it takes the form of standard or non-standard varieties, regional dialects, accented varieties, pidgins or creoles, is produced out of a particular set of past historical and political conditions, which continue to affect the way that variety of speech is regarded in the present.

How we speak—our specific speech practices—is influenced by a number of social and cultural dimensions. Bourdieu, in *Language and Symbolic Power* (1991a), suggests that speakers acquire a 'practical sense', which is the capacity to make our utterances relevant or appropriate in particular contexts. Acquiring this 'practical sense', or linguistic habitus, means acquiring a sense (so ingrained it is not conscious) of the conditions which attach to contexts, of what speech behaviour is appropriate and of the consequences of behaving appropriately or otherwise. This 'practical sense' guides us through what can sometimes be a minefield of social interactions, so that we know, for example, what kinds of things it is appropriate to say at a funeral, and in what tone of voice, and how to close off a telephone conversation. Whether the interaction is a self-consciously ritualised one, or a routine daily one, speakers' linguistic habitus enables them to negotiate these situations.

The ability to speak, then, is much more than the ability to use our physiological resources (vocal cords, lips, tongue, mouth) to produce a series of vocal sounds recognisable as a well-formed and meaningful utterance in a particular language known to our hearers (although this is no mean feat in itself!). Bourdieu identifies the linguistic habitus as both 'the capacity to generate grammatically correct discourse' and 'the social capacity to use this competence adequately in a determinate situation' (Bourdieu 1991a:37). Thus what Bourdieu refers to as a practical sense or habitus is part of the notion of literacy we have been developing throughout this book.

This literacy about how to speak in different contexts is not possessed equally by everyone, nor is what constitutes this 'practical sense' the same for all speakers of a language. Not everyone is equally proficient at speaking in public, and most people know someone who can never end a telephone conversation easily and without awkwardness (someone who never seems to notice hints such as 'OK, well, I'd better get going then . . .'). Linguistic literacy, or the ability to perform successfully in a wide range of speech contexts, is a resource which is differentially available. It constitutes a kind of 'cultural capital' (Bourdieu's term), a valuable resource which can give speakers a high degree of control over their social interactions.

Possession of a particular form of linguistic literacy does not automatically confer cultural capital. Bourdieu gives the example of the mayor of the regional city of Pau, in France, who makes a speech in the local French dialect (Béarnais) at a ceremony celebrating a famous local poet. The speech is enthusiastically applauded by the audience. Bourdieu makes the point that the local townsfolk were particularly impressed because although the mayor could speak the 'standard' French language (which would usually be the norm on official occasions), he chose to speak his (and their) native dialect. By virtue of his position as mayor and as a speaker of fluent standard French, he has acquired a form of capital by 'condescending' to speak the less prestigious local dialect. Bourdieu points out that 'what is praised as good quality Béarnais when issued from the mouth of the mayor would have been accorded a quite different (and no doubt much lower) value had it been uttered by a peasant who spoke mere fragments of French' (1991a:19).

When we learn to speak, we do so in particular contexts, including the family, the peer group and the school. There are many factors which exercise what Bourdieu calls a 'determining influence' (1991a:95) on speakers' linguistic habitus. These include:

- gender;
- level of education;
- social position;
- social origin (rural or urban); and
- ethnic origin.

None of these factors can completely define how a speaker will handle a particular speech event, but their influence is too strong to be ignored in any explanation of 'what is going on' here. Our gender, schooling, what our parents do/did for a living, whether we are city born or country born, where we live now, and our ethnicity are all influences which produce our orientations to meaning making, or *coding orientations* (Bernstein 1971).

The utterances speakers produce, according to Bourdieu, are the result of the relation between the linguistic habitus and a linguistic field or *market*. By the term market, he means a field of action or social context in which resources (different kinds of capital) are distributed and exchanged. Just as the stock exchange is a market for distributing and exchanging economic capital, other fields can be seen as linguistic markets.

Bourdieu gives the example of a pub landlord, whose 'possession of a talent for being "the life and soul of the party"' . . . is a very precious form of capital' (1991a:99):

> Thus a good pub landlord finds, in the mastery of the expressive conventions suitable for this market (jokes, funny stories and puns . . .), and also in his special knowledge both of the rules of the game and the peculiarities of each of the players (names, nicknames, habits, oddities, specialities and talents from which he can profit), the necessary resources for exciting, sustaining, and also containing . . . the exchanges capable of producing the effervescent social atmosphere which his clients come for and to which they must themselves contribute.
>
> Bourdieu 1991:99–100

A speaker's sense or expectation of the value that linguistic practices will have in different markets is thus also part of the linguistic habitus. Speakers attempt to position themselves to profit from the linguistic capital they possess (or at least, to minimise their losses). For some speakers, faced with a market for which they don't have the required linguistic capital, silence is the only possible response. To return to the example of Torres Strait creole, children who grow up with this as their first language and who enter the mainstream white education system may find themselves lacking the linguistic literacy to participate alongside middle-class white children speaking 'standard English', unless the school system is flexible enough to include their own culture and language in the learning process. What is more, in a market dominated by the values of the mainstream, any speech they might produce might be less valued and regarded as 'impoverished'. Similarly, a blue-collar worker wanting to defend themselves in a court of law would be strongly disadvantaged, not only because of a lack of detailed knowledge of, and expertise in, law, but because the worker would lack the linguistic capital of the expressions, demeanour and mode of argument appropriate to this 'market'.

We move now from a consideration of speech as a resource acquired by speakers, and from the broad social and cultural context in which the acquisition of speech takes place, to a consideration of the differences between speech and writing.

SPEECH VERSUS WRITING

Speech and writing are two of the primary means or mediums people use to communicate. They are two alternative ways people can communicate using language. Thus they share a common code (a particular language, for example English, Chinese, German). However, they also differ in four important ways, ways which can affect the purposes to which we put them:

1. Speech is transmitted as sounds, while writing is transmitted as marks.
2. Unlike written communication, oral communication is accompanied by paralanguage and bodily communication.
3. Speech is the usual medium of communication when the participants are face-to-face; writing is more commonly used when communicators are separated physically.
4. The medium of writing allows a message or text to seem like a product; speech is like a process.

We will discuss each of these in turn.

Speech is transmitted as sounds

Sounds are transient, not permanent, unless one of the various audio technologies (such as audiotape, compact disc) is used to make a more permanent record of them. So speech demands the hearer's immediate understanding and relies on memory.

In contrast, writing is usually produced in a more permanent form (on paper, walls, plaster casts), although there are exceptions (for example, sky writing, messages written on the sand as the tide is coming in, and so on).

Writing allows readers to re-read a text, to check their comprehension, find a piece of information that they missed the first time, and so on. On the other hand, listeners don't have the same kind of control over an oral message without the aid of technology such as recording devices. Instead, they may interrupt the speaker to ask for something to be repeated, clarified or explained.

Oral communication is accompanied by paralanguage and bodily communication

There are many resources available to speakers for making meanings. Speech involves not just sounds, which combine to form words, but the tone, pitch, rhythm, pace and volume of the voice (this is known as **paralanguage**). In fact, when speech takes place face-to-face, the whole body becomes a resource for making meaning.

In written communication, the reader is using a different set of resources to read meanings. Paralanguage is absent, although writers can use punctuation and lettering styles to 'reproduce' paralanguage. For example:

- a question mark can show rising intonation: 'Will you be back later?';
- capitals may indicate loudness: 'HEY, YOU!'; and
- italics may be used for emphasis: 'No, *I* don't want to go, *you* go instead.'

But writing as a form of communication does not employ the resources of the body to make meaning in the same way that spoken communication does.

Nevertheless, with the advent of new technologies, what seem to be fairly clear cut differences between the medium of speech and the medium of writing are becoming less distinct. For example, the Internet, a vast web of interactive computer networks which spans the globe, links individual users to other users, so that by typing a message into a home or office computer linked to this network, one user can 'talk' to another. Once a message is completed and sent, it travels almost instantaneously, and if the other user is using the network at the same time, that user can reply almost immediately. Communication via the Internet can thus take on the interactivity of a telephone conversation while allowing the option of keeping a permanent record of the message, like a letter.

Users of the Internet have even developed a common code to supply the paralanguage and bodily communication (the facial expressions, tones of voice and gestures) which supplement the verbal meanings in face-to-face interaction—see Figure 14). These are typographic symbols combined to form miniature icons for various emotions (to make sense of these read them sideways).

Speech is the usual medium of face-to-face communication

Written communication enables a message to be produced in the absence of the receiver and to be read in the absence of the sender. Although we often take writing very much for granted, its ability to cross barriers

Figure 14 Emotions on the Internet: 'Smileys' are faces turned sideways

Characters	Meaning
:-(	frown
;-)	wink (denotes a pun or sly joke)
:-O	yelling or screaming, completely shocked
:-P	sticking your tongue out
:-D	big smile
%-(	confused and unhappy
:'	crying
:'-)	crying happy tears
*	kiss
{{{***}}}	hugs and kisses
<g> or <G>	grin

Courtesy of Albion Books. Shea 1995

of space and time makes it a powerful technology; and for many centuries it was the only technology which could do this (before the invention of other technologies such as telephone, radio, television, audio recording, fax and computer).

Of course, there are contexts in which written communication does take place in the presence of both sender and receiver, for various reasons. For example, writing allows for private communication within the context of a group (passing a note to a friend in class), or for a degree of formality (handing an employer a letter of resignation), or to enable ideas or information to be put 'on display' for consideration or discussion (the use of blackboards, overhead transparencies or handouts by teachers and seminar presenters).

Speech is like a process

Although we are using the term 'speech', in everyday life we more usually talk about speaking to refer to the same activity. This signals a common way of thinking about talk as something people do (a *process*) rather than a thing (a *product*).

On the other hand, writing is commonly used to produce a finished text (product), a message which can be thought about as a discrete whole, rather than something experienced as a more or less continuous flow (process). Of course, to construct a piece of writing, writers have to go through a process, for example, writing multiple drafts of an essay or several versions of a personal letter.

Most written communication hides the processes that produced it (it's considered unacceptable to hand in an essay with paragraphs scratched out and rewritten, and sections cut and pasted on). Again, this relates to the function of the communication—its formality and its degree of permanence. For example, you might post a personal letter leaving in numerous crossed-out sections rather than copy it out neatly, but a published book (a much more permanent and public piece of writing) is checked and re-checked for errors before being printed.

Depending on the task that you are using speech or writing to perform, there will be differences in the ways you use the medium to achieve a similar purpose. For example, as part of your university assessment, you may be required to present your ideas on a particular topic to a class orally, and in writing to your tutor/lecturer. Let's compare the features of the oral task and the written task—we could expect them to differ in the ways shown in Figure 15.

The features of speech work well because we make sense of it through anticipation. The features of writing work well because we make sense of it retrospectively—we are able to look back over what we have already read. Speech is no less structured and organised than writing; it is just that it is structured and organised *differently*. It is important to remember that what works in writing won't always work orally, and vice versa.

The differences discussed above are partly to do with the limitations of each medium (the **materiality** of speech and writing), and partly to do with the purposes to which we put speech and writing within a culture (their social functions, their structuring as *social sign systems*). These purposes come to take on a particular value within a culture. Within Western culture (European and English-speaking cultures), it is conventional to presume that writing as a means of communication has been more highly valued than speech: those areas of a culture (such as law, science and literature) which primarily employ the medium of writing have often been highly regarded. Interestingly enough, the French philosopher Jacques Derrida suggests that, to a certain extent, speech is still valued over writing because it is understood as being more

Figure 15 Oral presentation versus written essay

Spoken text	Written text
• uses repetition of words and ideas	• uses variation in word choice
• ideas are introduced one at a time	• denser—packs ideas in more tightly
• ideas linked or strung together	• ideas joined together in complex ways (longer sentences)

spontaneous, and more 'honest' in that it is closer to the 'truth' of our intentions (Derrida 1976).

How do these features of speech work in relation to speech practices? Let's consider spoken language as a form of interaction, and look at the genre of spoken conversation.

SPEECH ACTS AND SPEECH GENRES

For many decades it was assumed, mainly as a result of the influence of formal linguistics, that studying writing was the best way of going about understanding language as a system of communication. Studying speech as a means of communication provides a very different perspective than can be gained from assuming that writing is the paradigmatic example of language as communication. This position is strongly developed by Mikhail Bakhtin.

For Bakhtin, the basic unit of speech communication is the **utterance**, a term which connects explicitly with spoken language, although for Bakhtin it applies equally to written communication. The utterance is not to be confused with the sentence. Unlike the sentence, which is a formal unit of written language, the utterance is a unit of 'living language'. The notion of 'living' language or speech is very significant here. Bakhtin often talks about 'speech life' or the 'life of signs', indicating first that language and communication cannot be understood only from an abstract perspective, but must be considered as part of what people do in their lives. Second, he is indicating that speech, words and signs take on 'a life of their own', not subject to the control of individual speakers and their wills. Speakers may attempt to bend speech to their will, but speech is an intersubjective phenomenon; that is, the meanings that speech takes on are the result of not just speakers but also listeners, and a variety of social forces.

This last point is an extremely important one for Bakhtin. Speech always involves both a speaker and a listener, and the listener is no less active in this process than the speaker. That is, the listener responds actively to the speaker's utterance, and is potentially a speaker in turn. Dialogue or conversation provides the clearest example of this, but whole texts can also be seen to be participating in a dialogue with other texts either directly, such as letters in a newspaper, or less directly, as when a film such as *Big Trouble in Little China* is produced partly as a (comic) response to earlier films in the same genre, such as the *Rambo* films (see the discussion of intertextuality in Chapter 4).

Unlike Saussure, who believed that what people actually did with language (what he referred to as *parole*, or actual speech practice) was

M.M. (Mikhail Mikhailovich) Bakhtin

Mikhail Bakhtin [pronounced buk-teen] was a Russian scholar, literary theorist and philosopher of language. He was born in 1895 and died in 1975. His work did not become well known in the west until the 1980s, largely because translations of his work from the Russian did not become available until this time. Bakhtin lived and worked in some very difficult times: the Bolshevik Revolution, the Stalinist purges and the Second World War (during which he made cigarette wrappers out of the pages of one of his manuscripts, owing to a paper shortage!). He worked with several other scholars, including V.N. Volosinov, in what has become known as the Bakhtin Circle. It is not quite clear whether some of the work produced by this circle belonged to Bakhtin or Volosinov, as members of the circle sometimes attributed their work to one another in order to protect themselves from persecution. He has been hailed as 'the most important Soviet thinker in the human sciences and the greatest theoretician of literature in the twentieth century' (Todorov 1984:ix).

too chaotic and unpredictable to be studied, Bakhtin argues that the choices speakers make are not completely free but are governed by broad regularities. Despite the enormous variety of uses to which we put language, Bakhtin points out that 'each sphere in which language is used develops its own *relatively stable types* of utterances' (1986:60). These he refers to as *speech genres*, a term which includes both written and spoken genres. Bakhtin's work is very useful, not only for thinking about speech, but because he makes the point that all language, whether spoken or written, is **dialogic**. To summarise our discussion of his work:

- the utterance is the basic unit of speech communication;
- speech genres are types of utterances developed for use in particular contexts; and
- speech, and indeed all language, is potentially dialogic (i.e. involves and anticipates a response).

The utterance as a unit of interaction

We now move to a consideration of the ways and extents to which this responsiveness can take place, and how it is tied up with the issue of different contexts. According to Bakhtin, any utterance is shaped with a listener in mind, and with the expectation that that listener will be in some way responsive. This may mean that the listener becomes a speaker in turn, in speech genres which are overtly dialogic, such as conversation, dramatic dialogue (plays, films, TV), school debates, question time in parliament, and so on. Other, more apparently monologic texts, that is, texts shaped by a single speaker/writer, nevertheless always implicitly address some audience. Newspaper articles, poems and political speeches all address an audience. Some speech genres may shift between these two modes of interaction; for example, conversations are usually dialogues, but may also involve chunks of monologue, where a single speaker tells an anecdote or story. The distinction between dialogue and monologue, then, is not absolute—monologue is, in a sense, simply an extreme pole in a range of modes of linguistic interaction.

Bakhtin's notion of the utterance has some similarities with the concept of the speech act. Speech act theory (first developed by the English philosopher J.L. Austin, in his 1962 book *How to Do Things With Words*) argued that language did not merely represent or describe something in the world of experience but could also be used to perform actions. Austin identified a special class of utterances which he called **performatives** because of their function in performing the action they name. For example:

'I christen this child Mary Joe' (uttered by a priest in a christening ceremony).

'I name this ship the *Lazy Slob* (uttered while smashing a champagne bottle against the hull of a vessel).

'I pronounce you husband and wife' (uttered by a minister of religion or marriage celebrant in a marriage ceremony).

Other speech acts include threatening, promising, cursing, blessing, warning and congratulating.

The utterance, then, is an act performed in saying something, an act performed through language. Bourdieu picks up on Austin's work and points out that the effectiveness of a performative utterance is totally dependent on the institution which authorises the speaker to pronounce it. Not just anyone can pronounce two people 'husband and wife' and make it stick. The utterance must be uttered by an authorised speaker, who expresses the authority of the institution, but does not create it:

> The power of words is nothing other than the delegated power of the spokesperson, and his [or her] speech . . . is no more than a testimony, and one among others, of the guarantee of delegation which is vested in him [or her].
>
> Bourdieu 1991a:107

Bourdieu refers to this as 'authorised language'.

Now we move from a consideration of isolated speech acts, to a discussion of speech acts within the context of spoken dialogue, specifically the genre of conversation.

Conversation as speech genre

Participants in spoken interaction take turns to speak, thereby jointly producing a text. What is it that propels such interactions along? Some speech genres, such as casual conversation, appear to be 'about' very little—just talk for talk's sake, like this dialogue from a play:

Man:	You was a bit busy earlier.
Barman:	Ah.
Man:	Round about ten.
Barman:	Ten, was it?
Man:	About then.
	(*Pause*)
	I passed by here about then.
Barman:	Oh yes?
Man:	I noticed you were doing a bit of trade.
	(*Pause*)
Barman:	Yes, trade was very brisk here about ten.
Man:	Yes, I noticed.
	(*Pause*)
	I sold my last one about then. Yes. About nine forty-five.
Barman:	Sold your last then, did you?
Man:	Yes, my last *Evening News* it was. Went about twenty to ten.
	(*Pause*)
Barman:	*Evening News*, was it?
Man:	Yes.
	(*Pause*)
	Sometimes it's the *Star* is the last to go.
Barman:	Ah.
Man:	Or the . . . whatsisname.
Barman:	*Standard*.
Man:	Yes.
	(*Pause*)
	All I had left tonight was the *Evening News*.
	(*Pause*)
Barman:	Then that went, did it?
Man:	Yes.
	(*Pause*)
	Like a shot.
	(*Pause*)

Harold Pinter, *Last to Go*, 1961

And so it goes on, for another page and a half! The playwright, Pinter, is pushing to a comic extreme the capacity of conversation to be sustained when there seems to be very little information being exchanged. If you look at the conversation, the sum total of the information that emerges is that the Barman was busy around ten o'clock, and that the Man sold his last newspaper, the *Evening News*, at around twenty (or a quarter) to ten! Note also that both these items of information are provided first by the Man, and that the Barman cooperates in the conversation by replying to the Man's questions and confirming or acknowledging his statements, although in a very minimal way (reluctant? embarrassed, perhaps? bored?).

This kind of communication is known as **phatic communion**, where the function of communicating seems to be solely to keep the channel of communication open and to keep the conversation going. Much of our brief daily spoken interactions are like this: 'hello'—'isn't it hot/cold/humid', 'have a nice day', 'see you later'.

So what is at stake in this interaction? What keeps it going? It seems to involve utterances which are concerned not so much with exchanging information, as with using the exchange of information to negotiate the continuation of the interaction. It seems fairly clear that the Man is keener to negotiate this than the Barman.

At this point, it is useful to introduce some technical terms so we can be precise in our analysis of language as interaction. Halliday (1985a: 68–9) has suggested that when analysing utterances as interaction, we need to identify what he calls their **speech function**. Utterances, or **moves** (another term for the same concept) may function in a variety of ways for different participants, depending on their specific agendas. These agendas might include negotiating to obtain or to provide information, or seeking or offering a form of action. Figure 16 shows some possibilities, in table form, along with the names used for each speech function.

This gives a broad picture which encompasses most (but not all) of the basic ways in which speakers can use moves to interact. For each of these speech functions, there is also a range of possible responses, some more likely and more cooperative than others (see Figures 17 and 18).

Here we can see how Bakhtin's insight that all utterances anticipate a response operates in practice. While the speech function of a move does not completely determine the response, it sets up a range of possible or probable responses. The listener, who becomes speaker in turn, can be compliant, or can be less cooperative with the speaker by not negotiating along the lines set up by the speaker. The listener may not answer the question, or not do so directly, or may even challenge the

Figure 16 Basic speech functions

giving information:	statement
demanding information:	question
giving action:	offer
demanding action:	command

Figure 17 Speech functions and responses

Speech function	Compliant response	Non-compliant response
statement	acknowledgment	contradiction
question	answer	disclaimer
offer	acceptance	rejection
command	undertaking	refusal

Figure 18 Examples of speech functions

Statement	**Acknowledgment**	**Contradiction**
School sucks.	Sure does.	You've got to be kidding!
Question	**Answer**	**Disclaimer**
Where was Sally yesterday?	She had to go to a funeral.	None of your business! *or* I don't know.
Offer	**Acceptance**	**Rejection**
Want a beer?	Thanks *or* Why not?	No thanks *or* I'd better not (*or shakes head*).
Command	**Undertaking**	**Refused**
Help me lift this rhinoceros.	OK (or performs action).	No way *or* I can't, I've got a bad back.

speaker's right to ask the question. The listener may even avoid the question altogether, and ask another question instead.

But a participant in a conversation has to balance their own purposes against those of the other participant/s. In order to get what you want, you have to give the other person enough of what they want to keep the conversation going. If the conversation breaks down, negotiation stops.

Furthermore, speakers often use less than direct ways of framing their moves. Consider how often we frame negotiations for action in terms of information. For example:

- if we want someone to turn the television down, we might use the statement 'The TV is too loud'; or
- if we are trying to get a wealthy companion to buy us an expensive gift in a jewellery shop, we might say 'Isn't that diamond necklace fabulous?'.

Such indirect ways of negotiating speech purposes relate to cultural conventions concerning power differences and politeness. By expressing a request as a statement, a speaker allows the addressee the option of refusing the request less bluntly by simply treating it as a statement or question. For example, the addressee could respond to the examples above by saying, 'Yes it is, isn't it?', thereby refusing to enter into the negotiation on the speaker's terms. 'Escape clauses' like this allow the appearance of politeness and communicative harmony to be maintained—particularly important where there is a power differential between the participants.

Note here that we are not assuming that conversation is all about consensus and agreement. By talking about negotiation and moves that participants make, we are recognising that what is at stake for people in any interaction may differ among the participants, and that they are therefore involved in a process of negotiation in order to achieve either shared ends or different ends. The basic speech functions need to be interpreted quite differently when the interests of the two participants are in conflict, for example:

Question → *interrogation*
A: Where were you on the night of the robbery?
B: Having dinner with Elvis.
Statement → *insult*
A: You're an absolute loser!
B: Up yours!
Offer → *threat*
A: Want a gunshot wound to the head?
B: (terrified look, flees)

It is important not to assume that all participants in a conversation have equal power and thus equal control over what's going on. In casual conversation the power relations between the participants may not seem to be very marked or unequal. Nevertheless, this does not mean that the issue of power is not 'at stake' or 'under negotiation' in this speech genre. Having provided you with some tools for the analysis of dialogue, let's now address the question of speech and power.

SPEECH AND POWER

Magistrate: I'm putting it to you again—are you going to *make* another offer—uh—to discharge this debt. [1]

Defendant: Would you in my position? [2]

Magistrate: I—I'm not here to answer your questions [3]—you answer *my* question. [4]

Defendant: One rule for one and one for another—I presume. [5]

Magistrate: Can I have an answer to my question—please? [6] The question is—are you prepared to make an offer to the court—to discharge—this debt. [7]

Defendant: What sort of minimal offer would be required? [8]

Magistrate: It's not a bargaining situation [9]—it's a *straight* question, Mr H [10]—can I have the answer? [11]

Defendant: Well, I'll just pay the court a pound annually? [12]

Magistrate: That's not acceptable to us. [13]

Harris 1984:5

This dialogue takes place in the formal context of the courtroom, under the constraints of an institution—the legal system—which sets up power relations that are clearly defined and institutionally enshrined. In such a context, we expect to find that magistrates have greater power than defendants, and that this difference in power will be manifested in the magistrate's control over who speaks and when, and over the kinds of issues that will be discussed. We also expect that it will be the magistrate and the prosecution and defence lawyers who ask the questions and decide if the answers are adequate ones. After all, for the defendant, a great deal is at stake; her or his liberty (or good name, or bank balance) may depend on these answers.

In terms of these kinds of expectations, what is odd about the interaction above between the magistrate and the defendant? Using the categories of speech functions provided above, we can analyse what is going on in this interaction (italics indicate speech functions of moves). The magistrate asks a *question* of the defendant [1], but instead of complying by providing a direct *answer*, the defendant asks a *question* of the magistrate [2]. The magistrate points out that this is inappropriate behaviour [3]. Instead of accepting this *statement*, the defendant challenges it [4], forcing the magistrate to *command* him to answer, 'please' [6]. After repeating similar tactics, the defendant eventually makes an *offer* [12], which is *rejected* by the magistrate [13].

Clearly, the defendant's speech behaviour is at odds with the compliant and submissive position a defendant in court might be expected to take (watch any TV courtroom drama series for dramatised examples of how defence lawyers 'coach' defendants in this respect). The defendant in the example above uses the resources of the system of speech function in language to challenge and resist the court's legal right to make him pay his debts. This interaction demonstrates that while institutions constrain contexts and the types of speech interactions which can take place within those contexts, they do not completely determine them. Participants can and do attempt to challenge and negotiate the power relations assigned to them in specific contexts. The extent to which they are able to do so depends chiefly on the institutional power which underlies the speech situation. In the law court, the defendant may challenge the power of the magistrate, but these tactics will probably merely delay the eventual result—the enforcement of the magistrate's judgment—rather than be ultimately successful.

Our analysis of the courtroom example demonstrates a number of the features that Poynton (1985) identifies in language where there is a power difference. Power is manifested in general by asymmetry in the meaning choices available to the powerful and the less powerful. Those who exercise power in a speech interaction tend to:

■   control turn-taking in dialogue;
■   interrupt;
■   control what is under negotiation (through speech function);
■   control the topic being discussed;
■   control the degree of directness or indirectness (indirectness, euphem-
     ism and 'watching your words' are associated with the less powerful);
     and
■   control the use of address terms (use of titles rather than first names
     shows status).

This is neatly summed up by Fairclough's statement that 'power in discourse is to do with powerful participants controlling and constraining the contributions of non-powerful participants' (1989:46).

It is revealing of the relative status of women and men in Western society that studies of women's and men's speech have shown that men interrupt women more frequently than vice versa, that indirectness is more characteristic of women's speech, and that in conversations between women and men, it is largely men who determine the topic (Poynton, 1985:26–7).

It is useful at this point to return to the notion of the linguistic habitus and the linguistic market introduced by Bourdieu. Bourdieu (1991a) makes the point that an important element of the habitus is the speaker's practical sense of the conditions which attach to markets; that is, of who can speak under what circumstances. Linguistic markets determine who can speak, whether or not they will be listened to and to what extent their speech will be valued or seen as legitimate. Here is a final example which illustrates the operation of a linguistic market; it concerns a study of the TV football viewing practices of a family and their friends:

> Competence to read the game well enough to participate in 'viewing' rituals may, apparently, be quickly taught (especially if the novice is familiar with any form of football). But the right to be 'heard' when you speak about the game depends on other initiatory rites. The level of competence appropriate to televised football spectatorship is reasonably openly shared with women by men. However, the competence of women to speak about the game is recognised by neither Richard nor Peter. In my interviews with Peter considerable time was spent establishing just whether or not women had been present during the observation and what the nature of their participation had been. Peter had 'defined' his viewing group as 'men only', even though all were accompanied by their wives and girlfriends. The wives and girlfriends offered beer, and watched them viewing from the sidelines. This positioning offers an interesting parallel with the positioning of the cheerleader squad during the televised game. On one occasion the women went to the movies while the men watched football. On another occasion they visited a friend. When the women did come into the room it was not registered in Peter's account. When women did speak about the game it was considered not significant for the study, even though all participating students had been asked to note down everything they observed, without exception. However, when the women spoke about the advertisements broadcast and the relationship of the advertisements to the program, their voice was noticed. And when the women commented on the viewing behaviour of the men their comments were also recognised. The women were granted the right to speak and be heard about consumer related matters and about their men, but not about the game.
>
> When I asked Peter how the women could comment on the advertisements and how they could notice the behaviour of the men if they were not present, he disclosed that the women had traversed the domestic space of viewing, the lounge room, and had often stopped long enough to notice and comment.

VN:	When the women would come into the room, did they ever make comments about the game or ask questions about what was happening?
Peter:	Maybe not so much about the game but particular players.
VN:	What would they say?
Peter:	I don't know.
VN:	So they knew the main footballers.
Peter:	Oh yes, well not all of them—but high profile players that are in the news all the time, on television and doing ads.

VN: What sort of things would they say?
Peter: Pretty critical things . . .
VN: Come on, I want to know . . .
Peter: Oh you know 'you log' or . . .
VN: So they were critical of the way a particular player was playing the game . . .
Peter: No, just critical of the player . . . and football . . .
VN: So they'd say 'oh, not so-and-so again' . . .
Peter: Yeah and that they considered . . . I suppose they looked at the players . . . like they looked at players a long time ago in the sense that there's nothing—all brawn and no brains.

The discursive space constructed around televised football is then gender-coded 'male', though male dominance of the space is certainly contested by some women. The women's authority to speak about football was considered to be based in the mediated authority of newspaper reports and spoof sporting programs on radio, though it remains unclear why women would want to read newspaper reports about football if they had no more than a passing interest in the game and never became involved in it. Peter was convinced that women are interested in footballers as individuals, but not in football itself.

Nightingale 1992:162–3

The author of this study, Virginia Nightingale, discovered that not only did women's equal knowledge of and literacy in the game of football (at least as spectators) not count according to the men, but their presence as part of the spoken interaction around football watching was actually ignored, or edited out in the men's report of the interaction. In this case the women's speech, no matter what their contribution, is discounted almost as if they had not spoken. Their literacy carries no capital, unlike the men's. They are rendered silent, metaphorically if not literally.

In both spoken and written communication practices, not speaking or not writing—silence—may be the only option for those lacking either institutionally or culturally sanctioned capital to speak or write within a particular cultural field. McCormack notes that an important literacy is knowing when not to write, or speak; when writing or speaking:

> can commit a breach of strategic power relations, when committing something to written record can make you the object of surveillance or coercion, when silence has more efficacy than speech or writing.

McCormack, cited in Luke 1996:325

SUMMARY

This chapter has examined the differences between speech and writing, in terms of:

- their materiality; and
- the values assigned to them.

We noted that writing is valued through its association with 'prestige' areas of Western culture, while speech is linked to a different set of values, such as sincerity and spontaneity.

Oral literacy is thus both valued and devalued. The values attributed to speech cannot be separated from the social and historical conditions which produce both dialects and speakers.

By analysing communication from the perspective of speech, we can apply the metaphor of negotiation to linguistic interaction, in which the utterance or move is the fundamental unit. All speech genres, and all genres, deploy moves in order to negotiate meanings. An analysis of the speech genre of conversation shows that this genre is as much constrained by rules as it is spontaneous.

Finally, the chapter dealt with the question of 'authorised language' and power in discourse, and in particular with the ways in which power is tied into control of, and also access to, particular linguistic markets, and different forms of speech which may or may not constitute capital within a market.

FURTHER READING

Bakhtin, M. 1986, 'The problem of speech genres', in *Speech Genres and Other Late Essays*, trans. V. W. McGee, ed. C. Emerson and M. Holquist, University of Texas Press, Austin, pp. 60–102

Bourdieu, P. 1991a, *Language and Symbolic Power*, ed. and introduced by J.B. Thompson, trans. G. Raymond and M. Adamson, Polity Press, Cambridge: Introduction by John B. Thompson (pp. 1–10) and Appendix: 'Did You Say Popular?' (pp. 90–102)

Fairclough, N. 1989, *Language and Power*, Longman, London & New York, Chapter 3

Chapter 9

Written genres

This chapter is concerned with writing and its literacies, practices and genres, beginning with a review of current attitudes to literacy and the future of written literacy. We will examine the constraints and possibilities of writing as a medium, and the way in which new communication technologies are reshaping these. We look at the cultural fields in which writing operates, and the different values and capital associated with written genres across these fields. Finally, we look at the notion of the author, a cultural construct strongly associated, until recently, with written texts.

Within many cultures, a high value has traditionally been placed on written texts and the ability to write. Currently, there is a perception in countries such as the US, the UK and Australia that literacy (in the conventional sense of 'competence in reading and writing') is in crisis. Governments are anxiously attempting to 'measure' written literacy by mass testing of school children, and newspaper reports talk of a serious decline in literacy standards. Clearly, possession of this kind of literacy is regarded as very important: governments, the media and educators agree that written literacy is 'fundamentally tied up with cultural and economic power' (Luke & Gilbert 1993:2). (Recently both the UK and the Australian governments have made moves to make unemployed people undertake compulsory literacy training.) While written literacy experts disagree over whether standards are really falling, most recognise that there are rapid changes affecting the uses to which we put writing and the ways we develop written and other kinds of literacies.

On the one hand, the information/communication revolution means that every day of our lives we experience (through infotainment, the workplace, and throughout the culture generally) a flow of images and information which is far greater than it was even one generation ago.

Children are now born into a culture mediated by the computer and the television as much as by books. The way this changes the kinds of literacies they develop is only beginning to be explored and understood—what it does suggest is that time spent acquiring and putting into practice the traditional literacies of good spelling, the ability to write complex and grammatically correct sentences etc. is fast becoming a luxury (since a decent computer can do most of these things for us).

On the other hand, Western economies are shifting from a basis on manufacturing and industrial production, to service and information work; this means, to be employable, people increasingly need the high level literacy skills once irrelevant in unskilled labouring work. So relatively high standards of written and other forms of literacy become, for more and more people, the passport to basic economic capital—such as a job. New technologies such as the fax machine, email, word processing and even the photocopier have increased the speed and volume at which written information and documents can be produced and circulated, demanding from workers a greater capacity to produce, process and manage this information flow. Written literacy is thus not becoming any less important, but what constitutes written literacy—and its place within a wider configuration of literacies—is shifting. Instead of an emphasis on the detailed study of aspects of form (spelling, punctuation, etc.) there is a greater concern with and emphasis on the ability to deploy a range of genres, mediums and discourses, and to handle complex ideas and information. Written literacy must now function alongside other forms of literacy, such as oral, visual and information literacies.

WRITING AS A MEDIUM

We noted briefly in Chapter 8 some of the characteristics of writing as a medium, compared to speech. Let's look at these in more detail, under the following headings:

- written text as object and as commodity; and
- writing as a resource and as a technology.

Written text as object and commodity

Written texts are experienced as objects or products rather than as processes. Most written texts hide their processes of production; they are circulated in a final form that does not show obvious traces of the drafting and editing which is part and parcel of the writing process. This also enhances their status and value within a culture (or is it the other way around—their status within a culture requires this careful attention, because more is at stake in the meanings of such texts?). Written texts are subjected to 'gatekeeping' processes to various degrees; the more durable the written product is expected to be, the more it is subjected to checking and filtering. Book publishing exemplifies this.

The written text, in the form of the book, is one of the most important commodities in what is known as the cultural industry. As an object, it can be not only commoditised but aestheticised. Specialist bookbinders produce beautifully crafted editions of books, bound in hand-tooled calf leather with gold leaf on the pages and marbled end-papers. The contents of the book become insignificant in relation to its handsome appearance on a library shelf in a 'private residence'.

Within Western culture, the book was for centuries a symbol of knowledge and thus power, a status object because it represented cultural capital. It progressively lost this status when the production of books shifted from the intensive labours of monks in monasteries, which were centres of learning accessed by a privileged few, to the mass production of books enabled by the invention of the printing press in the fifteenth century. This status has been further eroded in the twentieth century with the coming of the electronic age and the information superhighway.

The status of written texts as objects thus enables them to be commoditised—packaged as products which can be bought and sold (in a literal sense), but which also carry cultural capital for their owner. Commoditisation is increasingly a feature of all forms of communication in contemporary post-capitalist cultures.

Writing as a resource and a technology

Writing is a relatively permanent, durable form of text, and therefore a re-usable resource. It is used by cultures for keeping records, storing knowledge and putting memories into permanent form, so that these can be consulted again and again if desired. This durability is important for genres such as tax records, financial bookkeeping, history books, personal diaries, library catalogues, reference books and many others. Not all written genres place a high value on permanence. Some types of written text are ephemeral, and have relatively short 'lifespans' of use. They include bus tickets, shopping lists, phone messages, emails and junk mail. The mass print media—newspapers, pulp fiction and magazines—fall somewhere in between.

Information retrieval is another important function which writing has had for centuries (since writing was invented, in fact). The capacity to store and retrieve information is shifting increasingly from print to computers, with a rapid expansion in the range and volume of information which can be accessed (for example via computer databases and the World Wide Web).

Writing can be regarded as a technology which enables a text to be produced in the absence of the reader and to be read in the absence of the sender. This gives the potential for achieving both physical and social distance (in terms of tenor) between writer and reader. Thus writing is often used for contexts involving impersonal, distant or formal tenor relations. Examples are genres such as job applications, job advertisements, government policy documents and petitions.

Body language and paralanguage, semiotic systems which realise interpersonal (tenor-related) meanings, are not available to readers of written genres. These systems are generally regarded as less easy for speakers to consciously control than their words. Hence writing is also used sometimes to 'control' or even to attempt to 'edit out' some kinds of interpersonal meanings we might (unconsciously) express through bodily communication in a face-to-face interaction, such as affect, the dimension of tenor which relates to emotionality or attitude. Writing allows the writer to avoid the interactivity of speech and its tendency to reproduce existing power relations because of participants' difficulty in speaking reflectively and in not reproducing habitual patterns of interaction. Writing enables a participant to attempt to negotiate a situation that the writer may think is loaded against them because of the greater power of the addressee.

Examples of genres and contexts in which writing might function in this way are writing a letter to break off a relationship, or a teenager writing a note to her parents to announce she won't be in for Sunday dinner with the grandparents. Writing can also be a way of avoiding responsibility (literally, being answerable) for the potential effects of one's message. Writing is thus a way to introduce distance into otherwise relatively intimate situations in which the expression of affect would usually be prominent.

Kress concludes that 'writing as a medium and writing as an activity both encourage and permit distancing—from the immediate context, from the audience and from the subject matter' (1988b:97).

Speech and writing are not just different ways of making the same meanings, nor is writing a better way of communicating than speech. But each tends to be used for different purposes within a culture. As different technologies of communication, each constitutes a different set of resources for meaning. Written language has a number of characteristics directly related to the material possibilities and limits of the medium, as well as to its functions. Writing is often:

- informationally dense;
- explicit; and
- structurally and grammatically complex.

The first characteristic, *informational density*, relates to the fact that written texts are usually in a more or less permanent form and so can be read and re-read at the reader's own pace, giving the opportunity to reflect on the meanings of words.

The second characteristic, the *explicitness* of written texts, relates to their use in contexts in which writer and reader are not both present (unlike speech). The lack of deixis is one example of this need to be explicit. **Deixis** is where language is used to point or refer to something else. **Deictic** words are meaningful to the extent that they set up a relation between the speaker/writer of a text and the time ('now'), place ('here'), people ('I', 'you', 'we') or things ('this', 'that', 'yours') being referred to. Deictics can refer to items within the text or outside it, but when they refer outside the text, in order to be unambiguously inter-preted they require both speaker and hearer to be present. (A classic example is that of a person walking on the beach who picks up a message in a bottle. The message reads 'Meet me here tomorrow'.)

Written texts are not as likely to make use of the first and second person pronouns ('I' and 'you') and other deictic items as often as spoken discourse does, because their meaning is not so easy to retrieve when the context is not an immediate, shared one. Nevertheless, deictic items still occur in written language, particularly the first and second person pronouns, which function to make explicit the writer's position as 'speaker' and the text's function in directly addressing a reader.

Written texts therefore function by anticipating 'what the reader needs to know'. They construct what is shared context and what is not by making some meanings implicit and others explicit. Implicit meanings might be things like not needing to explain what some words mean, because the writer assumes the reader will share an understanding of what a cat or a table is. On the other hand, in this textbook we explicitly define the technical terms we don't expect readers to be familiar with (such as deixis). By making such assumptions, writers position readers in particular ways. It is important to make the point here that such positioning is one of the ways in which *ideology* works, because it sets up assumptions about what meanings can be taken for granted, or treated as naturalised, and what meanings have to be explicitly negotiated (see Chapter 5).

The third characteristic, *structural complexity*, is closely linked to the feature of informational density. Like informational density, complexity is possible in written texts because they are able to be read and re-read at the reader's discretion. Therefore meanings can be structured into longer and more complex information chains (sentences, paragraphs) without the reader 'losing track'.

Two types of discourse which exemplify the features of written language are legal discourse and scientific discourse, both of which are often characterised by high informational density, long and complex sentences, and the avoidance of deictics and personal reference. Most written texts fall somewhere between the extremes of much legal and scientific discourse and written texts which approximate features of casual speech. (An exception in legal discourse is the recent trend toward using 'plain English' in legal documents such as insurance policies and contracts. These avoid the more confusing qualities of traditional legal discourse and are designed to be more clearly understood by their non-expert users.)

Figure 19—a contribution to an email discussion on the subject of the distribution of knowledge via the Internet—is an example of a written text which shows some of the 'typical' features of written language. It packs in a lot of information and argument, explicitly describes and categorises the various subjects and ideas being discussed, and uses a number of long and complex sentences (see Figure 21 for examples).

Compare this text to Figure 20—an exchange of personal emails between family members Meg and Bob. Although it is a much shorter text, it is also not nearly as densely packed with information. There are references to people and things familiar to the two correspondents, but not to 'outsiders' (such as the readers of this textbook). Meg and Bob have a shared background which enables their email dialogue to be relatively inexplicit (for example, through the use of personal deixis). Their sentences are quite short and often incomplete or punctuated by dashes and '. . .', indicating a simple linking of ideas (see Figure 21 for examples). This gives the text a spontaneous feel, almost as if this was a spoken conversation.

The two texts clearly differ in a number of ways and demonstrate different types of 'written' literacies. The writers are negotiating the written medium to achieve different purposes—in one case, primarily to present a set of arguments in a 'public' forum, in the other, to 'stay in touch' and exchange personal information (family photos). The cultural fields, genres and audiences are in each case quite different. The Figure 19 text is basically a 'public' text, participating in a forum on a matter of global concern, addressing an on-line audience which is large and predominantly unknown to the writer. Generically, it is similar to a conference paper or a feature article/opinion piece in the 'serious' press. Use of the 'traditional' forms of print literacy are appropriate to the function of such a text, as well as carrying cultural capital within this field.

On the other hand, the Figure 20 text is a 'private' text—similar to the genre of a personal letter. The audience is 'one-to-one', a dialogue

Figure 19 Email to an on-line discussion list

```
Date:        Sat, 15 May 99 14:37:47 EDT
Sender:      <omitted>
Precedence:  bulk
From:        Judyth_Mermelstein@babylonmontreal.qc.ca
             (Judyth Mermelstein)
To:          <omitted>
Subject:     [IRNTECH:861] Technology, Publishing and
             On-line Communities [text omitted]


TECHNOLOGY
We humans are generally very bad at learning the
lessons of history, and even worse at remembering
them. Current activities within the 'Internet
industry' in  the developed world reveal this very
clearly. The primary reason the Internet evolved so
rapidly from a system used by the American
military and a select group of 'computer geeks'
was its aptness for cheap, rapid, two-way
information exchanges and 'on-line conference'
activities, all of which were conducted in standard
text mode and were therefore accessible regardless
of the particular computer and software used by
any given individual. Only a decade after the
Internet became useful to all kinds of people all
around the world for this very reason, we are now
living in a world where that universal agora has
not only been heavily commercialized and encroached
upon by the North American 'entertainment industry'
with its demands for 'special effects' and 'groovy
graphics', but has also been subverted by
commercial thinking—to the point where governments
are economizing by ceasing to print much public
information and choose to distribute public
information electronically, but do so via Web sites
which are not accessible to most citizens and post
it as huge proprietary .PDF or Word 97 for Windows
files which require the newest powerful computers
and the latest versions of expensive software to
be used.

I am not terribly surprised that some members of
this group have taken the latest developments for
granted in the discussion of on-line publishing. I
AM determined to remind people that this method of
distribution is guaranteed to PREVENT access by
most of the non-affluent world. Amongst other
things, this approach entails a constant upgrading
of equipment and software, modern speeds and access
lines which simply cannot be maintained by
developing nations ... and is not really affordable
```

to most Canadian universities except at the cost
of eliminating courses and faculty in favour of
new computers every year or two.

Meanwhile, however, almost anyone anywhere can be
given some form of text access at a very small
cost. As has been discussed, truly incredible
numbers of perfectly functioning computers are
scrapped routinely in the quest for the latest
upgrades and can be collected and redistributed for
the costs of shipping and a little basic training
at the receiving end. 'Open source' software is
available for the cost of a download (or a $5
CD-ROM) as compared to the $1000 or so involved in
buying the most heavily-marketed brand. Working on
the Internet in text mode can be done as quickly
and efficiently on a vintage 1980 IBM XT as on a
486 in graphic mode. Where full-fledged Internet
access is not possible, one can still use email
(and such tools as Gopher and FTP) through a
gatewayed BBS reached by a local telephone call.
With this type of 'low-tech' approach, there is no
good reason why universal Internet access should
not be possible within the next 5 years—except
lack of political will to commit funds to such an
'old fashioned' approach when the same money would
buy more glamorous 'cutting edge' equipment for a
select few ... [email continues ...]

Mermelstein 1999

between two people whose tenor relations are close and who are using
the medium to maintain that contact. The text, while exchanging
information (about the family photos, about Bob's new scanner etc.) is
predominantly tenor-oriented, unlike the first text, which is strongly
field-oriented. The writers deploy literacies to negotiate this tenor focus,
literacies which pick up on 'speech-like' qualities rather than the formal
qualities of writing.

What both texts exemplify (to a different extent) is the way in which
new forms of electronic communication have the potential to change
traditional genres and characteristics of writing—and are already doing
so. Kress makes the point that:

> The newer form [of writing], as it appears in electronic forms of
> communication for instance, is moving in the direction of the structures
> of speech, in its basic syntactic and grammatical organization: less
> complex, less hierarchical syntax; shorter units; simpler sentence
> structures; and so on.

Kress 1997:123

Figure 20 Personal email

```
Date:        Wed, 11 Mar 1998 14:27:17 -0800
From:        Bob <address omitted>
To:          Meg <address omitted>
Subject:     Re: Christmas Photos

>Hi Meg,
>At last a worthwhile reason to send you an email!
>I thought you might like to see the family photos
taken on Dick's disposable camera. They really came
out well. The mysterious 3rd one is a bit of a
puzzler though ... nobody seems to remember who
actually took this one.
>Let me know if you are unable to view them as
.BMP - I'll resend in another format (JPEG or
something).
>100% fun,
>Bob.

>Hi Bob
>Thanks for sending these - I was only talking to
Mum on the phone last night and she was describing
them to me (someone's head on the watering can??).
Unfortunately I can't open them in this format, so
can you send them in jpeg?
>Hope everything's going OK at work. I'm Acting
Manager this week ... the power!!:).
>See you.
>Meg.

Meg,
That's slightly spoiled the anticipation of horror
or revulsion at seeing your sibling propped up in
watering drum ... anyway, here they are - family
photos Christmas 97.
I bought a Canon image scanner recently. Using A4
photo paper in my printer, I've been able to
produce some really excellent photo enlargements.
So if you have anything you'd like to do this
way, just send it on down.
Bye
Bob
```

While this suggests that electronic forms of communication are becoming more 'accessible', Mermelstein's email (Figure 19) also makes the point that 'first world' decisions about the technology have the potential to place severe limits on the Internet's capacity to revolutionise and universalise access to information (a frequent claim).

Figure 21 Comparison of the two emails

Email to an on-line discussion list (Figure 19)	Personal email (Figure 20)
Informational density	
• introduces several new ideas in each sentence	• fewer ideas developed in each sentence, compared to Figure 19 text
• develops an argument and presents facts/information to support this (e.g. 'The primary reason the Internet evolved so rapidly . . . was . . .')	• mix of everyday language and a small amount of technical discourse ('.BMP', 'JPEG', 'image scanner')
• technical discourses of communication ('two-way information exchanges', 'on-line conference') and computing ('standard text mode', '.PDF or Word 97 for Windows files', '"Open source" software')	
Explicitness	
• technical language functions to identify and categorise subject matter precisely	• assumption of a shared context means language is not fully explicit: 'the family photos' assumes the reader will know which family and which photos are being referred to; 'Mum' makes sense only in relation to the identity of the speaker (c.f. 'Mrs June Brown')
• use of many detailed descriptive terms that are specific rather than general ('cheap, rapid, two-way information exchanges', 'latest versions of expensive software', 'more glamorous cutting-edge equipment for a select few')	• preciseness of technical terms is sometimes modified and made vague ('JPEG or something')
• few deictics, although the writer makes some direct personal references to present her opinion ('I am not terribly surprised . . .') and to refer to a shared problem/characteristic ('We humans are generally very bad at learning the lessons of history . . .')	• lots of personal deixis ('you', 'me', 'I')
	• little explicit description (e.g. the vagueness of 'someone's head on the watering can??')
Structural complexity	
• long, relatively complex sentences (e.g. 'With this type of "low-tech" approach, there is no good reason why universal Internet access should not be possible within the next 5 years—except lack of political will to commit funds to such an "old-fashioned" approach when the same money would buy more glamorous "cutting edge" equipment for a select few.')	• mostly short, single-clause sentences (e.g. 'They really came out well.')
	• short paragraphs, often one sentence long
	• structured in terms of a dialogue (message → reply → reply to reply)
• paragraphs where a point is introduced then elaborated over several sentences	• incomplete sentences (e.g. 'At last a worthwhile reason to send you an email!', 'Hope everything's going OK at work!')

GENRE, THE PUBLIC SPHERE AND THE PRIVATE SPHERE

These two genres appear to function, then, in two different social domains: the public and the private. What do we mean when we speak of the public sphere and the private sphere?

The sociocultural world has been theorised as consisting of two interlocking domains: the public and the private. The public sphere is typically seen as the world of:

- work;
- politics;
- business;
- citizenship;
- legality; and
- rationality.

Traditionally, the public sphere has been the world of men, a world implicitly supported by the private sphere, the 'natural' domain of women according to a patriarchal model of social structure. The private sphere concerns itself with:

- the family;
- child education;
- morality;
- sensuality and pleasure;
- domesticity;
- reproduction; and
- the personal.

The distinction between the public sphere and the private sphere is an influential one which has structured many Western practices. Kress has argued that the values of the private sphere are closely aligned with speech, and those of the public sphere with writing: 'Participation in public life and the power which that distributes depend on access to and mastery of the forms of writing' (Kress 1985:46).

While it is certainly the case that this kind of literacy is a vital skill in the public sphere, we will qualify that statement by arguing that access to the particular genres and discourses associated with the public sphere, in both their spoken and written forms, is a form of literacy which empowers individuals. The ability to speak in public contexts (such as meetings, political rallies, television interviews) is a literacy which carries a great deal of cultural capital. Conversely, being able to write really comprehensive shopping lists and highly entertaining and intimate personal letters is a form of literacy which does not carry as much prestige and power within the culture. Speech and writing are not discrete activities in themselves but activities whose forms and values are inflected (shaped) by their functions within the public or private sphere respectively.

While the division of the social world into public and private has been motivated by the sexual division of labour (women in the home, men in the 'workplace'), as a result of the social change which has been accelerating in the last thirty years under the influence of feminism, this division is no longer quite so clear cut. We have argued throughout this book that language and other semiotic systems actively symbolise the social, and that social change is negotiated through textual practices. We would therefore expect that these changes could be identified in specific texts. The print media are a linguistic market (in Bourdieu's terms) in which the distinction between public and private is frequently at stake. Let's examine some print media texts to see how particular written genres negotiate these changes.

The print media as cultural field

The print media target various social groups differentiated largely on the basis of gender but also in terms of socioeconomic status. All the print media are 'public' in the sense that they are published and mass distributed, but some sectors of the print media are oriented to the public sphere (newspapers, news magazines, business magazines) and others (specialist magazines, women's magazines) are oriented toward the private sphere.

The picture becomes slightly more complex, however, when we examine these print media forms in terms of their component genres. Newspaper genres include:

- the public sphere genres: 'hard' news articles (with their discourses of business, law and order, and politics), opinion or comment articles, editorials, classified advertisements, real estate and employment sections; and
- the lifestyle, leisure and entertainment sections, the social pages, the comics.

The categories newspapers use to define what is news largely reproduce the values of the public sphere: 'hard' news is the serious stuff and traditionally a field reported by men, while the social pages and the lifestyle sections were (and in some cases still are) seen as the province of female reporters, who were 'more suited' to deal with private-sphere issues (see Steiner 1992). A further complexity arises from the different markets of the 'quality' press and the tabloid (popular) press. The quality press is regarded (and regards itself!) as the archetypal voice of the public sphere. The tabloid press mediates public-sphere issues through a perspective and a mode of address which personalise issues and reduce the sense of distance between the public world and the private world (with stories about celebrities, tragedies involving children, the sex lives of politicians, and so on).

Magazines, more than newspapers, are oriented to the private sphere of leisure, sexuality and the home. Yet they too address both private and public sphere issues, through a variety of genres. For example, generalist women's magazines (which comprise the bulk of the magazine market) include genres such as:

- feature articles;
- how-to articles;
- recipes;
- agony columns; and
- fiction (including romance).

The print media as a cultural field is thus hierarchically organised around distinctions such as public/private, quality/tabloid, information/ entertainment and serious/popular. The cultural capital within this field is negotiated around these terms. For example, a journalist may acquire cultural capital and status within the field by moving from a tabloid paper to a 'quality' paper (the *Australian*, the *Guardian*, the *New York Times*). This journalist would probably feel 'superior' to someone working for a mass women's magazine such as *Elle* or *Hello*, yet the profitability and popularity of these magazines earns them more economic capital, and thus also cultural capital.

Not surprisingly, however, the written genres found in the pages of women's magazines are not those most highly valued by authoritative institutions (such as the education system) within Western culture. In fact, they are frequently devalued and regarded as trivial, by both women and men. Yet contemporary women's magazines, aimed at working women, introduce discourses of business and employment alongside those of home, domestic skills, family, relationships, beauty and fashion. Figure 22 shows part of a text which addresses working mothers.

This text deals with an issue concerning a traditionally private-sphere activity—childcare—which also impinges on the public sphere through legislation enabling mothers (and, more recently, fathers) to take leave from work to look after their babies. How does this text negotiate the minefield that this intersection of public and private represents? It begins by invoking the public sphere, announcing that 'Australian women have officially had the right to maternity leave since 1979'. This is the discourse of the law and of industrial regulation, presented without qualification in a reporting mode which—so far—would not be out of

Figure 22 'The (offfice) politics of pregnancy'

AUSTRALIAN WOMEN HAVE OFFICIALLY HAD THE RIGHT TO MATERNITY LEAVE SINCE 1979. BUT IN PRACTICE, TAKING TIME OFF IS TRICKY BUSINESS. CLAUDIA BOWE EXPLAINS HOW TO PLAY OFFICE POLITICS FROM THE MOMENT YOU ANNOUNCE YOUR PREGNANCY TO THE DAY YOU RETURN TO WORK.

Liz never thought she would hate her job, but that's exactly how she felt upon returning to her real estate firm after having a baby. She had expected to enjoy working again; instead she became a guilt-wracked wreck.

After a year, she quit in disgust. 'I wasn't getting a feeling of success from any part of my life,' she recalls.

It *sounds* so simple: the career woman who wants to 'have it all' becomes pregnant, takes maternity leave and then returns to work—only now she has *both* a satisfying career and a delightful little bundle waiting for her at home. In reality, returning to work after a baby is a delicate dance of negotiation among newly competing demands and identities. There's the practical side of life to be worked out: you have to respond to the suddenly doubled demands on your time and energy. And there are the more thorny emotional dilemmas, such as how you weave in the tremendous importance of the new baby with your dedication to work. You're being called upon to play two very different roles, and shifting identities several times a day can begin to wear on you.

Even for devoted careerists, going back to work after giving birth is often difficult; not every woman will be able to make good on her intentions to do it all. But for those who want to try, planning ahead and knowing how to play the office politics can make the road smoother.

Baby-love can come as a shock Baby-love is unlike any love you've ever known and it can bowl you over; in its grip, many new mothers find themselves questioning goals that formerly were set in concrete. For career women who've been very driven for years, having a baby can be a shock. All of a sudden you realise you really love being with this baby and it may never have occurred to you that you would—you thought you'd just go back to work right away and get someone to take care of the baby for you. Instead, you become very attached. It's a real conflict.

When baby-love kicks in, it may prompt you to re-evaluate your life scheme. Quite a few women end up deciding that, at this point in their life, mothering is more worthwhile than working. These women probably will—and *should*—quit working for a time if it's financially feasible. The important thing to remember is that you most likely will want or need to return to work at some point, so take care not to burn any bridges.

There's no right or wrong about whether to return to work after having a baby—it's a decision that each new mother must make for herself. Remember, the women's movement was about freedom of *choice*, so don't let other women make you feel like you're letting down the sisterhood by choosing motherhood over work at this point in your life.

Be aware that in some people's eyes, you will be compromising your professional reputation by abandoning your career mid-stream. There will always be those women who feel you've let down the female contingent with your about-face concerning your career, and there will be male employees who will take your defection as further proof that time spent grooming women for upper management is time wasted.

> THERE'S A SIGNIFICANT EXIT FROM THE LABOUR FORCE BY WOMEN AFTER THEIR FIRST CHILD IS BORN. THE WOMEN MOST LIKELY TO RETURN? THOSE WITH HIGH-STATUS OCCUPATIONS, HIGH EARNING POTENTIAL, HUSBANDS WITH A LOW INCOME, WHO WORKED UNTIL JUST UP TO THE BIRTH AND HAVE BEEN WITH THE SAME EMPLOYER FOR A LONG PERIOD.

Courtesy of Murdoch Magazines. Bowe 1992:3

place in a newspaper article. The qualification comes in the next breath: 'But in practice, taking time off is tricky business'. The phrase 'tricky business' and the reference to 'how to play office politics' are not part of the serious, 'straight' public sphere discourses of business and politics. Instead, these are metaphors for the 'business' of managing interpersonal relations, traditionally women's field of expertise and now applied to the workplace.

The body of the article begins with a (hypothetical?) anecdote about Liz, a mother who went back to work but left again after a year because she 'became a guilt-wracked wreck'. The anecdotal style immediately personalises the issues—a characteristic of private sphere discourse, with its focus on the personal and private. The tone of the article is that of motherly or 'sisterly' advice: familiar in terms of social distance, with the frequent use of 'you' to directly address and involve the reader. 'Make use of my wisdom, I have been there and done that (or someone I know has)', the writer seems to imply.

Juxtaposed against the main text, and set in bold, are a set of 'industrial facts' whose tone is not easily assimilated into the body of the article. Their inclusion functions to give the seriousness and authority of the public sphere to the issue, but is not allowed to intrude upon the article's generic function of 'giving advice'. To incorporate public sphere discourses into the advice genre would be to depersonalise the tenor and thus to destabilise the genre, which depends on personalised address to be successful.

Yet the article must still deal with the field and the subject matter of the workplace and its roles and activities. By looking at the lexical choices in it, we can see how it weaves together the two strands of office work and mothering (see Figure 23).

Each of these discourses is represented either in every sentence or in every alternate sentence, constructing the conflict between the competing demands of the two spheres. Apart from the repetition of 'baby-love', 'baby' and 'love', the text spends few words expounding the joys of motherhood, which are taken for granted (an ideological assumption? definitely!). On the other hand, the positive affect associated with the

Figure 23 Discourses of work and mothering

Discourse of work	Discourse of mothering
career	delightful little bundle
leave	home
work	emotional dilemmas
careerists	giving birth
financially feasible	baby-love [repeated]
professional reputation	new mother
male employees	baby [repeated]
upper management	love [repeated]

world of work needs to be explicitly constructed; much of the lexis associated with work is coupled with terms that associate work either with female identity or with a positive attribute:

- career *woman*;
- *satisfying* career;
- *maternity* leave;
- *dedication* to work; and
- *devoted* careerists.

The text tries to be open in terms of emphasising that the choice between going back to work or quitting to stay at home with the baby is the reader's. However, subtle shifts suggest that it is oriented more towards those women who continue to work (predictable given the readership *New Woman* is targeting—young career women). Throughout the text, women are directly addressed as 'you', or referred to in the third person in their roles as mothers or 'career women'; but there is a shift to the more distant, less inclusive phrases 'quite a few women' and 'these women' (implying, 'but probably not you') in references to women who choose mothering over paid work. But the even more distant 'those women' is reserved for women who criticise mothers who give up their career (the 'sisterhood' musn't criticise 'motherhood'). (It is worth noting that the distinction between paid work and the unpaid work of mothering is never made in the text—throughout, there is an opposition between real work and the joys of motherhood, which is an ideological binary based upon a capitalist, patriarchal social and economic structure in which women's work in the home has no economic value.)

What we hope to have demonstrated in this analysis is that the modes of private discourse have a strong influence upon the way in which both public sphere and private sphere issues and discourses are organised textually (and that this has ideological effects). There is no way that readers familiar with and literate in print media texts could read this article in the same way as, say, a hard news story in a newspaper. The genre of advice, so typical and pervasive in women's magazines, constrains the ways in which this text means, individualising the issues and framing them as a matter of personal choice.

Is there anything wrong with this? Maybe not, but it does constitute an ideological move, since by personalising and individualising an issue, it also becomes depoliticised. The text plays down the roles of institutions like the workplace, the legal system and industrial regulations in determining what individuals can and can't do and how they can live their lives. A personal view of a problem is what advice columns provide, and the typical solution is to 'talk about it'. The problem and the solution are addressed locally. The social power structures which may underpin the personal problem are thus unlikely to be addressed or changed.

The different discourses and genres of the print media thus inflect the notions of public and private in complex ways. The print media function as multidiscursive and multigeneric institutions. That is, they employ a variety of genres, and these genres express a variety of discourses. These in turn constrain not only *what* we read but *how* we read and require literacies in and across these genres and discourses.

WRITERS, AUTHORS AND TEXT PRODUCTION

We noted earlier in this chapter that writing makes possible what Kress has called the 'effacement of the writer from the text' (1988b:95). Written texts may or may not explicitly identify their writers. Why are some written texts anchored to the name of an author and not others? What is at stake for texts in their anchoring to authors? Why are academics so concerned about plagiarism? Does it matter 'whose words' they are in written texts? If we accept Bakhtin's argument that all texts are composed of *heteroglossia*, the 'many voices' of a language, and bear traces of 'where they've been'—the innumerable contexts which words carry with them (intertextuality)—then can anyone ever claim to be the author of a text, or its sole original source?

Michel Foucault has pointed out the apparently idiosyncratic use of the term author within Western cultures:

> the name of an author is a variable that accompanies only certain texts to the exclusion of others: a private letter may have a signatory, but it does not have an author; a contract can have an underwriter, but not an author; and, similarly, an anonymous poster attached to a wall may have a writer, but he cannot be an author.

Foucault 1977:124

It is clear, then, that not all writers are regarded as authors. Kress argues that a writer's function is that of an 'assembler of text. That is, out of her or his experience of other texts, he or she creates a new text which meets the demands of a particular social occasion' (1985:47). Yet the role of author is clearly regarded as more than this. What is at stake in this distinction between authors and writers?

A key cultural value at stake here is the concept of originality. Written texts which are the works of an author are judged to have qualities of creativity and uniqueness. Such values are attributed in particular to literary genres, such as novels, plays and poems. (This is closely tied to notions of the individual subject who expresses themself through unique utterances. This conception of the subject is an ideological one, which corresponds to (small 'l') liberal beliefs in free will and the importance of self-expression, an ideology which fails to recognise the ways in which social structure constrains behavioural and linguistic systems. Kress (1985) points out how disempowering this model of writing is for children learning to write, since they are expected to express themselves 'in their own words', yet their ability to do so depends on a wide experience of a variety of other texts.

The term author is applied not only to poems, plays and novels, but to most published books of whatever genre, with the exception of reference works such as dictionaries and encyclopaedias. However, the same genres have not always required attribution to an author. In the past, literary texts did not need to be attributed to an author to gain their value.

Genres which require an author are those in which the identity of the writer contributes to the authority and value of the text (and this applies not just to written genres but also to films—critics study the films of Coppola, Eisenstein, or John Ford). The author is a function of our way of handling texts.

Other written genres gain their credibility from anonymity. Just as the naming of an author implies a particular writing position and an individualised style, genres which don't acknowledge their writer/s, such as dictionaries, encyclopaedias, 'hard' news stories (which often acknowledge a news agency but not a journalist), lay claim to values such as 'objectivity', 'fact', 'universality' or 'truth'.

Yet other texts, such as bus tickets, road signs and jar labels, are regarded as too 'generic' (read as the opposite of 'original') or too ephemeral to require attribution to a source.

Naming an author has another function: it identifies the person who has legal rights to a text and takes legal responsibility for its content. Authors are writers who own their texts; that is, who hold legal copyright for them. The term author thus belongs not only to cultural criticism (of literature, films) but to legal discourse. The author is the individual who can be sued for libel and who can receive royalties from the sale of the commodity, the written text.

Plagiarism is thus the sin of failing to recognise the copyright holder—in effect, 'stealing' the copyright holder's work. Plagiarism sometimes surfaces publicly as a legal issue, in the form of court cases where one author sues over the claimed use of that author's work by another (the former Beatle George Harrison was successfully sued when a court decided that in his 1970s hit 'My Sweet Lord' he had made unacknowledged use of the tune of the 1960s Chiffons hit 'He's So Fine'). In academic discourse, however, what is at stake is, among other things, intellectual honesty and giving due acknowledgment to the work of other writers. Elaborate methods of acknowledgment, in the form of various systems of referencing, are used to identify who wrote what, and when.

The functions of acknowledging authorship here are slightly different, at least as they relate to the humanities disciplines. An author may be cited to give authority to an argument or to demonstrate that a range of positions or approaches are possible. Finally, by using a referencing system to identify the source of their material, students are being explicit about their function as writers—their role as 'assemblers of text'.

The agent of production could be an amorphous institution, a team of writers, a writer or an author. In certain fields, such as bureaucracies, the 'actual' author of a text (say, a research officer) is 'absent' from the body of the text. In other fields, such as film making, a director is responsible for only a part of the finished text (along with camera operators, actors etc.) but it becomes acknowledged as the director's 'work'. The concept of 'authorship' is thus differently handled within different cultural fields, but is largely tied to the degree to which capital is attached to a particular written genre; fields in turn regulate who is allocated this capital (and the 'credit' for authorship) according to their position within the field/institution.

SUMMARY

Writing as an activity, and written genres as types of texts, are shaped in part by the materiality of the medium, a materiality which is rapidly changing because of the impact of new communication technologies.

Writing is a resource and a technology which acquires value and capital through the uses made of it within a culture.

Writing as a practice is determined and influenced by the discourses and genres it realises, and the institutions which underpin these discourses and genres. For example, many of the differences we assume exist between speech and writing are not so much essential differences between the two mediums as differences that arise from the uses to which we put speech or writing within our culture. In particular, many written texts function in contexts which are formal and impersonal in their tenor relations, whereas speech is often the favoured mode in personal, informal interaction. To understand more fully the role of written language in our culture, we need to ask:

- Which genres are written genres and which are spoken?
- Which institutions, fields and markets make use of writing?
- What tenor relations attach to these genres and institutions?
- What forms of capital attach to these genres?

FURTHER READING

Foucault, M. 1977, *Language, Counter-Memory, Practice*, ed. and trans. D.F. Bouchard and S. Simon, Cornell University Press, Ithaca, New York

Kress, G. 1997, *Before Writing: Rethinking the Paths to Literacy*, Routledge, London & New York

Luke, A. 1996, 'Genres of power? Literacy education and the production of capital', in R. Hasan and G. Williams, *Literacy in Society*, Longman, London & New York

Pateman, C. 1989, 'Feminist critiques of the public/private dichotomy', in *The Disorder of Women*, Polity Press, Cambridge, pp. 118–40

Chapter 10

Visual mediums

The main focus of this chapter is on visual mediums and genres. Speech and writing genres are increasingly involved in a smaller proportion of communication practices in contemporary Western cultures, which is dominated by visual genres and mediums: photographs, television, film, video, cartoons, posters, t-shirts, comics and computer simulations, to name just a few. Increasingly, an argument can be mounted that a literate person in contemporary Western cultures is, first and foremost, someone who is able to recognise, read, analyse and deploy a variety of visual genres and mediums.

THE VISUAL AS REAL

Perhaps the first thing we can say about a number of contemporary visual mediums—photographs or film, for instance—is that they have gained a high level of credibility as means of communication precisely because they seem to be able to reproduce reality in an apparently objective way. Visual texts do not appear to be mediated: there appears to be no obvious difference between the image the text provides and the 'reality' it stands in for.

Unlike visual mediums, speech and writing are quite obviously mediated: there is an obvious difference between their own materiality (sounds, words on a page) and the materiality they stand in for or deliver up (people, events). The same argument could be made, of course, for older visual communication mediums, such as drawing and painting. The images to be found in paintings—at least in 'realist' paintings—seem very close to the 'original' image that is being represented. But are such images any more real than words or sounds?

The French painter René Magritte produced a picture which consisted of a remarkably realistic looking smoking pipe; the painting's title, which appeared on the image, was (as it translates into English) 'This is not a Pipe'. What was the point of giving that title to an extremely realistic painting of a pipe? It draws attention to the constructed and mediated nature of any kind of representation, whether it is 'realistic' or otherwise. 'This is not a Pipe' is exactly what it claims to be—it is not the object it represents. Just like sounds and words, however, it presents itself as being a genuine or faithful substitute for 'the real thing'.

There are other issues related to the 'reality' of visual representations which we need to address before we move on to a more detailed consideration of visual communication mediums and genres. First, what do we mean when we describe a representation as realistic? Second, paintings, drawings and other less technologically sophisticated and advanced forms of visual representations may be no more real than speech or words, but what about those mediums (such as photographs or film) which seem to directly reproduce reality? And is there any form of visual representation or reproduction that is completely unmediated and objective?

When discussing the 'realistic' aspects of some visual mediums and genres, it is worth bearing in mind that the notion of realism is not something that we can take for granted, nor do all cultures agree on what is realistic. To give an example, in ancient Egyptian culture, people and things were usually drawn using hard, straight lines, which made their features look rigid and geometric. Moreover, those representations did not make use of the same notion of perspective or balance that characterises most contemporary Western visual representations. People in a drawing were not represented according to their relative physical size, nor could people be positioned just anywhere within the drawing. The Pharaoh was generally represented as being much larger than her or his subjects, and was also usually positioned above them (see Figure 24).

This might seem rather strange and unrealistic to us, but it would probably not have appeared that way to most ancient Egyptians. Different cultures have different ideas of what is realistic, because what is accepted as real depends very much on specific cultural contexts, literacies and ideologies. In Chapter 5, we made the point that ideologies were produced by groups within a culture in order to make it appear as if their world view was the only possible and natural, the only real, world view.

Claude Lefort suggests that in pre-capitalist cultures, ideologies were presented as if they came directly from, and were sanctioned by, God or the supernatural world (Lefort 1986). For most ordinary people living in ancient Egypt, the world and all its activities were seen and understood

Figure 24 Akh-en-Aton and family worshipping the Sun-Disk

Illustration by Pat Goon

in terms of the ideology of the rule of the God-Pharaoh. This meant that the Pharaoh was far more powerful and important than mere mortals, and therefore it was only realistic to represent the Pharaoh as bigger—that is to say, greater—than anyone else except some gods.

What about the geometric and rigid faces and bodies? Again, it is worth recalling Volosinov's argument, also discussed in Chapter 5, that every representation is a sign that has been ideologised, and Laclau's suggestion that this process also applies to those signs that are subjects/identities. In ancient Egypt, the ruling ideologies would have produced a series of identities that grouped people within the culture according to their function in relation to the Pharoah. The identity of each person referred, in some way, to the identity of the Pharoah.

In visual texts, these identities corresponded to different styles of representation; different angles, geometric shapes, sizes and the inclusion or exclusion of different material details all had significance within the culture. A high priest, for instance, had a very different identity from a peasant or a soldier, and so it was only natural—and realistic—that they be represented differently.

In ancient Egypt, as in every culture, materiality or reality and the cultural production of that reality could not be divided from one another. Put simply, ancient Egyptians saw reality—both literally and metaphorically—differently from us, precisely because the ideological meanings available to them were different. As a result, their pictures and drawings were probably realistic to them, but seem stylised and un-realistic to contemporary viewers.

OBJECTIVITY

Our argument about the relativity of representations might apply to Egyptians who lived and communicated four thousand years ago, but they never had access to photographs, television, film or computers. Can we make the same argument in an age when technology enables us to reproduce reality quickly, and in remarkable detail? Have advances in communication technology enabled us to reproduce objective reality?

It has been argued, ever since photographs first appeared, that at last a medium of representation was available which produced only the truth or reality; that is, what was really there. The first objection to this proposition is a simple one: photographs can be 'doctored'—that is, they can be tampered with. During the late 1960s, when long hair was fashionable but often frowned upon by school principals, a school magazine editor at a high school took the liberty of trimming the hair of male students in class photographs! Perhaps a little more serious and sinister was the 'editing' of photographs and films that took place in Eastern European countries in the 1950s and 1960s. A powerful politi-cian would appear in official photographs until she or he fell from grace; after they had been disposed of, those same official photographs were edited to remove any sign of the now disgraced politician. In other words, according to the official photographic record, they had never existed: 'So you say comrade Chekhov was at the opening of the sports stadium in 1956? Look, here is the photograph of the opening, and he isn't in it.'

That is one argument against the objectivity of the new visual mediums. But surely those doctored photographs were objective and faithful before they were tampered with?

'EDITING' THE VISUAL

The answer is that visual mediums, like other communication mediums, are produced through processes of selection and omission. Anyone taking a photograph always makes decisions, sometimes quite unconsciously, about:

- what to include and what to leave out;
- how close to get to the material being photographed;
- the angle from which the photograph is to be taken; and
- when to take the shot.

Moreover, how is the photograph going to be used? Is it to be placed in an album or pinned on a wall? Will it accompany an article in a newspaper, or be used to blackmail a politician? These, and the almost infinite number of other possibilities we haven't mentioned, constitute the contexts that will produce and constrain possible readings of the photographs.

Let's address this question of the 'editing' of the visual through reference to some examples. First, what is included in and excluded from any photograph or film shot is significant because it constrains how the text can be read. This was demonstrated in a commercial for a television news show screened in the early 1990s. The channel was not attracting viewers to its news, so it ran an ad with a voice-over which said, 'Some news services only show you part of the picture.' Accompanying this voice-over was film of a woman, getting out of a car, who is startled and frightened when she sees a man running towards her.

From what we saw in this particular version ('not the complete picture'), it looked as if the woman was about to be assaulted or robbed by the man. However, the so-called 'complete picture' showed details, not included in the first version, which changed our reading of what was happening; there was an object about to fall onto the woman, and the man had seen it and was attempting to push her to safety.

The 'real' and complete picture, then, was to be seen on Channel X; but its commercial was as guilty of giving us an incomplete picture as its rivals' ads. Why? Because if the commercial had widened its perspective even further, it would have shown us television cameras filming the commercial. In other words, in order to claim to be giving us the complete picture ('here is a man saving a woman from an accident'), the TV station's commercial had to edit out its own involvement in the activity ('here is a television company shooting a commercial about a man saving a woman from an accident—which didn't really happen').

The distances and angles involved in taking photographs and shooting film also work to produce the end product. This is all reasonably straightforward: a shot from above or below, or from near or far, can influence how people read the 'captured' material, precisely because:

- those aspects determine what other material is included in the shot;
- angles and distances change the place from where we see the material (viewing position); and
- different angles and distances often have specific cultural meanings.

In many films it is customary to open with a long shot which gives the viewer the 'macro-picture', and then to zoom in to a close-up of the more specific action or scene (the 'micro-picture'). In *Blade Runner*, for instance, the opening shots are of a huge metropolis dominated by skyscrapers and electronic billboards; these are followed, however, by closer shots of crowds of people (made up of mixed races) going about their business in a market area. The first shots can be read as producing a sense of the inhuman character of the city (all buildings and billboards), while the next shots seem to reverse that notion, providing plenty of evidence of humanity, although the shots of the crowd tend to reinforce the earlier sense of depersonalisation.

The position from which we view is equally important in determining what we view. There is a famous scene in the Alfred Hitchcock film *Lifeboat* where a German survivor of a battle between a U-boat and an Allied ship is pulled onto the lifeboat by people he has just finished attacking. This is how the cultural theorist Slavoj Zizek describes the scene, and the importance of viewing position in film analysis:

> Let's take a small detail from *Lifeboat*, from the scene where the group of Allied castaways welcome on board their boat a German sailor from the destroyed submarine: their surprise when they find out that the person saved is an enemy. The traditional way of filming this scene would be to let us hear the screams for help, to show the hands of an unknown person gripping the side of the boat, and then not to show the German sailor, but to move the camera to the shipwrecked survivors: it would then be the perplexed expression on their faces that would indicate to us that they had pulled something unexpected out of the water. What? When the suspense was finally built up, the camera would finally reveal the German sailor. But Hitchcock's procedure is the exact contrary of this: what he does not show, precisely, is the shipwrecked survivors. He shows the German sailor climbing on board and saying, with a friendly smile, 'Danke schon!' Then he does not show the surprised faces of the survivors; the camera remains on the German. If his apparition provoked a terrifying effect, one can only detect it by his reaction to the survivors' reaction: his smile dies out, his look becomes perplexed.

> Zizek 1991a:144

By showing the German's reaction to the other survivors' reactions, Hitchcock changes things around, as Zizek suggests. Normally, the subjects in such a scene, and the people we (that is, English-speaking audiences) would be expected to identify with, would be the survivors. The German would be the object we gazed at—in fear, hatred and horror. Hitchcock makes the German the subject, however, which works to personalise and humanise him—particularly when we are able to see, as Zizek points out, the very human emotions displayed across his face.

Angles and distances are also important because they have specific cultural meanings which change from one context to another. In an introduction to a program which replays American football games, one of the opening shots is of a group of football players shot closeup and from waist height. The shot gives you the impression that the players are huge (which they are) and towering threateningly above you. In other words, the idea is to suggest that American football is a frightening and intimidating physical contest.

A second example is a commercial about an insurance company. The company featured in the commercial wanted to give the impression that it treated policy holders in a courteous, friendly and personalised way. It did this by showing a smiling employee standing side-by-side with another man making a claim, then offering him a seat and sitting a comfortable distance from the claimant (about two metres, which was politely close but not intrusively so; the claimant still had plenty of personal space). This was juxtaposed with a scene of what other insurance companies supposedly do. The employee remained seated when the claimant entered, but when he (the claimant) sat down the employee stood over him and stuck his face next to and above his head, interrogating him.

The meanings that are associated with angles and distances within a culture are used by photographers and filmmakers to add to the meanings that can be read into their shots: we have seen examples of this with the football show and the insurance commercial. However, it is important to remember two points about angles, distances and meanings. First, there are always a variety of ways of reading angles and distances. Extreme closeness need not suggest intimacy; it might simply mean that there isn't much space available (for example, a scene in a lift). And second, angles and distances can always be re-contextualised, which can change their meanings.

There is a famous poster of 1950s actor James Dean, shot full-length in the foreground, walking alone along a street, while in the background crowds of people are milling around, seemingly inhabiting the same space. One reading of this deployment of space is that Dean is a loner but also somebody different and special who stands out from the everyday, ordinary crowd.

If that shot had been taken from a different angle and distance, however, it could be read differently. A shot from within the crowd (full of happy faces and personalised interactions), for instance, which only picked up Dean as a tiny figure on his own in the background, could produce him negatively, as being excluded from human company and activities. In other words, the meaning of the relation of the two groups (Dean and the crowd) would depend to a large extent on how those two groups, and the distance between them, were positioned by the camera.

INTERTEXTUALITY AND VISUAL NARRATIVES

The photograph of Dean was famous enough to be used by Nike to advertise its footwear. In the newer version, James Dean is replaced by former tennis star John McEnroe, and the text has been re-titled 'Rebel with a Cause', a reference to Dean's film *Rebel Without a Cause*. Nike is using the Dean photograph to say something both about John McEnroe (he's a righteous rebel) and itself (its a company whose products are endorsed by that righteous rebel). Dean carries cultural capital, which is connected, and 'passed on', to McEnroe (and by extension, Nike) through the 'intertextuality' of the photograph.

Intertextuality refers, broadly, to the different cultural literacies we bring to any reading of a text. When we watch a film, for instance, we usually make sense of it in terms of other films we have watched. Audiences watching John Carpenter's 1980s remake of *The Thing* could have had at least three intertexts available to them as they watched the film:

1. they could have been familiar with previous Carpenter films; and/or
2. they could be highly literate in Hollywood science fiction films; and/or
3. they could have seen the earlier 1950s version of the film.

Any or all of these intertexts—and a lot more we could have mentioned—will predispose us to pick up on some features of scenes from Carpenter's film, and to miss or ignore others. Intertexts provide us with reading patterns and dispositions which we don't have to adhere to, but which do influence our view of 'what is there'.

It is important to emphasise that all visual texts, from photographic stills to film shots, constitute, and are usually read as, narratives. That is, the choice and arrangement of objects and the use of space in a visual text are all potentially meaningful, and when those meanings are brought together or integrated (either through reference to a single image or multiple images) we have a narrative. Films, for instance, may look as if they are 'occurring naturally', but they are just as much 'narrated stories' as novels.

The process, in films, where individual shots and scenes are 'stitched together' is called *montage*. Slavoj Zizek writes that:

> Montage is usually conceived as a way of producing from fragments of
> the real—pieces of film, discontinuous individual shots—an effect of
> 'cinematic space' . . . It is universally acknowledged that 'cinematic
> space' is never a simple repetition or imitation of external . . . reality,
> but an effect of montage.
>
> Zizek 1991a:116

In 'horror' or 'thriller' genres, for instance, we are usually made to
feel that 'something is wrong', and that 'terrible things will happen'. Part
of this comes from intertextuality: something is supposed 'to be wrong'
in those genres (a psychotic killer is on the loose, or something like
that). But it also comes from the way the director puts different shots
together, or uses close-ups and strange camera angles. We usually know
in advance where the 'unexpected' attack will come from, because shots
of the person to be attacked are followed by shots of the place that holds
the threat (a locked door, bushes); or again, the shot of the victim will
be from the 'point of view' of the attacker. This effectively constructs a
narrative: it says something like 'the victim walked towards the psychotic
killer, who was hidden in the bushes'.

Montage is one way that visuals work to 'tell a story'. Quite often,
however, the narrative is 'helped along' by sound. In order to understand
just how large a part sound plays in 'making sense' of, and naturalising,
the flow of visual images, French film critic Michel Chion 'rewinds'
several scenes from Ingmar Bergman's film *Persona*, and plays them
without sound:

> First, the shot of the nail impaling the hand: played silent, it turns out
> to have consisted of three separate shots where we had seen one,
> because they had been linked by sound. What's more, the nailed hand
> in silence is abstract, whereas with sound, it is terrifying, real. As for
> the shots in the mortuary, without the sound of dripping water that
> connected them together we discover in them a series of stills, part of
> isolated bodies, out of space and time. And the boy's right hand,
> without the vibrating tone that accompanies and structures its exploring
> gestures, no longer 'forms' the face, but just wanders aimlessly. The
> entire sequence has lost its rhythm and unity.
>
> Chion 1994:4

The same applies to the use of music in film. The horror film genre
doesn't just use montage to let you know that something is about to
happen: shrill or discordant violin music, for instance, usually suggests
that the bloodletting is about to begin. And there are musical sounds
which signal, and are associated with, characteristics, emotions and states
such as heroism (trumpets!), romance (tenor sax) and sexual orgasm
(frenzied piano).

The details of a visual text are usually read in terms of different cultural meanings, even in something as 'meaningless' as an abstract painting, or a succession of apparently random images in a music video.

VISUAL LITERACIES AND ECONOMIES OF PLEASURE

Visual mediums are similar to other communication mediums mainly because the meanings and realities we produce and read into them are connected to, and based upon, different cultural literacies and contexts. Visual mediums are different from other communication mediums, however, mainly because their materiality produces a different kind of relationship between the medium and its audiences.

Different visual mediums constitute a cultural context of their own; for instance, telephone conversations will become quite different communication practices when the technology for accompanying voice with visuals becomes commonly available. Similarly, watching a film or television is not the same kind of experience as reading a book. They are different kinds of experiences, not because you have to do more work or be more imaginative reading a book (this is the usual story put out by those who privilege written literacies), but because different mediums require different reading practices and literacies. While reading a book is usually a private experience, watching a film is often a more communal activity: you travel to a theatre, buy a ticket, and sit with a group of people who may be reacting to the film (say, if it is a comedy) in a very audible way. In other words, whereas reading a book is usually a self-contained exercise, watching a film is often done together with other people whose reactions become part of the experience.

Moreover, there is a huge time difference or commitment that differentiates the two activities. Reading a book can take several hours, days or months, while watching a film takes a couple of hours. That is, books and films are characterised by different economies of pleasure. This is not to say that one activity is better than the other; what it does mean is that people may take this factor into account when they choose between the two.

It could be argued, for instance, that films deliver a quicker, more intense and 'economical' pleasure fix than, say, conventional novels. After all, in a film you can be kidnapped, fight off a vampire, escape, fall in love, have sex, break up, become rich, save someone's life and expose crooked politicians with Winona Ryder or Jeff Bridges, all within two hours of committed time. The same time commitment to the novel *Anna Karenina* might leave you with the impression that all happy families are very similar to each other, while all unhappy families are unhappy in their own way.

If more happens in a shorter time in a film, and if the pleasure fix is more intense, why do people read books? Simply because there are different kinds of pleasure that can't be quantified. As Bourdieu argues, what counts as pleasure, or as legitimate pleasure, depends very much on habitus. People who share a particular habitus can spend days reading a book because they are disposed to experience, appreciate and legitimise the pleasures associated with reading. The same people might dismiss the pleasures associated with film watching as superficial, trivial or worthless.

In contemporary Western cultures, however, and particularly in youth cultures, visual mediums and genres are becoming increasingly popular at the expense of other mediums. We referred, in our previous chapter, to the ways in which people 'commoditise themselves': visual mediums such as film, television and videos are sites where people often 'shop' for body fashions, attitudes, hairstyles, and personalities to identify with. At the same time visual texts (particularly television, film and advertising) function to regulate and influence the kinds of subjectivities available to us.

VISUAL TEXTS AND SUBJECTIVITY

In Chapter 6 we referred to three different theories of the production of subjectivity:

1. the psychoanalytical theory of subjectivity based on a lack;
2. the Foucauldian notion of the institutional regulation of subjects based on discipline—based knowledge; and
3. the notion, developed by Judith Butler, that subjectivity is based on repeated performances of bodily genres.

The following series of photographs have been taken from a sunscreen lotion advertisement (see Figure 25). They have written texts that help contextualise them, the most explicit of which reads as follows:

> Smart people don't even think about stepping outside without
> protection. Lucky Ambre Solaire has got you covered. Whether you're
> shopping, socialising or working up a sweat at tennis, we've got the
> product to suit you!

Let's consider these photographs, and this written text, as a 'regulatory narrative': people who use this sunscreen lotion are 'smart' both in the sense that they are intelligent (they won't get sunburnt), and in the sense that, because they are intelligent, they will (naturally enough) wear

Figure 25 Visual construction of subjectivity

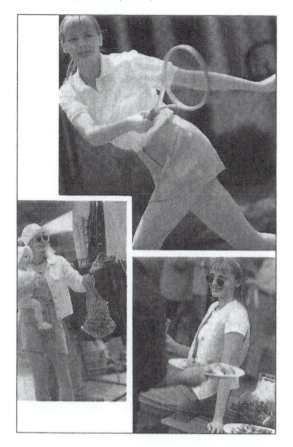

Courtesy of Ambre Solaire

attractive clothes and do trendy things (smart here refers to them being fashionable). What we are dealing with here is a form of interpellation: the advertisement is suggesting that smartness is connected to the use of sunscreen lotion, and in particular to the use of the advertiser's product. The reader is not so much being given advice about how to become smart—that the readers are smart is already presumed and communicated in the written text through the implied connection between 'Smart people' and 'Whether you're shopping . . . we've got the product to suit you'.

What kind of subjectivity is being called up here, and how is it produced visually? Let's return to our three theories of subjectivity and see how they can be used to analyse these photographs. In psycho-analytical terms, the notion of subjectivity based on the need to fill in a lack works in all three photographs through what is called the fetishising of objects. The fetish, in psychoanalytical terms, stands in for the lack that defines subjectivity. In the top photograph the fetishised object could be read as the tennis racket (and perhaps the sports clothes that go with it), while in the photograph on the left it might be the baby or the clothes the woman is considering buying (there is a certain truth to the saying 'I shop, therefore I am'). These objects are used to fill up the lack or complete the person because they stand in, metonymically, for generic identities. In other words, the tennis racket, clothes and/or the child function as proof of your (rightful) place in an ideologised narrative of subjectivity: here is a healthy sportswoman, successful, sexually attractive, stylish and vital, and a loving, caring mother who has kept her figure; both narratives produce the woman as attractive and valuable.

In Foucauldian terms, this advertisement is an excellent example of the regulation of subjectivity through deployment of the (visual) discourses of health and sexuality. The written and visual texts specifically prescribe a regime of activities (shopping, socialising, tennis) which a normal, healthy person would follow. Moreover, that emphasis on a varied, active and healthy lifestyle ties in with the notion of sexual normality. The woman in the photographs obviously exercises and eats well, and as a result she has a classically attractive figure. This suggests that she recognises the necessity of producing herself as sexually attractive and desirable (presumably for men or, more specifically, for her husband or partner).

Finally, for Butler subjectivity is culturally inscribed on the materiality of the body through the repeated performance of bodily genres, so that the body literally comes into being (that is to say, comes to mean) by learning to (successfully) perform itself! All three photographs provide examples of this. In the top photograph we recognise a sportswoman because of the way her body is configured: the leg stretched across her body, the left arm extended for balance, head held steady and eyes on the ball. Of course, in practical terms, this is only a performance of tennis, and a bad one at that—try actually hitting a proper tennis shot in this obviously staged position! The point, however, is not that she is a tennis player—she wouldn't want to be, since actually playing tennis would get in the way of the performance of subjectivity. Why? The written text may refer to 'working up a sweat at tennis', but there isn't any sweat evident in this photograph; sweat is messy, unstylish and unfashionable, and would spoil the effect!

Much the same process is at work in the photograph on the right. Here we have a controlled and very deliberate simulation of casual, stylish attractiveness. The sunglasses lowered to connote visual attentiveness, the raised eyes, the half smile, the wine glass held ready, but not so close it gets in the way, the left arm carefully balancing the body: the marvellous integration of these bodily gestures testifies to a successful performance of the 'real' of subjectivity.

The photographs we have referred to here are obviously staged, and do not convincingly pass themselves off as unmediated, objective reproductions of reality. At the same time, this staging (and the ideologising and subjectivising that go with it) is not just characteristic of the genres of visual advertising, but is to be found, to some extent, in all visual texts. To demonstrate this point, we will move from advertisements to an analysis of the supposedly more objective visual genre of news photographs.

VISUAL GENRES: THE NEWSPAPER PHOTOGRAPH

The photographs we are analysing were published in the same edition of a regional newspaper, the *Morning Bulletin*, on Friday, 16 December 1994. They are part of the news genre, but that generic categorisation doesn't get us very far, since there are considerable generic differences within that very broad term. We will therefore pitch our descriptions/analyses at a more specific generic level—at the 'soft' news photography genre.

'Soft' news usually refers to stories that are:

- 'positive';
- of local rather than international importance;
- not characterised by violence, antagonism or conflict; and
- meant to act as a balance to more sensationalised, serious and 'negative' stories.

All the articles and photographs we make use of fit neatly into this genre, which is not unexpected considering that the *Morning Bulletin* is a 'local' (rather than state or national) paper, which usually identifies its main function or rationale as being a form of community service. Part of that function would be to provide stories (and photographs) which reflect positively on the community.

Let's look at the four photographs from the *Morning Bulletin*, (see Figures 26–29). We can label them according to their accompanying headlines:

A. 'Firefighters get funds' (1994:2) (Figure 26);
B. 'Exchange student off to Germany' (1994:3) (Figure 27);
C. 'Mobile screening unit' (1994:4) (Figure 28); and
D. 'Week's leave, 50 years service' (1994:5) (Figure 29).

Figure 26 'Firefighters get funds'

Courtesy of Capricorn
Newspapers Pty Ltd

Figure 27 'Exchange student off to Germany'

Courtesy of Capricorn
Newspapers Pty Ltd

Figure 28 'Mobile screening unit'

Courtesy of Capricorn
Newspapers Pty Ltd

Figure 29 'Week's leave, 50 years service'

Courtesy of Capricorn
Newspapers Pty Ltd

The first point to make is that every photograph functions as little more than an adjunct to an article. All the pertinent details are in the written text, which means that these photographs are deployed primarily as evidence or support for ('yes, it did happen, here is a picture to prove it), and as a means of personalising ('here are some smiling faces'), the article. These photographs do not make wide demands on our cultural literacy, mainly because there is an expectation that the audience will recognise and share the paper's strong communal values.

We can be more specific. In photograph B, three people are arranged together, smiling. They are part of the same 'community' (Rotarians) and share a common purpose (the young girl's trip to Germany as an exchange student is supported by Rotary, which values this kind of activity). There is no obvious conflict, ambiguity or unintegrated meaning in this photograph. Much the same is true of photograph A (again, three people working together, a worthy cause, smiles all round), C (the narrative is almost a perfect copy of A's) and D (which features a couple celebrating their wedding anniversary). With D, we move away from the public sphere (the other photographs involve community work) to the private (a long-married couple still in love), but the reporting of the story gives it a public dimension (it functions as an example of communal values at work).

Why do these photographs seem unambiguous? The answer, to a certain extent, can be found in the way each photograph has been edited—more specifically, in the way details (the subject matter) within the shot have been arranged. First, notice that all four photographs are carefully 'staged': in each there is a narrative theme represented by a physical object which is placed in the foreground or the centre of the photograph:

- In A, the narrative relates to the generosity of community groups in raising money for the fire brigade. The physical object is the cheque, which is located in the middle of the photograph.
- In B, the Rotarian's trip and the values associated with it are represented by the blazer held in the foreground.
- In C, the theme of bringing resources to outlying parts of the community is represented by the breast cancer screening unit, which is again centrally located.
- In D, the foregrounded photograph of the couple's wedding testifies to, and provides evidence of, their successful 50-year-old marriage.

What we wrote previously about these photographs functioning as adjuncts testifying to the reality and humanity of the articles they accompany can be applied to the 'special' objects within the photographs. The written pieces require a 'little piece of the real'—a photograph—to provide them with credibility. However, these photographs are themselves arranged as narratives (handing over the cheque or blazer, delivering resources to the outback, celebrating an anniversary). They give the article credibility, but require another 'piece of the real' (the cheque, the blazer, the equipment, the photograph in the photograph) to 'ground' their own, photographic, narratives.

The mirroring of narratives between articles and photographs requires very close and careful editing—hence the lack of ambiguity or spontaneity in the photographs. In A, the written narrative is about members of a caring community pitching in to help others, and every detail in the photograph works to reinforce this:

- the national flag—an obvious marker of community—is located in the background;
- the three people are situated below the flag and all are smiling broadly;
- they are grouped quite close together: the two donors are active (holding up the cheque, playing the guitar), while the recipient looks appreciative (or just plain deliriously happy).

There are few other details to detract from this careful production of communal cooperation and goodwill.

The tendency to keep the space between subjects to a minium functions as another marker of community. In B, for instance, the angle from which the photograph has been taken means that the three figures seem to overlap with one other as they share what looks like a small park bench. Photograph C is more generous in its deployment of space, but this is largely because the article's focus is on machinery. Consequently, the three subjects couldn't be in each other's pockets without getting in the way of the focal point of the story. Moreover, the subject matter of C is slightly more formal than that of the other narratives (this is a government delivery of a resource, not a community inspired effort), and the subjects have professional status (a politician and two health management professionals). Hence a certain distance (literal and metaphorical) is evident in this photograph.

The use of space in D is, of course, the most intimate: the couple are touching and take up nearly all the space in the photograph. The reproduction of this private moment projects the intimacy of the couple's personal life into the community as a public spectacle, testifying to the practical, everyday human reality of the community and its values.

Let's recap:

- reading these photographs does not require a wide cultural literacy;
- there is an expectation that the audience will identify closely and unambivalently with the values that inform the articles;

- the subject matter is predominantly concerned with highly 'positive' representations of the community;
- the photographs are all staged;
- the photographs function as 'pieces of the real', which testify to the truthfulness of the written articles;
- within those photographs some object is foregrounded as a 'piece of the real', which testifies to the truthfulness of the photographic narrative; and
- the photographs tend to erase or minimise the distance between subjects, reinforcing the communal theme of the articles.

Why this commitment to the notion of community? People will be inclined to buy a local newspaper only if they identify, to a certain extent, with the community it promotes. People who think of their identity in terms of a wider sense of community—say at a state or national level—are unlikely to be particularly interested in, or read, the local newspaper. Most local newspapers can only survive as viable businesses if there is a market for them. In a sense, any local paper needs to promote a notion of local identity and community in order to make a place, if you like, for a community newspaper. This explains why, in the *Morning Bulletin*, articles and photographs are carefully arranged so as to mirror one another, and also explains the need for those 'little bits of the real' of the community to be held up for our inspection. A community comes into being, in a sense, when newspaper articles and photographs 'call it up'; and as we have seen, the soft news genre and its accompanying photographs are ideally suited for this purpose.

SUMMARY

In this chapter we suggested that conventional notions of literacy have tended to emphasise and value verbal and written, rather than visual, mediums of communication and representation. At the same time contemporary Western cultures, and the communication practices that characterise them, are making increasing use of visual mediums and genres.

Visual mediums are sometimes privileged over other mediums because they seem to be able to represent reality in an unmediated way. Visual mediums, however, selectively reproduce, rather than faithfully mirror, reality.

FURTHER READING

Bourdieu, P. 1998, *On Television and Journalism*, Pluto Press, London

Bourdieu, P. with L. Boltanski, R. Castel, J-C. Chamboredon and D. Schnapper, 1990, *Photography*, trans. S. Whiteside, Polity Press, Cambridge

Chion, M. 1994, *Audio-Vision: Sound on Screen*, ed. and trans. C. Gorbman, Columbia University Press, New York

Kress, G. and T. van Leeuwen 1990, *Reading Images*, Deakin University Press, Geelong, Victoria

Afterword

In the General Introduction to his 1988 book *The Practice of Everyday Life*, Michel de Certeau describes his work as:

> a continuing investigation of the ways in which users—commonly assumed to be passive and guided by established rules—operate. The point is not so much to discuss this elusive yet fundamental subject as to make such a discussion possible; that is, by means of inquiries and hypotheses, to indicate pathways for further research. This goal will be achieved if everyday practices, 'ways of operating' or doing things, no longer appear as merely the obscure background of social activity, and if a body of theoretical questions, methods, categories and perspectives, by penetrating this obscurity, make it possible to articulate them. (xi)

De Certeau makes two explicit points here:

1. People's practices cannot be explained in terms of the overt rules and regulations of a culture. In other words, people do not simply lead passive, consumption-oriented lives.
2. While practices cannot be fully explained in terms of cultural rules and regulations, at the same time research needs to be conducted in order to devise ways ('theoretical questions, methods, categories and perspectives') of understanding and describing those practices.

This book has attempted to follow de Certeau's lead by approaching the notion of communication as a practice. At no stage do we suggest that individual communication practices are objectively reducible to any one theoretical explanation or perspective. What we have attempted to do is to describe and work through a variety of different ideas or positions associated with contemporary cultural theory in order to analyse communication as a practice.

It is probably fair to say that this book has introduced and made use of a very wide variety of cultural theories. The reason for this was that no one body of theory struck us as being adequate to the task of satisfactorily addressing or assimilating all the issues we felt we needed to cover. One theorist, the French sociologist Pierre Bourdieu, is represented extensively, but his work, comprehensive and admirable as it is, does not deal in any detailed way with certain concepts (subjectivity, ideology, genre theory) that we felt were important. Moreover, neither Bourdieu's work nor any of the other bodies of theory we have referred to are without their weaknesses—something we have attempted to address through our 'mix and match' approach.

Bourdieu's work has provided us with a particularly important set of theoretical categories—habitus, cultural capital, distinction, dispositions, cultural field—which we have condensed into a general notion of cultural literacy. Literacy, as we understand it, enables us to make sense of how and why certain types of communication practices occur and not others—which in itself is a significant step. But the notion of literacy—at least the version derived from Bourdieu—enables us to go even further and analyse the 'politics' of communication; that is, it helps us understand the relationship between communication practices, on the one hand, and the uses and evaluations made of those practices, on the other.

It is perhaps appropriate to explain our extensive use of popular cultural texts as examples of communication practices, literacies and politics. Analysing Marxist notions of ideology through reference to *Gilligan's Island*, or habitus through *The Flintstones*, might be convenient (after all, these and other popular cultural texts are likely to be familiar to many of the readers of this text), but is it justifiable? In other words, how can we translate from specific cultural products (a television series, films) and the practices they represent to 'real life'? The answer we would put forward is that there is no essential difference between the two. There are, of course, specific generic and material differences between, say, a film about a romance between two people, and a 'real' romance, but the point is that both romances are 'framed' in terms of the same cultural values, rituals, rules and regulations. Indeed, the old saying that 'life imitates art' might be modified to read 'people's practices are often influenced or determined by the literacies they acquire from popular cultural texts'.

Finally, we wish to make the point that this text is itself a cultural product and an example of a communication practice; one which, like all communication practices, is informed by notions such as habitus and cultural politics—a cultural politics which has, we hope, been 'openly and without embarrassment' presented as our 'politics, not someone else's' (Frow 1995:169).

Glossary

affect: A term used in the analysis of tenor relations to refer to the attitudes, emotions and values produced or expressed as part of the textual interaction. See *tenor*.

agency: The ability to exercise control over social processes and events. Agency is generally regarded as a human attribute, but may be attributed to non-human entities through the operation of discourses. An unqualified belief in individual human agency is part of the doctrine of subjectivism. See *discourse; subjectivism*.

binary/binaries: Binary oppositions, or binaries, are pairs of terms whose meaning is produced in opposition to one another. The meaning of one term is produced through what that term is not (its opposing binary term). Binaries are always hierarchical, that is, one term is considered good (or natural, valuable, strong) while the other is considered bad (or artificial, insignificant, weak).

bio-power: A term from Foucault used to describe the process whereby scientific knowledge of the subject is used as a means of categorising, evaluating, disciplining, regulating and reforming the subject.

capital, cultural: A set of resources which have cultural value within a specific cultural field. Like economic capital (wealth, material assets) cultural capital can be distributed and exchanged. What constitutes cultural capital and how it is to be valued are determined within and by specific cultural fields.

citation: The speaker's or writer's introduction of another's speech into a text, either by quoting their words directly ('direct speech') or reporting their meanings (paraphrase, 'indirect speech').

code: A system of signs organised according to a set of rules or conventions. The term can also be used to refer to these organising rules or principles.

commodity, commoditisation: A commodity is anything which is 'packaged' to be bought, sold or otherwise exchanged. Commoditisation (a term from Appadurai) is the process of producing an object in terms of its 'exchangeability'. Signs and texts become commoditised when their most socially relevant feature is their exchangeability.

communication: The practice of producing meanings, and the ways in which systems of meanings are negotiated by participants in a culture.

contact: A term used in the analysis of tenor relations to refer to the degree of social distance or level of intimacy constructed as an aspect of the tenor relation between the participants. See *tenor*.

context: A set of circumstances in which communication practices (texts) are produced and read. The particular environments in which communication, texts and meaning making occur, and in which they function as meaningful.

cultural capital: See *capital, cultural*.

cultural field: See *field, cultural*.

cultural literacy: See *literacy, cultural*.

cultural practice: See *practice, cultural*.

cultural trajectories: See *trajectories, cultural*.

culture: The totality of communication practices and systems of meaning.

deixis, deictic: Deixis is Greek for 'pointing'. Deictic items are items used to point or refer to something else. They are meaningful to the extent that they set up a relation between the speaker/writer of a text and the time, place, people or things being referred to. Deictics can refer to items within the text or outside it, but when they refer outside the text in order to be unambiguously interpreted they require both speaker and hearer to be present.

dialogism, dialogic: The principle that all language, whether spoken or written, indeed all communication, is structured as dialogue. That is, all texts (or utterances, in Bakhtin's terms) function to respond to a prior text and to anticipate a response; they do not mean in isolation from other texts or utterances.

discourse: One meaning of discourse is simply as an alternative term for text, regarded as a social process. The sense in which we generally use the term discourse in this book, however, is as a type of language or way of speaking/meaning associated with a particular institution. Such discourse types are not merely sets of texts but groups of ideas, statements and ways of thinking which express particular institutional values.

dispositions: Dispositions are the tendencies we have to hold certain attitudes and values, and to act in specific ways, because of the influence of 'where we've been' in the culture. See *habitus*.

economies of pleasure: The relationship between the time and energy consumers/readers expend in reading texts as against the pleasure they gain from this. Different mediums (e.g. watching a film or listening to a CD compared to reading a book) provide different economies of pleasure.

field, cultural: A cultural field is both a set of institutions and rules which constitute an objective hierarchy, and the interaction between these institutions and rules, on the one hand, and cultural practices, on the other. Cultural fields produce and authorise specific practices, and attempt to determine what constitutes cultural capital within specific fields, and how that capital is to be distributed. See *capital, cultural.*

field (of discourse): A semiotic dimension of context which concerns the relation between a text and the social action it is performing or participating in. Analysis of field pays attention to the subject matter of the text and also to the discourse/s involved.

genre: Genres are ways of making sense of texts as particular types. Genres are text types which structure meanings in certain ways, through their association with a particular social purpose and social context. In social semiotic terms, genres can be analysed as culturally defined and expected combinations of field, tenor and mode.

habitus: A term from Bourdieu. Can be understood as a 'feel for the game' that is everyday life. More technically, habitus is a set of dispositions gained from our cultural history that stays with us across contexts. See *dispositions.*

hegemony: A dominant group's rule by ideological consent. Hegemony is achieved by an ideological process whereby the dominant group achieves power and control over other groups by representing to them that this state of affairs is in their best interests.

ideology/ideological process: A practice whereby a particular group within a culture attempts to naturalise their own meanings, or pass them off as universally accepted and as common sense.

imaginary, the: In psychoanalytic terms, the imaginary is the stage in a child's formation as a social identity when it still identifies closely with the mother.

intentionality: This refers to the concept that the intention of the producer/ sender of the message/text is crucial or intrinsic to its meaning. Intentionality is assumed to be essential by various models of communication, particularly process school models, and is very prevalent in 'common sense' notions of communication. This assumption has been critiqued by semiotics as the 'intentional fallacy'.

interpellation: The hailing or calling up of a person as a particular cultural identity so that the person accepts that identity as given.

The term comes from Althusser, who strongly linked interpellation to the workings of cultural institutions. See *subjectivity*.

intertextuality/intertexts: The meaning relations which exist between texts and the process of making sense of texts in reference to their relations with other texts. Intertextuality may involve one text making direct reference to another text, or may refer more generally to the ways in which texts embody meanings that have already been made, in one form or another, in other texts. See *dialogism*.

literacy, cultural: A knowledge of meaning systems combined with an ability to negotiate those systems within different cultural contexts.

materiality: This refers to the physical (as opposed to purely conceptual) aspect of communication practices. Materiality or material conditions affect or constrain communication practices in three ways: the physical nature of the medium involved and its possibilities and limitations, the participation of bodies in communication, and the material dimension of all social and cultural contexts.

meaning potential: The possibilities for meaning provided by sign systems such as language. Meaning potential is a way of viewing sign systems as constituted by the set of actual options for meaning making (what the speaker can mean). The term comes from Halliday.

medium: A general term referring to the means of communication. Communication media or mediums (we take either form of the plural as acceptable) are generally identified in either physical (oral, aural, visual, spoken, written, digital) or technical categories (print, radio, film, television, compact disc, the Internet etc.).

mirror stage, the: In psychoanalytic terms, the point at which the child recognises itself as a coherent identity (for example, by seeing its reflection in a mirror) but at the same time realises that it is also separate from itself (it is not its reflection) and separate from everything around it, including the mother.

mode (of discourse): A semiotic dimension of context which concerns the formation of the communication as a text. Analysis of texts and contexts in terms of mode pays attention to the ways in which the code and the medium constrain the meanings which can be made. See *code; medium*.

move: A unit of speech communication which can be equated approximately with the utterance in speech and the sentence in written language. The move is an utterance viewed as a communicative act. Moves perform various speech functions. See *performative; speech function*.

narrative: A way of structuring meanings in the form of a story. Narratives relate a sequence of events, implying a temporal order and often causal relations between events. Narratives work to structure cultural meanings in specific ways, and can come to constitute culturally ratified stories about social experiences (for example, the romance narrative, the capitalist success story, the ANZAC myth). Such widely accepted narratives are also known as *myths*.

Oedipus complex, the: In psychoanalytic terms, the Oedipus complex refers to the child's (necessarily repressed) desire for the mother and hatred of the father as a rival for the mother's affections.

objectivism: See *subjectivism*.

objectivity: The concept that a stable reality or truth exists independently of the means used to signify or represent that reality or the producer or reader of the representation/text. The notion of objectivity (the 'mirror model' of representation) is often invoked by the media when they claim to be reporting events objectively or providing 'faithful' visual images.

paradigm/syntagm: Two terms from semiotics. A paradigm is a set of possible meanings which could be selected in a particular context. A syntagm is the linking of signs together, their combination to form (part of) a text.

paralanguage: The vocal resources available to speakers in addition to spoken words. Paralanguage includes the tone, pitch, pace, rhythm and volume of the voice.

performative: A term from speech act theory used to refer to a class of utterances which function to perform the action they name (e.g. christening, warning, naming, blessing). See *speech function*.

phatic communication: Communication whose primary function is to make and maintain social contact, and which therefore relies mainly on the 'exchange' of already shared meanings or common information.

power: A general term in semiotic and cultural analysis which refers to unequal relations between individuals and groups. Power relations are arguably part of every communicative event or practice, and every social relation, whether or not they are explicitly or overtly at stake. More specifically, the analysis of power in tenor relations refers to the extent to which participants are positioned as equal or unequal. Power can be seen to relate directly to the possession of cultural and economic capital. See *bio-power; capital, cultural; tenor*.

practice, cultural: The activities performed in everyday life and their relationship with cultural rules, conventions and structures. Cultural practice can be considered as the performance of cultural literacy. See *literacy, cultural*.

semiology/semiotics: The 'science of signs' or study of sign systems. Semiotics is used to refer to theoretical approaches to the production of meaning which argue that meaning is produced through the interrelation of signs within a socially produced system.

sign, signifier, signified: In semiotic theory, according to Saussure, the basic unit of meaning is the sign. The sign is composed of the relation between the signifier and the signified. The signifier is the material or physical form of the sign (a sound, visual image or written word). The signified is the mental concept it invokes.

speech function: A term used to refer to the concept of the function or act performed by an utterance or move. The speech function of a move may be classified broadly as statement, question, offer or command. See *move; performative.*

subjectivism/objectivism: Subjectivism is the theoretical doctrine that human behaviour and the decisions people make at particular moments are largely the result of the individual's exercise of free will. Objectivism describes the opposing position; that is, that what people do (their practice) is basically determined by 'objective' structures such as institutions, laws and systems of relationships.

subjectivity, subject positions: Subjectivity is a concept derived from psychoanalytic theory and used in cultural studies to replace commonsense notions of the self/individual. Subjectivities are the cultural identities produced through discourses and ideologies. These are also referred to as subject positions. See *interpellation.*

syntagm: See *paradigm/syntagm.*

tenor (of discourse): A semiotic dimension of context which concerns the interaction the text is constructing or taking part in. Tenor concerns the relations between participants, and the positions they are taking up or being assigned. The analysis of tenor involves paying attention to the coding of power relations, social distance, and attitudes, values and emotions. See *affect; contact; power.*

trajectories, cultural: The paths through a culture that a person has taken and which can be understood as a map of that person's cultural history.

unconscious, the: In psychoanalytic terms, the unconscious is the site of repressed desires, desires which the split subject cannot consciously admit and must therefore be censored (e.g. the child's desire for the mother).

utterance: See *move.*

Bibliography

Adams, D. 1980, *The Restaurant at the End of the Universe*, Pan Books, London

Adas, M. 1992, *Machines as the Measure of Men*, Cornell University Press, Ithaca, New York

Althusser, L. 1977, *Lenin and Philosophy and Other Essays*, trans. B. Brewster, New Left Books, London

Appadurai, A. (ed.) 1988, *The Social Life of Things*, Cambridge University Press, New York

——1997, *Modernity at Large*, University of Minnesota Press, Minneapolis

Austin, J.L. 1962, *How to Do Things With Words*, Clarendon Press, Oxford

Australian, 1995, 10 March, News Limited, Sydney

Australian Magazine, 1994, 28–29 May, News Limited, Sydney

Bakhtin, M.M. 1981, 'Discourse in the novel', in *The Dialogic Imagination*, University of Texas Press, Austin, pp. 259–422

——1986, 'The problem of speech genres' in *Speech Genres and Other Late Essays*, trans. V. W. McGee, ed. C. Emerson and M. Holquist, University of Texas Press, Austin, pp. 60–102

Ballaster, R., M. Beetham, E. Frazer & S. Hebron, 1991, *Women's Worlds: Ideology, Femininity and the Woman's Magazine*, Macmillan, London

Barthes, R. 1977, *Image-Music-Text*, trans. S. Heath, Fontana, Glasgow

Baudrillard, J. 1975, *The Mirror of Production*, trans. M. Poster, Telos Press, St Louis

——1981, *For a Critique of the Political Economy of the Sign*, trans. C. Levin, Telos Press, St. Louis

——1983, *Simulations*, trans. P. Foss, P. Patton and P. Beitchman, Semiotext(e), New York

——1995a, *The Gulf War did not take place*, trans. P. Patton, Power Publications, Sydney

——1995b *The Illusion of the End*, trans. C. Turner, Polity Press, Cambridge

Bernstein, B. 1971, *Class, Codes and Control*, vol. 1, Routledge & Kegan Paul, London

Birch, D. 1991, *The Language of Drama: Critical Theory and Practice*, Macmillan, London

Bourdieu, P. 1962, *The Algerians*, Beacon Press, Boston

——1986, *Distinction*, trans. R. Nice, Routledge, London

——1990a, *In Other Words*, trans. M. Adamson, Polity Press, Cambridge

——1990b, *The Logic of Practice*, trans. R. Nice, Polity Press, Cambridge

——1991a, *Language and Symbolic Power*, ed. and introduced by J. B. Thompson, trans. G. Raymond and M. Adamson, Polity Press, Cambridge

——1991b, *Outline of a Theory of Practice*, trans. R. Nice, Cambridge University Press, Cambridge

——1993a, *The Field of Cultural Production*, trans. R. Johnson, Polity Press, Cambridge

——1993b, *Sociology in Question*, trans. R. Nice, Sage, London

——1996a, *The Rules of Art*, trans. S. Emanuel, Stanford University Press, Stanford

——1998a, *Acts of Resistance*, trans. R. Nice, Polity Press, Cambridge

——1998b, *On Television and Journalism*, trans. P. Ferguson, Pluto Press, London

——1998c, *Practical Reason*, Polity Press, Cambridge

——1998d, *The State Nobility*, trans. L. Clough, Polity Press, Cambridge

Bourdieu, P. with L. Boltanski, R. Castel, J-C. Chamboredon and D. Schnapper 1990, *Photography*, trans. S. Whiteside, Polity Press, Cambridge

Bourdieu, P. and J-C. Passeron 1990, *Reproduction in Education, Society and Culture*, trans. R. Nice, Sage, London

Bowe, C. 1992, 'The office politics of pregnancy', *New Woman*, Murdoch Magazines, Sydney, July, p. 3

Burton, D. 1980, *Dialogue and Discourse: A Sociolinguistic Approach to Modern Drama Dialogue and Naturally Occurring Conversation*, Routledge & Kegan Paul, London

Butler, J. 1990, *Gender Trouble*, Routledge, New York

——1993, *Bodies that Matter*, Routledge, New York

——1997a, *Excitable Speech*, Routledge, London

——1997b, *The Psychic Life of Power*, Stanford University Press, Stanford, California

Candlin, C.N. 1987, 'Explaining moments of conflict in discourse', in *Language Topics: Essays in Honour of M.A.K. Halliday*, vol. 2, ed. R. Steele and T. Threadgold, Benjamins, Amsterdam

Certeau, M. de 1986, *Heterologies*, trans. B. Massumi, University of Minnesota Press, Minneapolis

——1988, *The Practice of Everyday Life*, trans. S. Rendell, University of California Press, Berkeley, California

——1997a, *Culture in the Plural*, trans. T. Conley, University of Minnesota Press, Minneapolis

——1997b, *The Capture of Speech*, trans. T. Conley, University of Minnesota Press, Minneapolis

Chion, M. 1994, *Audio-Vision: Sound on Screen*, ed. and trans. C. Gorbman, Columbia University Press, New York

Chomsky, N. 1968, *Language and Mind*, Harcourt Brace, New York & London

Christie, F. (ed.) 1990, *Literacy for a Changing World*, ACER, Melbourne

Coulthard, M. (ed.) 1985, *An Introduction to Discourse Analysis*, 2nd edn, Longman, London

Danaher, G., T. Schirato and J. Webb 2000, *Understanding Foucault*, Allen & Unwin, Sydney

Davies, B. and R. Harre 1990, 'Positioning: the discursive production of selves', *Journal for the Theory of Social Behaviour*, vol. 20, no. 1

Derrida, J. 1976, *Of Grammatology*, trans. G.C. Spivak, Johns Hopkins University Press, Baltimore

——1988, *Limited Inc*, trans. S. Weber and J. Mehlman, Northwestern University Press, Evanston, Ill.

Dolly, 1993, September, Australian Consolidated Press, Sydney

Eco, U. 1979, *A Theory of Semiotics*, Indiana University Press, Bloomington

Fairclough, N. 1989, *Language and Power*, Longman, London

——1992, *Discourse and Social Change*, Polity Press, Cambridge

Fiske, J. 1990, *Introduction to Communication Studies*, 2nd edn, Routledge, London & New York

Foucault, M. 1971, *Madness and Civilisation*, trans. R. Howard, Tavistock, London

——1972, *The Archaeology of Knowledge and the Discourse on Language*, trans. A.M. Sheridan Smith, Pantheon, New York

——1973, *The Order of Things*, Vintage Books, London

——1975, *The Birth of the Clinic*, trans. A. Sheridan Smith, Vintage Books, New York

——1977, *Language, Counter-Memory, Practice*, ed. and trans. D.F. Bouchard and S. Simon, Cornell University Press, Ithaca, NY

——1980, *The History of Sexuality Volume 1: An Introduction*, trans. R. Hurley, Vintage, New York

——1986, *The Use of Pleasure: The History of Sexuality Volume 2*, trans. R. Hurley, Vintage Books, New York

——1988, *The Care of the Self: The History of Sexuality Volume 3*, trans. R. Hurley, Vintage Books, New York

——1997, *Michael Foucault: Ethics The Essential Works 1*, ed. P. Rabinow, Penguin, London

——1998, *Michael Foucault: Aesthetics, Method, and Epistemology*, ed. J. Faubion, trans. R. Hurley et al., The New Press, New York

Freud, S. 1977, *Case Histories 1,* ed. and trans. J Strachey, Penguin, Harmondsworth

——1986a, *On Sexuality*, ed. and trans. J. Strachey, Penguin, Harmondsworth

——1986b, *The Interpretation of Dreams*, ed. and trans. J. Strachey, Penguin, Harmondsworth

——1986c, *The Origins of Religion*, ed. and trans. J. Strachey, Penguin, Harmondsworth

——1987a, *Case Histories 2*, ed. and trans. J. Strachey, Penguin, Harmondsworth

——1987b, *Civilization, Society and Religion*, ed. and trans. J. Strachey, Penguin, Harmondsworth

——1987c, *On Metapsychology*, ed. and trans. J. Strachey, Penguin, Harmondsworth

——1987d, *The Psychopathology of Everyday Life*, ed. and trans. J. Strachey, Penguin, Harmondsworth

Frow, J. 1988, *Marxism and Literary History*, Basil Blackwell, Oxford

——1995, *Cultural Studies and Cultural Value*, Clarendon Press, Oxford

——1997, *Time and Commodity Culture*, Clarendon Press, Oxford '

Gatens, M. 1991, *Feminism and Philosophy: Perspectives on Difference and Equality*, Polity Press, Cambridge

Gilbert, P. and S. Taylor 1991, *Fashioning the Feminine: Girls, Popular Culture and Schooling*, Allen & Unwin, Sydney

Goodall, H. 1993, 'Constructing a riot: television news and Aborigines', *Media Information Australia*, no. 68, pp. 70–7

Gramsci, A. 1986, *Selections from Prison Notebooks*, ed. and trans. Q. Hoare and G. Smith, New Left Books, London

Grosz, E. 1989, *Sexual Subversions*, Allen & Unwin, Sydney

——1990, *Jacques Lacan: A Feminist Introduction*, Allen & Unwin, Sydney

——1994, *Volatile Bodies*, Allen & Unwin, Sydney

Halliday, M.A.K. 1978, *Language as Social Semiotic*, Edward Arnold, London

——1984, 'Language as code and language as behaviour', in *The Semiotics of Culture and Language*, vol. 1, ed. R.P. Fawcett et al., Frances Pinter, London

——1985a, *An Introduction to Functional Grammar*, Edward Arnold, London

——1985b, *Spoken and Written Language*, Deakin University Press, Geelong, Victoria

Halliday, M.A.K. and R. Hasan 1976, *Cohesion in English*, Longman, London

——1985, *Language, Context and Text: Aspects of Language in a Social-semiotic Perspective*, Deakin University Press, Geelong, Victoria

Harker, R., C. Mahar and C. Wilkes 1990, *An Introduction to the Work of Pierre Bourdieu*, Macmillan, London

Harris, S. 1984, 'Questions as a mode of control in magistrates' courts', *International Journal of the Sociology of Language*, 49, pp. 5–27

Hasan, R. 1986, 'The ontogenesis of ideology: an interpretation of mother–child talk' in *Semiotics Ideology Language*, Sydney Studies in Society and Culture no. 3, Sydney Association for Studies in Society and Culture, Sydney, pp. 125–46

Hasan, R. and G. Williams 1996, *Literacy in Society*, Longman, London & New York

Hawkes, T. 1977, *Structuralism and Semiotics*, Methuen, London

Hodge, R. and G. Kress 1988, *Social Semiotics*, Polity Press, Cambridge

hooks, bell 1990, 'Feminism: a transformational politic', in *Theoretical Perspectives on Sexual Difference*, ed. D.L. Rhode, Yale University Press, New Haven

Innis, R. (ed.) 1985, *Semiotics: An Introductory Anthology*, Indiana University Press, Bloomington

Johnston, E. 1992, 'Evonne goes back to the beginning' *Australian Women's Weekly*, July, Australian Consolidated Press, Sydney, pp. 12–13

Knapp, P. 1997, 'Home on the planes', *Southern Review*, vol. 30, no. 3, pp. 345–53

Kress, G. 1985, *Linguistic Processes in Sociocultural Practice*, Deakin University Press, Geelong, Victoria

——(ed.) 1988a, *Communication and Culture: An Introduction*, University of New South Wales Press, Sydney

——1988b, 'Language as social practice', in *Communication and Culture*, ed. G. Kress, University of New South Wales Press, Sydney, pp. 79–129

——1997, *Before Writing: Rethinking the Paths to Literacy*, Routledge, London & New York

Kress, G. and T. van Leeuwen 1990, *Reading Images*, Deakin University Press, Geelong, Victoria

Kress, G. and T. Threadgold 1988, 'Toward a social theory of genre', *Southern Review*, vol. 21, no. 3, pp. 215–43

Lacan, J. 1977, *Ecrits: A Selection*, trans. A Sheridan, Norton, London

——1979, *The Four Fundamental Concepts of Psycho-analysis*, ed. Jacques-Alain Miller, trans. Alan Sheridan, Penguin, Harmondsworth

Laclau, E. 1987, *Politics and Ideology in Marxist Theory*, Verso, London

——1990, *New Reflections on the Revolution of our Time*, Verso, London

——1996, *Emancipation(s)*, Verso, London

Laclau, E. and C. Mouffe 1990, *Hegemony and Socialist Strategy*, Verso, London

Lankshear, C. with J.P. Gee, M. Knobel and C. Searle 1997, *Changing Literacies*, Open University Press, Buckingham & Philadelphia

Laplanche, J. 1999, *Essays on Otherness*, Routledge, London

Lefort, C. 1986, *The Political Forms of Modern Society*, trans. J. Thompson et al., MIT Press, Cambridge, Massachusetts

——1988, *Democracy and Political Theory*, trans. D. Macey, University of Minnesota Press, Minneapolis

Legge, K. 1993, 'In the case of Pat O'Shane', *Australian Magazine*, 31 July–1 August, News Limited, Sydney, pp. 8–12

Lemke, Jay L. 1990, *Talking Science: Language, Learning and Values*, Ablex, Norwood, New Jersey

Luke, A. 1996, 'Genres of power? Literacy education and the production of capital', in *Literacy in Society*, eds R. Hasan and G. Williams, Longman, London & New York

Luke, A. and P. Gilbert 1993, *Literacy in Contexts: Australian Perspectives and Issues*, Allen & Unwin, Sydney

Martin, J.R. 1985, 'Process and text: two aspects of semiosis', in *Systemic Perspectives on Discourse*, eds J.D. Benson and W.S. Greaves vol. 1, Ablex, Norwood, New Jersey

——1986, 'Grammaticalising ecology: the politics of baby seals and kangaroos', in *Semiotics Ideology Language*, eds T. Threadgold et al. Sydney Studies in Society and Culture no. 3, Sydney Association for Studies in Society and Culture, Sydney, pp. 225–68

——1992, *English Text: System and Structure*, Benjamins, Amsterdam

Marx, K. 1976, *Capital: A Critique of Political Economy 1*, trans. B. Fowkes, Penguin, Harmondsworth

——1981, *Surveys from Exile*, ed. D. Fernbach, Penguin, Harmondsworth

——1984, *Grundrisse*, ed. D. Fernbach, Penguin, Harmondsworth

Marx, K. and F. Engels 1988 (1948), *The Communist Manifesto*, Penguin, Harmondsworth

Mattelart, A. 1991, *Advertising International: The Privatisation of Public Space*, trans. M. Chanan, Routledge, London

——1994, *Mapping World Communication: War, Progress, Culture*, trans. S. Emanuel and J. Cohen, University of Minnesota Press, Minneapolis

——1996, *The Invention of Communication*, trans. S. Emanuel, University of Minnesota Press, Minneapolis

Mattelart, A. and M. Mattelart 1992, *Rethinking Media Theory: Signposts and New Directions*, trans. J. Cohen and M. Urquidi, Media and Society 5, University of Minnesota Press, Minneapolis

McGregor, W. 1991, 'Photographs of Aborigines and police', *Social Semiotics*, vol. 1, no. 2, pp. 123–58

McGuinness, P. 1994, 'History of invasion ignores more balanced school of thought', *Australian*, 15 June, News Limited, Sydney, p. 15

Melrose, S. 1994, *A Semiotics of the Dramatic Text*, Macmillan, London

Mermelstein, J. 1999, 'Technology, publishing and on-line communities' [electronic message], *IRNTECH*, no. 861, 15 May

Mouffe, C (ed) 1992, *Dimensions of Radical Democracy*, Verso, London

——1993, *The Return of the Political*, Verso, London

Muller, V. 1991, 'Packaging the "New Woman": a look at some new women's magazines', *Australian Cultural Studies Conference 1990*, ed. D. Chambers and H. Cohen,

Faculty of Humanities and Social Sciences, University of Western Sydney, Nepean, pp. 79–90

Muspratt, S., A. Luke and P. Freebody (eds) 1997, *Constructing Critical Literacies: Teaching and Learning Textual Practice*, Allen & Unwin, Sydney

Nietzsche, F. 1956, *The Genealogy of Morals*, trans. F. Golffing, Doubleday Anchor, New York

Nightingale, V. 1992, 'Contesting domestic territory: watching rugby league on television' in *Stay Tuned: An Australian Broadcasting Reader*, ed. A. Moran, Allen & Unwin, Sydney

O'Sullivan, T., J. Hartley, D. Saunders, M. Montgomery and J. Fiske 1994, *Key Concepts in Communication and Cultural Studies*, 2nd edn, Routledge, London

O'Toole, M. 1992, 'Institutional sculpture and the social semiotic', *Social Semiotics*, vol. 2, no. 1

Pateman, C. 1989, 'Feminist critiques of the public/private dichotomy', in *The Disorder of Women*, Polity, Cambridge, pp. 118–40

Patton, P. (ed.) 1993, *Nietzsche, Feminism and Political Theory*, Allen & Unwin, Sydney

Pattow, D. and W. Wresch 1993, *Communicating Technical Information*, Prentice Hall, New Jersey

Pinter, H. 1961, 'Last to go', in *A Slight Ache and Other Plays*, Methuen, London

Poynton, C. 1985, *Language and Gender: Making the Difference*, Deakin University Press, Geelong, Victoria

——1990, *Address and the Semiotics of Social Relations*, unpublished PhD, Linguistics Department, University of Sydney

——1993, 'Grammar, language and the social: post-structuralism and systemic linguistics', *Social Semiotics*, vol. 3, no. 1

Pratt, M.L. 1987, 'Linguistic utopias' in *The Linguistics of Writing: Arguments between Language and Literature*, eds N. Fabb, D. Attridge, A. Durant and C. MacCabe, Manchester University Press, Manchester, pp. 48–66

Robbins, M. 1994, 'Philosopher's art escapes the duty of reality', *Australian*, 22 April, News Limited, Sydney, p. 6

Sanders, N. 1993, 'Azaria Chamberlain and popular culture' in *Nation, Culture, Text: Australian Cultural and Media Studies*, ed. G. Turner, Routledge, London

Saussure, F. de 1989, *Course in General Linguistics*, trans. R. Harris, Open Court, London

Schirato, T. 1997, 'Between practice and structure: cultural literacy and Bourdieu's notion of habitus', *Southern Review*, vol. 30, no. 3, pp. 259–67

Shea, V. 1995, *Netiquette*, Albion Books, New York

Shnukal, A. 1983, 'Blaikman Tok: changing attitudes to Torres Strait creole', *Australian Aboriginal Studies 2*, pp. 25–33

Silverstone, R. 1994, *Television and Everyday Life*, Routledge, London

Snyder, I. 1997, *Page to Screen: Taking Literacy into the Electronic Era*, Allen & Unwin, Sydney

Steiner, L. 1992, 'The construction of gender in news reporting textbooks 1890–1990', *Journalism Monographs*, No. 135, October

Stoler, A. 1995, *Race and the Education of Desire*, Duke University Press, Durham, North Carolina

Tannen, D. 1989, *Talking Voices: Repetition, Dialogue and Imagery in Conversational Discourse*, Cambridge University Press, Cambridge

Thibault, P. J. 1988, 'Knowing what you're told by the Agony Aunts: language function, gender difference and the structure of knowledge and belief in the personal columns', in *Functions of Style*, eds D. Birch and L.M. O'Toole, Frances Pinter, London

Thompson, J. 1990, *Ideology and Modern Culture*, Polity Press, Cambridge

Threadgold, T. 1986, 'Semiotics-Ideology-Language', Introduction to *Semiotics Ideology Language*, eds T. Threadgold et al., Sydney Studies in Society and Culture no. 3, Sydney Association for Studies in Society and Culture, Sydney, pp. 15–60

——1988a, 'Language and gender', *Australian Feminist Studies*, vol. 3, pp. 41–70

——1988b, 'Stories of race and gender: an unbounded discourse', in *The Functions of Style*, eds, D. Birch and L.M. O'Toole, Frances Pinter, London

——1989, 'Talking about genre: ideologies and incompatible discourses', *Cultural Studies*, vol. 1, no. 3, Jan. 1989, pp. 101–27

Thwaites, T., L. Davis and W. Mules 1994, *Tools for Cultural Studies: An Introduction*, Macmillan, Melbourne

Todorov, T. 1984, *Mikhail Bakhtin: The Dialogical Principle*, trans. W. Godzich, University of Minnesota Press, Minneapolis

Turner, G. 1988, *Film as Social Practice*, Routledge, London

——1990, *British Cultural Studies: An Introduction*, Unwin Hyman, Sydney

Tyner, K. 1998, *Literacy in a Digital World: Teaching and Learning in the Age of Information*, Lawrence Erlbaum Associates, Mawah, New Jersey and London

Unreich, R. 1993, 'Why he thinks you're desperate', *Dolly*, September, Australian Consolidated Press, Sydney, p. 109

van Leeuwen, T. 1986, 'The consumer, the producer and the state: analysis of a television news item', in *Semiotics Ideology Language*, Sydney Studies in Society and Culture no. 3, Sydney Association for Studies in Society and Culture, Sydney, pp. 203–24

——1991, 'The sociosemiotics of easy listening music', *Social Semiotics*, vol. 1, no. 1, pp. 67–80

Virilio, P. 1991, *The Lost Dimension*, trans. D. Moshenberg, Semiotext(e), New York

——1994, *The Vision Machine*, trans. J. Rose, Indiana University Press, Bloomington

——1997, *Open Sky*, trans. J. Rose, Verso, London

Volosinov, V. 1986, *Marxism and the Philosophy of Language*, trans. L. Matejka and I. Titunik, Harvard University Press, Cambridge, Massachusetts

Wallace, A. and S. Yell 1997, 'New literacies in the virtual classroom', *Southern Review*, vol. 30, no. 3, pp. 333–44

Williams, R. 1983, *Keywords*, Fontana, London

——1990, *Television, Technology and Cultural Form*, Routledge, London

Williamson, Dugald 1997, 'Media education, literacy and skills', *Southern Review*, vol. 30, no. 3, pp. 320–32

Windschuttle, K. 1990, *The Media*, 3rd edn, Penguin, Melbourne

Winship, J. 1987, *Inside Women's Magazines*, Pandora, London

——1991, 'The impossibility of *Best*: enterprise meets domesticity in the practical women's magazines of the 1980s', *Cultural Studies*, vol. 5, no. 2, May, pp. 131–56

Wright, J. 1991, 'Gracefulness and strength: sexuality in the Seoul Olympics', *Social Semiotics*, vol. 1, no. 1, pp. 49–66

Young, R. 1995, *Colonial Desire*, Routledge, London

Zizek, S. 1991a, *Looking Awry*, MIT Press, Cambridge, Massachusetts

——1991b, *For They Know Not What They Do*, Verso, London

——1992a, *Enjoy Your Symptom*, Routledge, New York

——1992b, *The Sublime Object of Ideology*, Verso, London

——1993, *Tarrying with the Negative*, Duke University Press, Durham, North Carolina

——(ed.), 1994a, *Mapping Ideology*, Verso, New York

——1994b, *The Metastases of Enjoyment*, Verso, London

——1996, *The Indivisible Remainder*, Verso, London

——1997, *The Plague of Fantasies*, Verso, London

Index